JOELLEN K. BLAND

MERIWETHER PUBLISHING LTD.
Colorado Springs, Colorado

Meriwether Publishing Ltd., Publisher
P.O. Box 7710
Colorado Springs, CO 80933

Editor: Arthur L. Zapel
Typesetting: Sharon E. Garlock
Cover design: Tom Myers

Printed in the United States of America
First Edition

Library of Congress Cataloging-in-Publication Data

Bland, Joellen.
Playing scenes from classic literature : short dramatizations of the world's most famous literature / Joellen Bland. -- 1st ed.
p. c.m.
Summary: Presents a collection of monologues and short scenes adapted from classic novels, stories, poems, essays, and plays.
ISBN 1-56608-024-X (pbk.)
1. Acting--Juvenile literature. 2. Young adult drama, American. 3. Literature--Adaptations--Juvenile literature. [1. Acting.] I. Title.
PN2080.B56 1996
812'.54--dc20

96-36386
CIP
AC

1 2 3 4 5 6 7 8 9 99 98 97 96

To my family,
with love and thanks for the time and
encouragement they have generously given me
to pursue the endless joys and challenges
of playwriting and theatre.

CONTENTS

INTRODUCTION

I have adapted scenes and excerpts from the classics for more than thirty years, selecting my favorite characters and episodes to share with readers and performers, and encourage them to explore and enjoy the complete literary works. The samples from classics in this book may be read for pleasure, acted out in performances, used in speech classes, for auditions, or rehearsal exercises; but regardless of how they are used, I hope that the characters will come alive for today's readers who may share the doubts, happiness, problems, predicaments, humor, terror, and love of these characters, and appreciate how they have endured over the centuries.

This broad selection of scenes and monologs, taken from novels, stories, poems, essays, and plays in the public domain, represents fifty-four authors from thirteen countries. You will find humor in such works as "Don Quixote," "The Adventures of Huckleberry Finn," "The Big Bear of Arkansas," and "Tyl Ulenspiegl"; drama and romance in "A Tale of Two Cities," "Anna Karenina," "Les Miserables," and "Wuthering Heights"; melodrama and adventure in "Treasure Island," "The Three Musketeers," "The Count of Monte Cristo," and "Rob Roy"; favorite stories for young people in "Heidi," "The Adventures of Tom Sawyer," "The Wizard of Oz," and "Hans Brinker"; terror and suspense in "Dracula," "Frankenstein," "The Telltale Heart," and "Dr. Jekyll and Mr. Hyde"; timeless fables in "The Decameron" and "The Panchatantra"; a war story, a detective story, a story of the American West, dramatized poetry, memorable short speeches, and much more.

Fascinating fictional heroes and heroines await you: Captain Ahab, Rip Van Winkle, Jean Valjean, Edmond Dantes, Ben-Hur, Cyrano de Bergerac, D'Artagnan, and King Arthur; Jane Eyre, Hester Prynne, Jo March, Lorna Doone, Daisy Miller, and Catherine Earnshaw, as well as real-life figures of note: Abigail Adams, Sojourner Truth, Benjamin Franklin, Henry David Thoreau, and Frederick Douglass.

These are only a few among the array of characters and cuttings from literature around the world. Some are familiar; some may have been lost to memory and recalled; some are new, coaxed from their hiding places in the pages of forgotten works.

Here are authors who live on through their writings: Mark Twain, Stephen Crane, Washington Irving, Herman Melville, Louisa May Alcott, and Edgar Allan Poe; Charles Dickens, Jane Austen, Robert Browning, Charlotte Brontë, and Oscar Wilde; Sir Walter Scott, Robert Louis Stevenson, Victor Hugo, Jules Verne, Anton Chekhov, Johanna Spyri, Cervantes, Boccaccio, Erasmus, and many, many more who have enriched our lives.

I invite you to use this book to the fullest extent, and thoroughly enjoy, as I do, these "old" literary treasures which firmly retain their place as world classics.

—JKB

Monologs

From

SELECTED LETTERS OF THE ADAMS FAMILY

While John Adams was away from his home on public business as a lawyer, and later as a central figure in the Continental Congress from 1774 to 1777, his wife, Abigail, ran the family farm in Braintree, Massachusetts, raised their children, and wrote many encouraging letters to John which helped him through weary and troubled times. Here are excerpts from some of her letters.

ABIGAIL ADAMS: *(She sits at a table, composing a letter, and thinking of what she is writing.)* **Dearest Friend, 'Tis a fortnight since I wrote you a line, during which I have been confined with the jaundice, rheumatism, and a most violent cold. Many, very many people who have had the dysentery are now afflicted both with jaundice and rheumatism. The great and incessant rains we have had this fall (the like cannot be recollected) may have occasioned some of the present disorders. We have lately had a week of very cold weather, as cold as January, and a flight of snow which I hope will purify the air of some of the noxious vapors. It has spoiled many hundreds of bushels of apples, which were designed for cider.**

• • •

Colonel Warren returned last week to Plymouth. He damped my spirits greatly by telling me your stay will be prolonged another month. I was pleasing myself with the thoughts that you would soon be upon your return. 'Tis vain to repine. I hope the public will reap what I sacrifice.

• • •

I wish I knew what mighty things were fabricating where you are. If a form of government is to be established here, what one will be assumed? Will it be left to our assemblies to choose one? And will not many men have many minds? And shall we not run into dissensions among ourselves?

• • •

I am more and more convinced that man is a dangerous creature, and that power, whether vested in many or a few, is ever grasping and like the grave cries, give, give. The great fish swallows up the small. The reins of government have been so long slackened that I fear the people will not quietly submit to those restraints which are necessary for the peace and security of the community; if we separate

from Britain, what code of laws will be established? How shall we be governed so as to retain our liberties? Can any government be free which is not administered by general stated laws? Who shall frame these laws? Who will give them force and energy?

• • •

I long to hear that you have declared an independency, and by the way, in the new Code of Laws which I suppose it will be necessary for you to make, I desire you would remember the ladies, and be more generous and favorable to them than your ancestors. Do not put such unlimited power into the hands of the husbands. Remember, all men would be tyrants if they could. If particular care and attention is not paid to the ladies, we are determined to foment a rebellion, and will not hold ourselves bound by any laws in which we have no voice or representation.

• • •

That your sex are naturally tyrannical is a truth so thoroughly established as to admit of no dispute, but such of you as wish to be happy willingly give up the harsh title of master for the more tender and endearing one of friend. Why, then, not put it out of the power of the vicious and the lawless to use us with cruelty and indignity with impunity? Men of sense in all ages abhor those customs which treat us only as vassals of your sex. Regard us then as beings placed by Providence under your protection, and in imitation of the Supreme Being, make use of that power only for our happiness.

• • •

I believe I have tired you of politics. I shudder at the approach of winter, when I think I am to remain desolate. Our little ones send duty to Papa and want much to see him. I must bid you good night. 'Tis late for one who am much of an invalid. Adieu.

From

LORNA DOONE

By Richard D. Blackmore

Richard Blackmore recalled many of his own childhood memories when writing *Lorna Doone*. Published in 1869, the novel is set in the wild Exmoor country of Devon in the 1670s, and traces the life of young John Ridd, a sheep farmer who tells, in his own words, the story of his love for the beautiful and mysterious Lorna Doone, despite the fact that she lives among a fierce band of gentlemen outlaws, one of whom had killed his father when he was very young. Hidden away in a well-guarded valley, the Doones were feared as thieves and murderers, and left alone. Only by chance does young John Ridd first penetrate the forbidden place, where he discovers Lorna and vows that she will one day love him as he loves her. In this scene, when he is twenty-one and Lorna sixteen, he has braved the threat of discovery by her family to meet her in a hidden bower. She appears sad and frightened, and when he asks her the cause of her distress, she tells him her story.

LORNA: I cannot go through all my thoughts, John Ridd, so as to make them clear to you, nor have I ever dwelt on things to shape a story of them. I know not where the beginning was, nor where the middle ought to be, nor even how at the present time I feel, or think, or ought to think. There are but two in the world who ever listen and try to help me. One of them is my grandfather, Sir Ensor Doone, and the other is a man of great wisdom, whom we call the Counsellor. My grandfather is very old and harsh of manner, except to me. He seems to know what is right and wrong, but not to want to think of it. The Counsellor treats my questions as of play and not worth his while to answer, unless he can make wit of them.

Among the women there are none with whom I can hold converse, since my Aunt Sabina died, who took such pains to teach me. She was a lady of high repute and lofty ways and learning, but grieved and harrassed more and more by the coarseness and the violence and ignorance around her. In vain she strove from year to year to make the young men listen, to teach them what became their birth and give them a sense of honor. Very often she used to say that I was her only comfort, and I am sure she was my only one. When she died, it was more to me than if I had lost a mother.

I have no remembrance of father or mother, although they say that my father was the eldest son of Sir Ensor Doone, and the bravest and best of them. And so they call me heiress to this little realm of violence, and in sorry sport sometimes I am their princess, or their queen.

But what I want to know is something none of them can tell me – what I am, and why set here in this beautiful valley, yet forbidden to see things in the world beyond? Meanwhile, all around me is violence and robbery, coarse delight and savage pain, reckless joke and hopeless death. There is none to lead me forward; there is none to teach me

right; young as I am, I live beneath a curse that lasts forever!

(After a moment) **You, John Ridd, who have a mother and sisters, and a quiet home, you cannot tell what a lonely nature is. How it leaps in mirth sometimes, with only heaven touching it, and how it falls away desponding when the dreary weight creeps in. Sometimes I am so full of anger, that I dare not trust to speech, at things they cannot hide from me, and perhaps you would be much surprised that reckless men would care so much to elude a young girl's knowledge. They used to boast to Aunt Sabina of pillage and cruelty, on purpose, to enrage her. But they never boast to me. It even makes me smile sometimes, to see how awkwardly they come and offer me shining packets of ornaments and finery, rings, or chains, or jewels, lately belonging to other people.**

Often I wonder at the odds of fortune which have made me heiress of this mad domain, this sanctuary of unholiness! Oftentimes I am so vexed by things I cannot meddle with, yet which cannot be kept from me, that I am at the point of flying from this dreadful valley and risking all that can betide me in the unknown outer world. If it were not for my grandfather, I would have done so long ago. But I cannot bear that he should die with no gentle hand to comfort him.

We are to be pitied greatly, rather than condemned by people whom we have wronged, for I have read of places where gentle peace and love of home prevail. But I shall never know these things, being born to turbulence. Once I had the offer to escape this valley with a Scottish kinsman, to go to a high place in the gay, bright world, and yet I dared not trust it. And it ended so dreadfully – when my cousin Carver Doone murdered him, brutally, within my hearing. The horror of that deed overwhelmed me. It changed my life, in a moment, at a blow, from childhood

and thoughts of flowers and trees, to a sense of death and darkness and a heavy weight of earth. Before this, I had not truly known the evil of our living, the scorn of law, the outrage and the sorrow caused to others.

And now I am watched and spied upon and followed, and half my little liberty seems to be taken from me. You must go, John Ridd, go home to your mother, for I will not have her cheated of you! And come not again until two months have passed, one for your sake, and one for mine. But be not afraid for me. While I have my grandfather to prevent all violence, I am safe. I am safe...for now.

From

A TALE OF TWO CITIES

By Charles Dickens

Sydney Carton is perhaps the most memorable character in *A Tale of Two Cities,* Charles Dickens' historical novel of the French Revolution. As Carton stands on the guillotine, ready to sacrifice his life to save that of Charles Darnay, husband of Lucie, the woman he loves but can never call his own, his countenance is peaceful. He utters these last words.

SYDNEY CARTON *(Stands in his shirt-sleeves, his hands bound behind him.)* **I see Barsad, and Cly, Defarge, the Vengeance, the Juryman, the Judge, long ranks of the new oppressors who have risen on the destruction of the old, perishing by this retributive instrument, before it shall cease out of its present use. I see a beautiful city and a brilliant people rising from this abyss, and, in their struggles to be truly free, in their triumphs and defeats, through long, long years to come, I see the evil of this time and of the previous time of which this is the natural birth, gradually making expiation for itself and wearing out.**

I see the lives for which I lay down my life, peaceful, useful, prosperous and happy, in that England which I shall see no more. I see *her* with a child upon her bosom, who bears my name. I see her father, aged and bent, but otherwise restored and faithful to all men in his healing office, and at peace. I see the good old man, so long their friend, in ten years' time enriching them with all he has, and passing tranquilly to his reward.

I see that I hold a sanctuary in their hearts and in the hearts of their descendants, generations hence. I see her, an old woman, weeping for me on the anniversary of this day. I see her and her husband, their course done, living side by side in their last earthly bed, and I know that each was not more honored and held sacred in the other's soul, than I was in the souls of both.

I see that child who lay upon her bosom and who bore my name, a man winning his way up in that path of life which once was mine. I see him winning it so well, that my name is made illustrious there by the light of his. I see the blots I threw upon it faded away. I see him, foremost of the just judges and honored men, bringing a boy of my name with a forehead that I know and golden hair, to this place, then fair to look upon, with not a trace of this day's

disfigurement, and I hear him tell the child my story with a tender and faltering voice.

It is a far, far better thing that I do, than I have ever done; it is a far, far better rest that I go to than I have ever known.

From

NARRATIVE OF THE LIFE OF FREDERICK DOUGLASS

Written in 1845, Frederick Douglass's compelling, articulate narrative of his own experience as a slave outlines the tragic facts of human bondage; how a man was made a slave, and how a slave was made a man who eventually became an advisor to President Lincoln and the diplomatic representative of the United States to Haiti and the Dominican Republic. He was extremely popular as a lecturer and spoke to audiences in a powerful voice, sharing his thoughts and deep feelings as he struggled to establish an identity and gain his precious freedom.

FREDERICK DOUGLASS: *(He begins to speak from a lectern, but moves freely across the stage as he continues, speaking directly and closely to the audience.)* **I was born in Tuckahoe, near Hillsborough in Talbot County, Maryland. I have no accurate knowledge of my age, never having seen any authentic record containing it. I was probably between seven and eight years old when I was sent from Colonel Lloyd's plantation on the eastern shore of Maryland to the city of Baltimore. Going to live at Baltimore laid the foundation and opened the gateway to all my subsequent prosperity. My new mistress, Mrs. Auld, was a woman of the kindest heart and finest feelings. She very kindly commenced to teach me the A B C. After I had learned this, she assisted me in learning to spell words of three or four letters. Just at this point of my progress, her husband, Mr. Auld, found out what was going on, and at once forbade Mrs. Auld to instruct me further, telling her that it was unlawful, as well as unsafe, to teach a slave to read. He said it would forever unfit me to be a slave. I would at once become unmanageable and of no value to him. It could do me no good, but a great deal of harm. It would make me discontented and unhappy. If I was given an inch, I would take an ell. I should know nothing but to obey my master.**

These words sank deep into my heart, stirred up sentiments within that lay slumbering, and called into existence an entirely new train of thought. I began to understand what had been to me a most perplexing difficulty – the white man's power to enslave the black man. From that moment I understood the pathway from slavery to freedom. Though conscious of the difficulty of learning without a teacher, I set out with high hope, and a fixed purpose, at whatever cost of trouble, to learn how to read.

What my master most dreaded, that I most desired. What he most loved, that I most hated. That which to him

was a great evil to be carefully shunned, was to me a great good to be diligently sought. In learning to read, I owe almost as much to the bitter opposition of my master, as to the kindly aid of my mistress. When my mistress ceased to instruct me, I read newspapers and books whenever I found the opportunity. But the plan which I adopted that was most successful, was that of making friends of all the little white boys whom I met in the street. As many of these as I could, I converted into teachers. With their kindly aid, obtained at different times and places, I finally succeeded in learning to read. I used to talk this matter of slavery over with them. I would say to them, I wished I could be as free as they would be when they got to be men. "You will be free as soon as you are twenty-one, but *I am a slave for life!* Have not I as good a right to be free as you have?"

These words used to trouble them. They would express for me the liveliest sympathy, and console me with the hope that something would occur by which I might be free.

The thought of being a slave for life began to bear heavily upon my heart. I got hold of a book entitled *The Columbian Orator* and read a bold denunciation of slavery and a powerful vindication of human rights. The more I read, the more I was led to abhor and detest my enslavers. I could regard them in no other light than a band of successful robbers who had gone to Africa, stolen us from our homes, and in a strange land reduced us to slavery. I loathed them as being the meanest as well as the most wicked of men. And as I read and contemplated the subject, behold! That very disappointment which my master had predicted would follow my learning to read had already come to torment and sting my soul to unutterable anguish! As I writhed under it, I would at times feel

that learning to read had been a curse rather than a blessing. It had given me a view of my wretched condition, without the remedy. It opened my eyes to the horrible pit, but to no ladder upon which to get out. In moments of agony I envied my fellow slaves for their stupidity. I often wished myself a beast – anything – no matter what, to get rid of thinking! But there was no getting rid of it. The silver trump of freedom had roused my soul to eternal wakefulness. Freedom now appeared, to disappear forever no more. I saw nothing without seeing it. I heard nothing without hearing it, and felt nothing without feeling it. It looked from every star, it smiled in every calm, breathed in every wind, and moved in every storm.

Sometimes I would look out over the Chesapeake Bay whose broad bosom was ever white with sails from every quarter of the habitable globe. Those beautiful vessels, robed in purest white, so delightful to the eye of free men, were to me so many shrouded ghosts, to terrify and torment me with thoughts of my wretched condition. I often stood all alone and traced, with saddened heart and tearful eye, the countless number of sails moving off to the mighty ocean. There, with no audience but the Almighty, I would pour out my soul's complaint, in my rude way: "You are loosed from your moorings and are free. I am fast in my chains and am a slave! You move merrily before the gentle gale, and I sadly before the bloody whip! You are freedom's swift-winged angels, that fly around the world; I am confined in bands of iron! O that I were free! O, that I were on one of your gallant decks, and under your protecting wing! O God, save me! God, deliver me! Let but the first opportunity offer and come what will, I am off! Get caught or get clear, I'll try it. I have only one life to lose. I had as well be killed running as die standing. Only think of it – one hundred miles straight north, and I am free!

Try it? Yes! God helping me, I will! It cannot be that I shall live and die a slave. I will take to the water. This very bay shall bear me into freedom. There is a better day coming!

My better day came on the third day of September, 1838, when I left my chains and succeeded in reaching New York. At last – I became free.

From

THE PRAISE OF FOLLY

By Desiderius Erasmus

The Praise of Folly, written in 1509 by the Dutch humanist Erasmus, presents a congenial feminine figure, Folly, who examines the issues of wisdom versus ignorance through a witty balance of satire and serious consideration.

FOLLY: *(A pretty young woman, beautifully dressed, cheerful, and perfectly at ease with the audience, enters and greets the audience with a radiant smile.)* **My name is Folly. And no matter what is ordinarily said about me (and I am not ignorant of how bad the name of Folly sounds, even to the biggest fools), I am still the one, the only one, I may say, whose influence makes Gods and men cheerful. Just as a new and youthful color reappears everywhere when the sun first shows its beautiful golden face to the earth, or when spring breathes softly after a hard winter, so your faces changed at the sight of me.**

• • •

I was born in the Fortunate Isles, where all things grow without plowing or planting; where there is no labor, no old age, and no sickness; where not a daffodil, onion, bean, or any other ordinary thing is to be seen, but where nose and eyes are equally delighted by sweet marjoram, ambrosia, lotus, rose, violet, hyacinth, and the gardens of Adonis.

• • •

Being born amidst these pleasant things, I did not begin life crying, but from the first laughed good-naturedly at my mother. I was nursed and attended by Drunkenness, Ignorance, Self-Love, Flattery, Forgetfulness, Laziness, Pleasure, Madness, and Sensuality. With the help of these faithful servants, I gain control of all things – even dictating to dictators.

• • •

I can show you that I am responsible for everything agreeable. Would life without pleasure be life at all? As a matter of fact, even the Stoics do not really dislike pleasure. They carefully pretend to, and they loudly denounce it in public, but only in order to deter others and thus have it all to themselves. Just let them explain to me what part of life is not sad, troublesome, graceless, flat, and

distressing without a dash of pleasure, or in other words, folly. This is very adequately proved by Sophocles, a person insufficiently appreciated, who has left this pretty eulogy of me: "Ignorance is bliss."

• • •

But one cannot acquire wisdom, which the wise call the secret of happiness, unless one follows the leadership of folly. First, everyone admits that all the emotions belong to folly. Indeed, a fool and a wise man are distinguished by the fact that emotions control the former and reason the latter. Emotions serve not only as a guide and teacher to those who are hastening toward the portal of wisdom, but also as a stimulus in all virtuous actions, as exhorters to good deeds.

• • •

By a timely mixture of ignorance, thoughtlessness, forgetfulness of evil, hope of good, and a dash of delight, I bring relief from troubles, so that men are unwilling to relinquish them. They are so far from being weary of existence, that the less reason they have for living, the more they enjoy life! Folly is the only key to happiness.

• • •

Is anyone happier than those we commonly call morons, fools, nitwits, and naturals – the most beautiful of names? These fools are free of the fear of death and free from the pangs of conscience. They are not terrified by ghosts and hobgoblins. They are not filled with vain worries and hopes. In short, they are not troubled by the thousand cares to which this life is subject. Shame, fear, ambition, envy, and love are not for them. They are always merry. Wherever they go, they bring pleasure, as if they were mercifully created by the gods to lighten the sadness of human life.

Compare the life of a wise man with that of a fool. Put

up against a fool some model of wisdom, one who lost his boyhood and youth in the classroom, who dissipated the best part of his life in continual worry and study, and who never tasted a particle of pleasure thereafter. He is always abstemious, poor, unhappy, and crabbed. He is harsh and unjust to himself, grim and mean to others. He is pale, emaciated, sickly, sore-eyed, prematurely old, dying before his time. Of course, it really makes little difference when such a man dies. He has never lived!

• • •

If Folly is any judge, the happiest man is the one who is most thoroughly deluded. May he maintain that ecstasy!

From

LES MISÉRABLES

By Victor Hugo

The most notable writer of the French Romantic Movement, Victor Hugo believed that he had a social mission to accomplish in his work. His great humanitarian novel, *Les Misérables* published in 1862, vividly portrays common life in France in the post-Napoleonic era, where his converted convict, Jean Valjean, struggles to redeem his unfortunate past. A former galley slave rescued from certain poverty and disgrace by the kindness of a churchman, Jean Valjean has made his way up to the position of mayor of a French village where he is known as Monsieur Madeleine. In this scene, Valjean has learned that another man is accused of being the escaped convict bearing his name, and is about to be sent back to the galleys. The real Valjean cannot allow this to happen. He goes to the courtroom at Arras where he shocks everyone assembled there with this speech.

JEAN VALJEAN: *(Stands straight and tall before the judge, jury, members of the court, and some convicts who have been brought in. His voice is strong.)* **Gentlemen of the jury, release the accused. Your honor, order my arrest. He is not the man whom you seek; it is I. I am Jean Valjean.** *(Pause)* **I am not mad. You shall see. You were on the point of committing a great mistake; release that man. I am accomplishing a duty. I am the unhappy convict. I am the only one who sees clearly here, and I tell you the truth. What I do at this moment, God beholds from on high, and that is sufficient. You can take me, since I am here.**

Nevertheless, I have done my best. I have disguised myself under another name. I have become rich. I have become a mayor. I have desired to enter again among honest men. It seems that this cannot be. In short, there are many things which I cannot tell. I shall not relate to you the story of my life; some day you will know it. I did rob Monseigneur the Bishop, that is true; I did rob Petit Gervais, that is true. They were right in telling you that Jean Valjean was a wicked wretch. But all the blame may not belong to him. Listen, your honors; a man so abased as I has no remonstrance to make with Providence, nor advice to give to society; but, mark you, the infamy from which I have sought to rise is pernicious to men. The galleys make the galley slave. Receive this in kindness, if you will. Before the galleys, I was a poor peasant, unintelligent, a species of idiot. The galley changed me. I was stupid, I became wicked; I was a log, I became a firebrand. Later, I was saved by indulgence and kindness, as I had been lost by severity.

But, pardon, you cannot comprehend what I say. You will find in my house among the ashes of the fireplace, the forty-sous piece of which, seven years ago, I robbed Petit Gervais. I have nothing more to add. Take me. *(Pause)*

Great God! The prosecuting attorney shakes his head. You say, "Monsieur Madeleine has gone mad."

You do not believe me. This is hard to be borne. Do not condemn that man, at least. *(Looks to one side.)* **What! These men here do not know me!** *(He steps to one side.)* **You must see clearly that I am Jean Valjean! See, I recognize these three convicts here! Brevet, do you remember those checkered, knit suspenders that you had in the galleys? Yes, you do! And you, Chenildieu, the whole of your left shoulder has been burned deeply from laying it one day on a chafing dish full of embers, to efface the three letters T. F. P., which yet are still to be seen there. Answer me, is this true? Of course, it is true! And you, Cochepaille, you have on your left arm, near where you have been bled, a date put in blue letters with burnt powder. It is the date of the landing of the emperor at Cannes, March 1st, 1815. Lift up your sleeve! Do you see? I know these men, and they know me, for we were together in the galleys!**

(He turns forward again.) **I will not disturb the proceedings further. I am going, since I am not arrested now. I have many things to do. Monsieur the Prosecuting Attorney knows where I am going and will have me arrested when he chooses.** *(He looks around the room.)* **You all, all who are here, think me worthy of pity, do you not? Great God! When I think of what I have been on the point of doing, I think myself worthy of envy. Still, would that all this had not happened!** *(He strides out of the room.)*

From

LES MISÉRABLES

By Victor Hugo

In Victor Hugo's great novel, *Les Misérables*, the character of Jean Valjean is foremost; but most of Valjean's troubles come from his pursuit by his dedicated and determined enemy, Inspector Javert, who is sworn to capture him and return him to the prison galleys. Javert has pursued Valjean relentlessly over many years and has failed to catch him. At the barricade, when Javert is made a prisoner by the revolutionaries, Valjean spares his life. And later, when Valjean is once again in his grasp, Javert spares him. Javert cannot understand how this has happened.

JAVERT: *(Standing on a bridge, he leans upon the railing.)* **I see two roads before me, both equally straight, and I am terrified! I have never in my life known but one straight line. These two roads are contradictory! One excludes the other. Which is the true one? How can it be that Jean Valjean has spared me, and I have spared Jean Valjean?**

What do I do now? Give up Jean Valjean? No! That is wrong! Leave Valjean free? No! That is wrong! I, the man of authority, cannot fall lower than the galley slave. A convict cannot rise higher than the law and set his foot upon it! In either case, it is dishonor to Javert.

I must have him arrested. But I cannot. Something bars the way. Something. What? There is nothing else in the world but tribunals, sentences, police, and authority. But something is penetrating my soul. Admiration for a convict? Respect for a galley slave? How can that be possible? *(He shudders.)* **Favor accepted and returned, respect of persons - no more final condemnation, no more damnation; a mysterious justice according to God going counter to justice according to men!**

This convict whom I have relentlessly pursued and who has had me beneath his feet and could have avenged himself, and who ought to have done so, granted me life! And what has he done? His duty? No. Something more. And I, in sparing him, what have I done? My duty? No. Something more. There is something more than duty.

All my life, since I have been the age of a man, and an official, I have been a spy. My superior has always been Monsieur Gisquet. But today – I wonder – if there is another superior. God. God! Unyielding! The true Conscience! I cannot comprehend this. I cannot penetrate it. I cannot form any idea of it! My head will burst!

I am no longer certain of anything. I am uprooted! The code I have always lived by is now but a stump in my hand.

I have to do with scruples of an unknown species!

This is unendurable! There are but two ways to get out of this. I can go to Jean Valjean, arrest him, and return him to the galleys. Or... *(He looks about him.)*

The darkness is complete. The clouds conceal the stars. The houses of the city no longer show a single light. Nobody is passing by. All that I can see of the streets and quays are deserted. The rains have swelled the river. Here I stand, above the rapids of the Seine, the formidable whirlpool which knots and unknots itself like an endless screw.

All is black. *(He takes off his hat and lays it at his feet.)*

Let it be known, if anyone should wish to know it, that Javert, Inspector of the First Class, on June the 7th, eighteen-hundred and thirty-two, at about one o'clock in the morning, chose the road he would take, and ended his pursuit of the galley slave, Jean Valjean. *(He looks down into the water, leans forward, spreads his arms and is about to jump as the lights black out on him.)*

From

THE TELLTALE HEART

By Edgar Allan Poe

American author Edgar Allan Poe is known as a master of suspense and terror. His tales deal with the sinister workings of the human mind, the effects of strange experiences on individuals, and all things macabre and mysterious to be found in gloomy halls, dark dungeons, tombs, and catacombs. In one of his more famous stories, *The Telltale Heart,* a murderer, who may be presumed to be confined in an asylum or a prison cell, describes the horrible crime he has committed.

SCENE: THE MURDERER sits on a bench, hunched forward, his hands folded together on his knees. At first he is silent, then he looks up, as if a visitor has appeared. He suddenly rises and moves about as he tells his story, in a defined narrow space, as if invisible cell walls confine him.

THE MURDERER: I will tell you my story. Observe how healthily, how calmly I tell you. It is impossible to say how the idea first entered my brain. But once conceived, it haunted me day and night. Object there was none. Passion there was none. I loved the old man. He had never wronged me. For his gold I had no desire. It was . . . his eye! He had the eye of a vulture, a pale blue eye with a film over it. Whenever it fell upon me, my blood ran cold! And so I made up my mind to take the life of the old man, and thus rid myself of the eye forever!

You fancy me mad? Madmen know nothing. But you should have seen how wisely I proceeded. With what caution, with what foresight I went to work! Every night for a week, about midnight, I turned the latch of the old man's door and opened it, oh, so gently! *(He mimes the motions as he speaks.)* **And then, when I had made an opening, I put in a dark lantern, closed so that no light shone out, and then I thrust in my head. Oh, you would have laughed to see how cunningly I thrust it in! And then I undid the lantern cautiously, oh, so cautiously, just so much that a single thin ray fell upon the vulture eye! And this I did for seven long nights, but I found the eye always closed – and so it was impossible to do the work, for it was not the old man who vexed me, but his Evil Eye.**

Upon the eighth night I was more than usually cautious in opening the door. Never before that night had I felt the extent of my own powers. To think that I was opening the door, little by little, and he not even dreaming of my secret

deeds or thoughts! I had my head in and was about to open the lantern, when my thumb slipped upon the tin fastening, and the old man sprang up in bed, crying out, "Who's there?"

I kept quite still and said nothing. For a whole hour I did not move a muscle, and I did not hear him lie down. He was still sitting up in bed – listening! Presently, I heard a slight groan and I know it was the groan of mortal terror – a low stifled sound that arises from the bottom of the soul when overcharged with awe. Death, in approaching him, had stalked with his black shadow before him, and enveloped the victim.

When I had waited a long time, very patiently, without hearing him lie down, I resolved to open a little – a very, very little crevice in the lantern. So I opened it - you cannot imagine how stealthily, until a single dim ray, like the thread of a spider, shot from out the crevice and fell full upon the vulture eye! It was open – wide, wide open, and I grew furious as I gazed upon it. I saw it with perfect distinctness – all a dull blue, with a hideous veil over it that chilled the very marrow in my bones.

And then there came to my ears a low, dull, quick sound, such as a watch makes when enveloped in cotton. It was the beating of the old man's heart, and it increased my fury, as the beating of a drum stimulates the soldier into courage. The hellish tattoo of the heart increased. It grew quicker and quicker, and louder and louder every instant! At the dead hour of the night, amid the dreadful silence of that old house, so strange a noise as this excited me to uncontrollable terror! I thought the heart must burst! And then a new anxiety seized me. The sound would be heard by a neighbor!

The old man's hour had come! With a loud yell, I threw open the lantern and leaped into the room. He shrieked

once – only once. I sprang upon him. In a moment, his eye troubled me no more.

If you still think me mad, you will think so no longer when I describe the wise precautions I took for the concealment of the body. First of all, I dismembered the corpse. I cut off the head and the arms and legs. I then took up three planks from the flooring and deposited all between the scantlings. Then I replaced the boards so cleverly, so cunningly, that no human eye – not even *his*, could have detected anything wrong. There was nothing to wash out, no stain, no blood spot. I had been too wary for that. A tub had caught all! *(Laughs.)*

When the police officers came and said a shriek had been heard by a neighbor, I smiled, for what had I to fear? I bade them welcome. The shriek, I said, was my own in a dream. The old man was away in the country, I told them, and in the enthusiasm of my confidence, I brought chairs for them to rest from their fatigues. And in the wild audacity of my perfect triumph, I placed my own seat upon the very spot beneath which reposed the corpse of the victim.

The officers were satisfied and we chatted of familiar things. But ere long my head ached and I fancied a ringing in my ears. I wished the officers gone, but still they sat and chatted. The sound increased. I talked more fluently and with heightened voice – yet the noise steadily increased to a low, dull, quick sound like a watch makes when enveloped in cotton! It grew louder – louder – louder – and still the men chatted pleasantly and smiled. And then I realized that the noise was not within my ears. Didn't they hear it? No! No! They heard! They suspected! They *knew*, and were making a mockery of my horror!

I felt that I must scream or die! And now, louder! Louder! Louder! It arose over all and continually increased! Louder! Louder! Louder! I could bear it no

more! "I admit the deed!" I shrieked. "Tear up the planks! Here! Here! It is the beating of his hideous heart!"

(He slowly returns to his seat, hunching forward and folding his hands together on his knees.) **Nervous. Dreadfully nervous I have been – and am now. Yet you say I am mad? Oh, no. The disease has sharpened my senses, not dulled them. Above all, the sense of hearing is acute. I have heard all things in the heavens and in the earth. I have heard many things in hell. Observe how healthily I have told you my story. How calmly. How then, am I mad?**

From

THE TRAVELS AND SURPRISING ADVENTURES OF BARON MUNCHAUSEN

By Rudolph Erich Raspe

The world of *Baron Munchausen* is a world turned upside down. His wild adventures flaunt every rule of logic and delight readers today as fully as they did two centuries ago. Rudolph Erich Raspe, who came from Hanover in Germany, just as the real Munchausen did, capitalized on the real Baron's penchant for telling tales in a ridiculously extravangant manner. Published in 1785, Munchausen's travels around the world offer an unforgettable series of "tall tale" adventures.

BARON MUNCHAUSEN: *(Enters, delighted to find an audience, and marches about with great precision, using expansive gestures and expressions to embellish his speech.)* **After we had resided in Ceylon about a fortnight, I accompanied one of the governor's brothers on a shooting party. Near the banks of a large piece of water I thought I heard a rustling noise behind me, and on turning about, I was almost petrified (as who would not?) at the sight of a lion approaching with the intention of satisfying his appetite with my poor carcass – and that without my consent! What was to be done in this horrible dilemma? My fowling piece was only charged with swan-shot, yet I had some hopes of frightening the lion by the report. I immediately let fly, but the report did but enrage him, for he quickened his pace and seemed to approach me at full speed. I attempted to escape, but that only added to my distress. The moment I turned about, I found a large crocodile with his mouth extended and ready to receive me. To my right was the water. To my left was a deep precipice, said to have (as I have since learned) a receptacle at the bottom for venomous creatures. In short, I gave myself up for lost, for the lion was now upon his hind legs and just in the act of seizing me. I fell to the ground with fear, and the lion sprang over me. I lay for some time in a situation which no language can describe, expecting to feel his teeth or talons in some part of me every moment. Then I heard a violent but unusual noise, different from any sound that had ever before assailed my ears. I ventured to raise my head and look round when, to my unspeakable joy, I perceived that the lion had jumped into the crocodile's mouth! The head of the lion was stuck in the throat of the crocodile, and they both were struggling to extricate themselves. Fortunately, I had my sword about me, with which I severed the lion's head at one blow and the body fell at my**

feet. With the butt end of my fowling-piece I rammed the head farther into the throat of the crocodile and destroyed him by suffocation.

This narrow and lucky escape was a chance turned to advantage by my presence of mind and vigorous exertion. But then, I have always been remarkable for the excellence of my horses, dogs, guns and swords, and luck at sporting. You have heard, I dare say, of the hunter's and sportsman's saint and protector, St. Hubert, and of the noble stag which appeared to him in the forest with the holy cross between his antlers. I have had a similar experience. One day, having spent all my shot, I found myself in the presence of a stately stag. I charged immediately with a handful of cherry-stones, for I had recently sucked the fruit as far as hurry would permit. Thus I let fly at him and hit him on the middle of the forehead between his antlers. It stunned him. He staggered, then ran off.

A year or two later, being with a shooting party in the same forest, I beheld a noble stag with a fine full-grown cherry tree, above ten feet high, between his antlers. I immediately recollected my former adventure, looked upon him as my property, and brought him to the ground with one shot – which at once gave me the haunch of venison and cherry sauce, for the tree was covered with the richest fruit I had ever tasted.

Another instance of incredible luck occurred one day in a Polish forest, when a terrible bear made for me at great speed, with open mouth. All my pockets were searched in an instant for powder and ball, but all I found were two spare flints. One I flung with all my might into the monster's open jaws and down his throat. It gave him pain and made him turn about, so I could level the second flint at his back door, which I did with wonderful success. It flew in, met the first flint in the stomach, struck fire and

blew up the bear with a terrible explosion. Though I came safe off that time, yet I should not wish to try it again. There is a kind of fatality in it.

For some unfathomable reason the fiercest and most dangerous animals generally come upon me when I am entirely defenseless, as if they had a notion or an instinctive intimation of it. Once a frightful wolf rushed upon me so suddenly and so closely, I could do nothing but follow mechanical instinct. I thrust my fist into his open mouth and pushed on until my arm was fairly in up to his shoulder. Now I assure you, I was not much pleased with my awkward situation, face to face with a wolf. If I withdrew my arm, he would fly the more furiously upon me. So I did the only thing I could do. I laid hold of his tail, turned him inside out like a glove, and flung him to the ground where I left him.

And so, for the proper manner of using my wits, as well as my sword and shooting piece, I may hope to be well remembered in the forest, upon the turf, and in the field!

(He bows and marches off.)

From

FRANKENSTEIN

By Mary Shelley

Since its publication in 1818, *Frankenstein* has inspired horror, awe and fascination in millions of readers. Mary Shelley, wife of the poet Percy Bysshe Shelley, was only nineteen when she created the story, which, in her own words, "would speak to the mysterious fears of our nature, and awaken thrilling horror — one to make the reader dread to look round, to curdle the blood and quicken the beatings of the heart." Dr. Victor Frankenstein tells his story in his own words, beginning with the creation of his unfortunate monster.

FRANKENSTEIN: Natural philosophy is the genius that has regulated my fate. When I had attained the age of seventeen, I became a student at the university of Ingolstadt. Chance, or rather the evil influence, the Angel of Destruction, which asserted omnipotent sway over me, led me first to Monsieur Krempe, professor of natural philosophy, deeply imbued in the secrets of his science. Professor Waldman offered a panegyric upon modern chemistry, the terms of which I shall never forget. "The modern masters promise very little; but these philosophers, whose hands seem only made to dabble in dirt, and their eyes to pore over the microscope or crucible, have indeed performed miracles. They penetrate into the recesses of nature and show how she works in her hiding places. They have discovered how the blood circulates, and the nature of the air we breathe. They have acquired new and almost unlimited powers."

I felt as if my soul were grappling with a palpable enemy; one by one the various keys were touched which formed the mechanism of my being; chord after chord was sounded, and soon my mind was filled with one thought, one conception, one purpose. Treading in the steps already marked, I would pioneer a new way, explore unknown powers, and unfold to the world the deepest mysteries of creation.

Professor Waldman took me into his laboratory and explained to me the uses of his various machines. He also gave me a list of books. From that day natural philosophy and chemistry became my sole occupation. I read with ardor those works so full of genius and discrimination. I attended the lectures and cultivated the acquaintance of the men of science at the university. My progress was rapid. My ardor was the astonishment of my fellow students, and my proficiency that of my masters.

One of the phenomena which had peculiarly attracted

my attention was the structure of the human frame. Whence, I often asked myself, did the principle of life proceed? I became acquainted with the science of anatomy. I observed the natural decay and corruption of the human body. I saw how the fine form of man was degraded and wasted; I beheld the corruption of death succeed to the blooming cheek of life. I examined and analyzed all the minutiae of causation, as exemplified in the change from life to death and death to life, until from the midst of this darkness a sudden light broke in upon me – a light so brilliant and wondrous, yet so simple. After days and nights of incredible labor and fatigue, I became capable of bestowing animation upon lifeless matter!

Although I possessed the capacity of bestowing animation, yet to prepare a frame for the reception of it, with all its intricacies of fibers, muscles, and veins, still remained a work of inconceivable difficulty and labor. I doubted at first whether I should attempt the creation of a being like myself, but my imagination was too much exalted to permit me to doubt of my ability. I began the creation of a human being.

I resolved to make the being of a gigantic stature, about eight feet in height and proportionably large. A new species would bless me as its creator and source; many happy and excellent natures would owe their being to me. But who shall conceive the horrors of my secret toil as I dabbled among the unhallowed damps of the grave or tortured the living animal to animate the lifeless clay? Frantic impulse urged me forward. I seemed to have lost all soul or sensation but for this one pursuit. I collected bones from charnel houses and disturbed, with profane fingers, the tremendous secrets of the human frame. In a solitary chamber at the top of the house, I kept my workshop of filthy creation. The dissecting room and the

slaughterhouse furnished many of my materials, and often did my human nature turn with loathing from my occupation, while, still urged on by an eagerness which perpetually increased, I brought my work near to a conclusion.

It was on a dreary night of November that I beheld the accomplishment of my toils. With an anxiety that almost amounted to agony, I collected the instruments of life around me, that I might infuse a spark of being into the lifeless thing that lay at my feet. It was already one in the morning, the rain pattered dismally against the panes, and my candle was nearly burnt out, when, by the glimmer of the half-extinguished light, I saw the dull yellow eye of the creature open. It breathed hard, and a convulsive motion agitated its limbs.

How can I describe my emotions at this catastrophe, or how delineate the wretch whom with such infinite pains and care I had endeavored to form? His limbs were in proportion, and I had selected his features as beautiful. Beautiful! Great God! His yellow skin scarcely covered the work of muscles and arteries beneath; his hair was of a lustrous black, and flowing; his teeth of a pearly whiteness, but these luxuriances only formed a more horrid contrast with his watery eyes that seemed almost of the same color as the dun-white sockets in which they were set, his shriveled complexion and straight black lips.

For this I had deprived myself of rest and health. I had desired it with an ardor that far exceeded moderation, but now that I had finished, the beauty of the dream vanished, and breathless horror and disgust filled my heart. Oh, no mortal could support the horror of that countenance. A mummy again endued with animation could not be so hideous as that wretch. It became a thing such as even Dante could not have conceived!

From

DRACULA

By Bram Stoker

In Bram Stoker's famous vampire novel, *Dracula*, the British lawyer, Jonathan Harker, has traveled to Castle Dracula in Transylvania to transact business with Count Dracula, who wishes to immigrate to England. At first he is cordially received, but soon Harker realizes that he is being totally controlled and held prisoner by the Count. His letters are intercepted; he sees no one in the castle but the Count; his door is kept locked, and one terrible night, he sees from his window how the Count crawls down the walls of the castle like a bat. He soon discovers that the Count is a vampire who sleeps by day in a coffin in a vault beneath the castle. Fearing for his own life, Harker recounts in his diary how he desperately attempts to escape from the castle by bravely climbing down the stone walls to the window of another room whereby he can make his way to the underground vault. There he hopes to find the key that will unlock the castle door and allow him to gain his freedom.

JONATHAN HARKER: The great box was in the same place, close against the wall, but the lid was laid on it, not fastened down, so I raised the lid and laid it back against the wall. And then I saw something which filled my very soul with horror. There lay the Count, but looking as if his youth had been half renewed, for the white hair and moustache were changed to dark iron-grey. The cheeks were fuller, and the white skin seemed ruby-red underneath; the mouth was redder than ever, for on the lips were gouts of fresh blood, which trickled from the corners of the mouth and ran over the chin and neck. Even the deep, burning eyes seemed set amongst swollen flesh, for the lids and pouches underneath were bloated. It seemed as if the whole awful creature were simply gorged with blood. He lay like a filthy leech, exhausted with his repletion.

I shuddered as I bent over to touch him, and every sense in me revolted at the contact, but I had to search, or I was lost. The coming night might see my own body a banquet. I felt all over the body, but no sign could I find of the key. Then I stopped and looked at the Count. There was a mocking smile on the bloated face which seemed to drive me mad. This was the being I was helping to transfer to London, where, perhaps for centuries to come he might, amongst its teeming millions, satiate his lust for blood and create a new and ever-widening circle of semi-demons to batten on the helpless.

The very thought drove me mad! A terrible desire came upon me to rid the world of such a monster. There was no lethal weapon at hand, but I seized a shovel which the workmen had been using to fill the cases he meant to take to England with him, and lifting it high, struck, with the edge downward, at the hateful face. But as I did so, the head turned and the eyes fell full upon me with all their glaze of basilisk horror! The sight seemed to paralyze me

and the shovel turned in my hand and glanced from the face, merely making a deep gash above the forehead. The shovel fell from my hand across the box, and as I pulled it away, the flange of the blade caught the edge of the lid which fell over again and hid the horrid thing from my sight. The last glimpse I had was of the bloated face, blood-stained and fixed with a grin of malice which would have held its own in the nethermost hell!

From

DRACULA

By Bram Stoker

In the horror novel *Dracula*, Bram Stoker traces the journey of the vampire, Count Dracula, from his home in Transylvania to London. The Englishman, Jonathan Harker, who escaped from the Count's castle in Transylvania, wrote a journal of his experience with the Count and with three horrible vampire women who threatened his life. Harker's wife, Mina, knows that the vampire is nearby, and that it has destroyed her dear friend Lucy Westenra. Although she and her husband have enlisted the aid of the famous Dr. Van Helsing, an authority on vampires, to overcome the monster, she is aware of something unusual that is beginning to affect her. She writes about it in her journal.

MINA HARKER: I feel full of devouring anxiety. I keep thinking over everything that has happened since Jonathan came back to London, and it all seems like a horrible tragedy, with fate pressing on relentlessly to some destined end. Everything that one does seems, no matter how right it may be, to bring on the very thing which is most to be deplored.

I can't quite remember how I fell asleep last night. I remember hearing the sudden barking of the dogs and a lot of queer sounds. And then there was silence over everything, silence so profound that it startled me, and I got up and looked out of the window. All was dark and silent, the black shadows thrown by the moonlight seeming full of a silent mystery of their own. Not a thing seemed to be stirring, but all to be grim and fixed as death or fate; so that a thin streak of white mist, that crept with almost imperceptible slowness across the grass towards the house, seemed to have a sentience and a vitality of its own.

When I got back to bed I found a lethargy creeping over me. I lay a while, but could not quite sleep, so I got out and looked out of the window again. The mist was spreading, and was now close up to the house, so that I could see it lying thick against the wall, as though it were stealing up to the windows. I felt frightened and I crept into bed and pulled the clothes over my head. I was not then a bit sleepy, at least so I thought; but I must have fallen asleep, for, except dreams, I do not remember anything until the morning when Jonathan woke me. I think that it took me an effort and a little time to realize where I was, and that it was Jonathan who was bending over me. My dream was very peculiar, and was almost typical of the way that waking thoughts become merged in, or continued in, dreams.

I thought that I was asleep and waiting for Jonathan to come back. I was very anxious about him, and I was powerless to act; my feet, and my mind and my brain were weighted, so that nothing could proceed at the usual pace. And so I slept uneasily. Then it began to dawn upon me that the air was heavy, and dank, and cold. I put back the clothes from my face, and found, to my surprise, that all was dim around. The gaslight which I had left lit for Jonathan, but turned down, came only like a tiny red spark through the fog, which had evidently grown thicker and poured into the room. Then it occurred to me that I had shut the window before I had come to bed. I would have got out to make certain on the point, but some leaden lethargy seemed to chain my limbs and even my will. I lay still and endured; that was all. I closed my eyes, but could still see through my eyelids. It is wonderful what tricks our dreams play us and how conveniently we can imagine.

The mist grew thicker and I could see now how it came in, like smoke – or with the white energy of boiling water – pouring in, not through the window, but through the joinings of the door. It got thicker and thicker, till it seemed as if it became concentrated into a sort of pillar of cloud in the room, through the top of which I could see the light of the gas shining like a red eye. Things began to whirl through my brain just as the cloudy column was now whirling in the room, and through it all came the scriptural words "a pillar of cloud by day and of fire by night." Was it indeed some such spiritual guidance that was coming to me in my sleep? But the pillar was composed of both the day and the night-guiding, for the fire was in the red eye, which at the thought got a new fascination for me, till, as I looked, the fire divided, and seemed to shine on me through the fog like two red eyes, such as Lucy told me of in her momentary mental wandering when, on the cliff, the dying sunlight struck the windows of St. Mary's Church.

Oh, if I hadn't gone to Whitby, perhaps poor dear Lucy would be with us now. She hadn't taken to visiting the churchyard till I came, and if she hadn't come there in the daytime with me, she wouldn't have walked there in her sleep; and if she hadn't gone there at night and asleep, that monster couldn't have destroyed her as he did!

Suddenly the horror burst upon me that it was thus that Jonathan had seen those awful women growing into reality through the whirling mist in the moonlight, in the monster's castle, and in my dream I must have fainted, for all became black darkness. The last conscious effort which imagination made was to show me a livid white face bending over me out of the mist!

I must be careful of such dreams, for they would unseat one's reason if there were too much of them. Last night tired me more than if I had not slept at all.

From

WALDEN

By Henry David Thoreau

Walden, published in 1854, is Henry David Thoreau's account of an experiment he made with the "simple life." While living alone on Walden Pond for two years, he learned what he wished to know — what real living was - and when he returned to his normal life, he was wiser and happier for his experience.

SCENE: THOREAU enters, comfortably dressed, carrying a straw hat which he places on his head from time to time, then removes as the notion strikes him. He could carry a tin bucket of huckleberries — or a fishing rod made from a sapling. He will "hunker down" to chat amiably with the audience, or sprawl out and recline on the ground. But he is as sincere and down-to-earth as any man you will ever meet.)

THOREAU: When I first took up my abode in the woods, on Independence Day, the Fourth of July, 1845, my house was not finished for winter, but was merely a defense against the rain, without plastering or chimney, the walls being of rough weather-stained boards with wide chinks – which made it cool at night. The frame, so slightly clad, was a sort of crystallization around me, and reacted on the builder. I did not need to go outdoors to take the air, for the atmosphere within had lost none of its freshness.

• • •

I was seated by the shore of a small pond, about a mile and a half south of the village of Concord, Massachusetts. I went to the woods because I wished to live deliberately, to front only the essential facts of life, and see if I could not learn what it had to teach, and not, when I came to die, discover that I had not lived. I wanted to live deep and suck out all the marrow of life, to live so sturdily and Spartan-like as to put to rout all that was not life; to cut a broad swath and shave close; to drive life into a corner and reduce it to its lowest turns, and if it proved to be mean, why, then to get the whole and genuine meanness of it and publish it to the world; or, if it was sublime, to know it by experience.

• • •

My nearest neighbor was a mile distant. I had my horizon, bounded by woods, all to myself. It was as solitary

where I lived as on the prairies. It was as much Asia or Africa as New England. I had, as it were, my own sun and moon and stars, and a little world all to myself. At night there was never a traveler who passed my house or knocked at my door, more than if I were the first or last man. I believe men are generally still a little afraid of the dark, though the witches are all hung, and Christianity and candles have been introduced.

• • •

It is remarkable how easily and insensibly we fall into a particular route, and make a beaten track for ourselves. I had not lived there a week before my feet wore a path from my door to the pond-side. The surface of the earth is soft and impressible by the feet of men, and so with the paths which the mind travels. How worn and dusty, then, must be the highways of the world; how deep the ruts of tradition and conformity! I did not wish to take a cabin passage, but rather to go before the mast and on the deck of the world, for there I could best see the moonlight amid the mountains.

• • •

I learned this, at least, by my experiment: that if one advances confidently in the direction of his dreams and endeavors to live the life which he has imagined, he will meet with a success unexpected in common hours. In proportion, as he simplifies his life, the laws of the universe will appear less complex and solitude will not be solitude, nor poverty poverty, nor weakness weakness. If you have built castles in the air, your work need not be lost; that is where they should be. Now put the foundations under them.

• • •

However mean your life is, meet it and live it; do not shun it and call it hard names. It looks poorest when you

are richest. The fault-finder will find faults even in paradise.

• • •

I left Walden on September 6, 1847. I left the woods for as good a reason as I went there. Perhaps it seemed to me that I had several more lives to live, and could not spare any more time for that one.

From

THE BIG BEAR OF ARKANSAS

By T.B. (Thomas Bangs) Thorpe

T. B. Thorpe wrote his famous American tall tale, *The Big Bear of Arkansas,* in 1841, and it quickly became the most famous tall tale of the pre-Civil War Southwest, and later became a favorite with storytellers throughout the country. The storyteller here is a braggart from Arkansas, who corrals a group of listeners on board the Mississippi River steamboat, *Invincible,* heading north from New Orleans, and tells his favorite story of a bear (or b'ar as he calls it) hunt. His story, however far-fetched, delights and entertains.

BIG BEAR: *(Enters, takes a seat and puts his feet up comfortably on another chair.)* **Strangers, how are you? I come from the State of Arkansas, the creation state, the finishing-up country, a state where the sile runs down to the center of the earth and government gives you a title to every inch of it. It's a state without a fault, and a state where the season for hunting bar is generally all year round, and the hunts take place about as regular. I read in history that varmints have their fat season and their lean season. That is not the case in Arkansas, feeding as they do upon the spontenacious production of the sile. They have one continued fat season the year round. They inhabit the neighborhood of my settlement, one of the prettiest places on old Mississippi. Let me just give you an idea of a hunt in which the greatest bar was killed that ever lived, *none excepted,* an old fellow that I hunted for two or three years.**

On a fine fall day, long time ago, I was trailing about for bar, and what should I see but fresh marks on the sassafras trees, about eight inches above any in the forests that I knew of. Now, the bar, you know, bites the bark and wood at the highest point from the ground they can reach, and you can tell by the marks the length of the bar to an inch. Says I, of these marks I saw, "Them marks is a hoax, or it indicates the longest bar that was ever grown." But I went on a ways and saw the same marks, at the same height, and I knew the thing lived! The conviction came home to my soul like an earthquake. Says I, "Here is something a-purpose for me. That bar is *mine*, or I give up the hunting business!"

Well, strangers, the first fair chase I ever had with that big crittur, I saw him no less than three distinct times at a distance. The dogs run him over eighteen miles and broke down. My horse gave out and I was as nearly used up as a man can be. That a bar runs at all is puzzling, but how this

one could tire down and bust up a pack of hounds and a horse that were used to overhauling everything they started after in no time, was past my understanding. And he done it over and over again!

That bar finally got so sassy, he used to help himself to a hog off my premises whenever he wanted one. Well, missing that bar so often took hold of my vitals and I wasted away. I would see that bar in everything I did. *He hunted me,* like a devil, which I began to think he was! While in this fix, I made preparations to give him a last brush and be done with it. I started at sunrise and to my great joy, found him in open country, very leisurely ascending a hill. Wasn't he a beauty, though! I loved him like a brother. On he went until he come to a tree, the limbs of which formed a crotch about six feet from the ground. Into this crotch he got and seated himself, the dogs yelling all around it, and there he sat, eyeing them as quiet as a pond in low water. Then a greenhorn friend of mine that I'd brought along, reached shooting distance before me and blazed away, hitting the crittur in the center of his forehead. The bar shook his head as the ball struck it, and then walked down from that tree as gently as a lady would from a carriage. 'Twas a beautiful sight to see him do that. He was in such a rage that he seemed to be as little afraid of the dogs as if they had been sucking pigs. Then the way his eyes flashed, why, the fire of them would have singed a cat's hair. In fact, that bar was in a *wrath all over!*

I came up, and taking deliberate aim as a man should do, at his side, just back of his foreleg, if *my gun did not snap,* call me a coward and I won't take it personal! Yes, it snapped! But the bar leaped over the ring formed by the dogs, and giving a fierce growl, was off, the pack in full cry of him, and he outrun them all! I was more than ever

convinced that I was hunting the devil himself.

I went home that night and took to my bed. I grew as cross as a bar with two cubs and a sore tail. I determined to catch that bar, go to Texas, or die, and I made my preparations accordin'. I had the pack shut up and rested. I took my rifle to pieces and iled it. I then told my neighbors that on Monday morning I would start that bar and bring him home with me, or they might divide my settlement among them, the owner having disappeared.

Well, on the morning previous to the great day of my hunting expedition, I went into the woods near my house, taking my gun, just from habit, and there, sitting down also from habit, what should I see, getting over my fence, but the bar! Yes, the old varmint was within a hundred yards of me and the way he walked over that fence, he loomed up like a black mist, he seemed so large, and he walked right towards me. I took deliberate aim and fired. Instantly, the varmint wheeled, gave a yell, and walked through that fence like a falling tree through a cobweb. I started after, but was tripped up by my inexpressibles which either from habit, or the excitement of the moment, were about my heels, and before I gathered myself up, I heard the old varmint groaning in a thicket nearby like a thousand sinners, and by the time I reached him, he was a corpse.

Strangers, it took six of us to put the carcass on a mule's back, and old long-ears waddled under the load as if he was foundered in every leg of his body. Now, with a common whopper of a bar, he would have trotted off and enjoyed himself.

T'would astonish you to know how big that bar was! I made a bedspread of his skin, and the way it used to cover my mattress and leave several feet on each side to tuck up, would have delighted you. It was, in fact, a creation bar,

and if it had lived in Samson's time and had met him in a fair fight, it would have licked him in the twinkling of a dice-box!

But strangers, I never like the way I hunted and *missed* him. There's something curious about it I could never understand. I never was satisfied at his giving in so easy at last. Perhaps he heard of my preparations to hunt him the next day, so he just come in to save his wind to grunt with in dying – but that ain't likely. My private opinion is that that bar was the *unhuntable bar and died when his time come!*

SPEECH ON WOMEN'S RIGHTS

By Sojourner Truth

A slave, born in the late eighteenth century, who eventually won her freedom in 1827, Sojourner Truth became a traveling preacher and lecturer who took up the causes of both abolition and women's rights. While she never learned to read or write, others took note of her unforgettable testimonies. When Sojourner was present at the Women's Rights Convention in Akron, Ohio, in 1851, the men who attended threatened to overwhelm the arguments of the women speaking out for their rights. Sojourner listened for a while and then stood up, a tall, stately woman who commanded the attention of everyone through her striking presence and the strong power of her voice. The president of the meeting, Frances Gage, later wrote down her words.

SOJOURNER TRUTH: Well, chilern, where there is so much racket, there must be somethin' out o' kilter. I think that 'twixt the negroes of the South and the women at the North, all talkin' 'bout rights, the white men will be in a fix pretty soon. But what's all this here talkin' 'bout?

That man over there say that woman needs to be helped into carriages, and lifted over ditches, and to have the best place everywhere. Nobody ever helps me into carriages, or over mud puddles, or gives me any best place! And a'nt I a woman? Look at me! Look at my arm! *(She bares her right arm to the shoulder, showing her muscle.)* **I have ploughed and planted and gathered into barns, and no man could head me! And a'n't I a woman? I could work as much and eat as much as a man – when I could get it – and bear the lash as well! And a'n't I a woman? I have borne thirteen chilern, and seen 'em 'most all sold off to slavery, and when I cried out with my mother's grief, none but Jesus heard me! And a'n't I a woman?**

Then they talks 'bout this thing in the head – what do they call it? *(Leans forward, as if waiting for an answer from the audience.)* **Intellect! That's it, honey. What's that got to do with women's rights or negroes' rights? If women want any rights more'n they's got, why don't they just take 'em, and not be talkin' about it?**

S'pose a man's mind hold a quart, and a woman's don't hold but a pint? If her pint is full, it's as good as his quart! That little man in black there, he say women can't have as much rights as men, 'cause Christ wan't a woman! Whar did your Christ come from? *(Louder)* **Whar did your Christ come from? From God and a woman! Man had nothin' to do with him!**

If the first woman God ever made was strong enough to turn the world upside down all alone, these women together here ought to be able to turn it back, and get it

right side up again! And now they is asking to do it, the men better let 'em!

I'm 'bleeged to ye for hearin' on me, and now ole Sojourner han't got nothin' more to say.

From

THE ADVENTURES OF HUCKLEBERRY FINN

By Mark Twain

In his novel of the outcast boy, Huck Finn, and runaway slave, Jim, journeying down the Mississippi River on a raft, Mark Twain has captured the essence of man's search for freedom and adventure. The two meet with all sorts of adventures and fall into the hands of two scheming rascals, The Duke and The King, who, to save their own necks, eventually sell Jim into slavery again. When Huck learns that Jim is a prisoner on a nearby farm, he vents his frustration and helplessness in a lonely spot along the river bank.

HUCK: After all this long journey, and after all we done for them scoundrels, here it's all come to nothing! Everything all busted up and ruined because they had the heart to serve Jim such a trick as that and make him a slave again all his life, and amongst strangers, too, for forty dirty dollars! *(He paces a moment, thoughtfully.)*

Well, maybe it'd be a thousand times better for Jim to be a slave at home where his family is, as long as he's got to be a slave. I better write a letter home to Tom Sawyer and tell him to tell Miss Watson where he is. *(Pacing)* **No, that won't work. Miss Watson would be mad and disgusted at his rascality and ungratefulness for leaving her and she'd sell him straight down the river again, and even if she didn't, everybody naturally would despise Jim and he'd feel ornery and disgraced. And then, think of me! It would get all around that Huck Finn helped Jim get his freedom, and if I was ever to see anybody from that town again I'd be ready to get down and lick his boots for shame. That's just the way: a person does a low-down thing, and then he don't want to take no consequences of it. Thinks as long as he can hide, it ain't no disgrace. That's my fix exactly!**

Here is the plain hand of Providence slapping me in the face and letting me know my wickedness is being watched all the time from up there in heaven, whilst I'm stealing a poor old woman's slave that hadn't ever done me no harm! Well, I can't help it! I was brung up wicked!

(He is suddenly very frightened.) **I...I... I got to pray! I got to see if I can't try to quit being the kind of a boy I am and be better.** *(He kneels down and closes his eyes tightly, clasps his hands together and makes a great effort to pray, then drops his hands and sighs.)* **The words won't come! It ain't no use to try and hide it from Him! Nor from me, neither.** *(He scrambles to his feet.)* **I know why the words won't come. It's because my heart ain't right. I ain't square! I'm playing**

double! I'm letting on to give up sin, but away inside of me I'm holding on to the biggest one of all. You can't pray a lie!

(He paces again.) **Well, I will write the letter and then see if I can pray.** *(He takes a scrap of paper and a pencil from his pocket, sits down, and writes carefully.)* **"Miss Watson, your runaway Jim is down here two mile below Pikesville, and Mr. Phelps has got him and he will give him up for the reward if you send. Huck Finn." There! Now then! I feel good and all washed clean of sin for the first time in my life! Just think how near I come to being lost and going to hell! And all because Jim and me come on this long trip down the river...** *(His expression slowly changes)* **...Jim and me...** *(He puts the letter down)* **...just Jim and me all the time, in the day and in the nighttime, sometimes moonlight, sometimes storms, and we a-floating along, talking and singing and laughing. I just don't see no place to harden me against him. I can see him standing my watch on top of his'n, 'stead of calling me, so I could go on sleeping, and see how glad he was when I come back out of the fog, and when I come to him again in the swamp, up there where the feud was, and suchlike times, and he would always call me honey and pet me, and do everything he could think of for me, and how good he always was – and the time I saved him by telling the men we had smallpox aboard and he was so grateful and said I was the best friend he ever had in the world, and the only one he's got...** *(He looks at the letter, then slowly picks it up. His hand trembles.)* **All right, then, I'll go to hell!** *(He tears up the letter.)*

I'll take up wickedness again, which is in my line, being brung up to it! And for a starter, I'll go to work and steal Jim out of slavery again, and if I can think up anything worse, I'll do that, too; because as long as I'm in, and in for good, I might as well go the whole hog!

Scenes for Two Performers

From

LITTLE WOMEN

By Louisa May Alcott

Little Women, completed by Louisa May Alcott in 1869, has remained a family classic loved by young and old for its warmth, affection, and domestic humor. Using herself and her own three sisters as models, Alcott created Meg, Jo, Beth, and Amy March, who lived in Concord, Massachusetts in the 1860s. Next door to the March family lived Mr. Laurence and his grandson, Laurie, who was a devoted, spirited friend and confidant to the March girls, especially Jo, who always called him Teddy, "her boy." As they grew older, Jo sensed that Laurie had a deeper interest in her than simple friendship, and she left home for a year to devote herself to her writing and hopefully allow time for Laurie, who was attending college, to forget her. When she returned, however, Laurie eagerly welcomed her, and she was delighted to see him again. In this scene, they take a walk in the garden, arm and arm.

CHARACTERS: JO MARCH, LAURIE

LAURIE: **Oh, by the way, Jo, you may thank Hannah for saving the cake for tonight's dessert from destruction. I saw it going into the house, and if she hadn't defended it manfully, I'd have had a pick at it!**

JO: *(Laughing)* **I wonder if you will ever grow up, Teddy.**

LAURIE: **I'm doing my best, ma'am, but can't get much higher, I'm afraid, as six feet is about all men can do in these degenerate days.**

JO: *(Gives him a friendly poke, then looks at him critically.)* **Is it the fashion now to be hideous? To make your head look like a scrubbing brush and wear orange gloves, and clumping square-toed boots? I'm not aristocratic, but I do object to being seen with a person who looks like a young prizefighter.** *(She sits on a garden bench with two bright pillows at each end.)*

LAURIE: *(With mock stuffiness)* **This unassuming style promotes study. That's why we adopt it.** *(Sits beside her.)* **By the way, Jo, that little fellow Parker is really getting desperate about Amy. He talks of her constantly, writes poetry, and moons about in a most suspicious manner. He'd better nip his little passion in the bud, hadn't he?**

JO: **Of course he had! We don't want any more marrying in this family for years to come! I could hardly bear to lose Meg. Mercy on us, what are the children thinking of?**

LAURIE: *(In a fatherly tone)* **It's a fast age and I don't know what we're coming to, ma'am. You are a mere infant, but you'll go next, Jo, and we'll be left lamenting.**

JO: **Don't be alarmed, I'm not one of the agreeable sort. Nobody will want me, and it's a mercy, for there should always be one old maid in a family.**

LAURIE: *(After a moment)* **You won't give anyone a chance. You won't show the soft side of your character, and if a fellow**

gets a peep at it by accident and can't help showing that he likes it, you treat him as Mrs. Gummidge did her sweetheart, throw cold water over him and get so thorny no one dares touch or look at you.

JO: I don't like that sort of thing. I'm too busy to be worried with such nonsense as lovers and other absurdities. And I think it's dreadful to break up families so.

LAURIE: *(With a shake of his head)* **Mark my words, Jo, you'll go next.** *(JO picks up one of the pillows and flings it at him. He laughs.)* **Oh, come Jo, do you suddenly hate your boy and want to fire pillows at him?**

JO: *(With an impish grin)* **How many bouquets have you sent Miss Randal this week?**

LAURIE: Miss Randal? Not one, upon my word. She's engaged. I never cared two pins for her anyway. Now then! *(Throws pillow back at her.)*

JO: Well, I'm glad of it. That was always one of your foolish extravagances, sending flowers and things to girls for whom you don't care two pins.

LAURIE: Sensible girls, for whom I *do* care whole papers of pins won't let me send them flowers and things, so what can I do? My feelings must have a *went*!

JO: Then if you must have a *went*, Teddy, go and devote yourself to one of the pretty modest girls whom you do respect and not waste your time with the silly ones.

LAURIE: *(Seriously)* **Do you really advise it?**

JO: Yes, I do. *(Rising)* **Now, go inside and sing to me. I'm dying for some music and I always like yours.**

LAURIE: *(Catching hold of her apron string)* **I'd rather stay here, thank you.**

JO: Well, you can't! *(She tugs at the apron string, but he keeps his hold.)* **I thought you hated to be tied to a woman's apron string.**

LAURIE: Ah, that depends on who wears the apron! *(He suddenly takes her hand.)*

JO: *(Seeing the change in his manner)* **No, Teddy, please don't.**

LAURIE: I will, and you must hear me. It's no use, Jo, we've got to have it out, and the sooner the better for both of us.

JO: *(Seeing that he is serious; patiently)* **Say what you like then. I'll listen.**

LAURIE: *(Drawing her back to the bench beside him, he looks at her intently, clears his throat, and begins.)* **I've loved you ever since I've known you, Jo. Couldn't help it. You've been so good to me. I've tried to show it, but you wouldn't let me. Now I'm going to make you hear and give me an answer, for I can't go on so any longer.**

JO: *(Gently)* **I wanted to save you this. That's why I went away.**

LAURIE: I know you did, but girls are so queer, you never know what they mean. They say no when they mean yes and drive a man out of his wits just for the fun of it.

JO: ***I*** **don't. I never wanted to make you care for me so.**

LAURIE: It was like you, but it was no use. I hoped you'd love me, though I'm not half good enough... *(He chokes a little, turns away a moment, then collects himself.)*

JO: Yes, you are. You're a great deal too good for me, and I'm grateful to you and so proud and fond of you, I don't see why I can't love you as you want me to. I've tried, but I can't change the feeling, and it would be a lie to say I do when I don't.

LAURIE: *(Taking her hands in his, looking at her earnestly)* **Really, truly, Jo?**

JO: Really, truly, dear. *(He drops her hands and buries his head in his arms.)* **Oh, Teddy, I'm sorry, so desperately sorry. I could kill myself if it would do any good. I wish you wouldn't take it so hard. I can't help it. You know it's impossible for people to make themselves love other people if they don't.** *(She pats his shoulder.)*

LAURIE: *(Not raising his head, his voice muffled)* **They do sometimes.**

JO: But I don't believe it's the right sort of love, and I'd rather not try it. *(He is silent.)* **You'll learn to love someone else, like a sensible boy, and forget all about me.**

LAURIE: *(Raising his head)* **I *can't* love anyone else and I'll *never* forget you, Jo, never, never!** *(He stamps his foot in his passion.)* **I don't believe you've got any heart!**

JO: *(Almost a sob)* **I wish I hadn't!**

LAURIE: *(Taking her hand again, urgently)* **Jo, everyone expects it, and I can't get on without you. Say you will love me and let's be happy!**

JO: *(With great tenderness, but firmly)* **I can't say yes truly, so I won't say it at all. You'll see that I'm right by and by and thank me for it.**

LAURIE: I'll be hanged if I do! *(He jumps up and turns away, pacing.)*

JO: Yes, you will! And besides, I don't believe I shall ever marry. I'm happy as I am and love my liberty too well to be in any hurry to give it up for any mortal man.

LAURIE: I know better! You think so now, but there'll come a time when you *will* care for somebody, and you'll love him tremendously and live and die for him. I know you will, it's your way, and I shall have to stand by and see it! *(He flings his hat to the ground.)*

JO: *(Jumping up, losing her patience)* **Yes, I will live and die for him if he ever comes and makes me love him in spite of myself, and you must do the best you can! I've done my best, but you won't be reasonable, and it's selfish of you to keep teasing me for what I can't give. I shall always be fond of you, very fond indeed, as a friend, but I'll never marry you, and the sooner you believe it, the better for both of us. So now!**

LAURIE: *(He looks at her steadily.)* **You'll be sorry someday, Jo!** *(He starts off.)*

JO: *(Alarmed)* **Teddy! Where are you going?**

LAURIE: To the devil! *(He strides out.)*

JO: *(Takes a few steps after him, then stops.)* **Oh, how can girls like to have lovers and then refuse them? I think it's dreadful!** *(She starts off in the opposite direction, looking after him once, then going on.)*

From

PRIDE AND PREJUDICE

By Jane Austen

Pride and Prejudice, Jane Austen's delightful comedy of manners first published in 1813 gives us one of literature's most spirited young heroines, Elizabeth Bennet. In this scene, Elizabeth receives an unexpected call from Lady Catherine de Bourgh, the haughty aunt of Mr. Darcy, a young gentlemen in whom Elizabeth has considerable interest. Lady Catherine requests that they walk in the garden where they may have a private conversation.

CHARACTERS: ELIZABETH BENNET, LADY CATHERINE DE BOURGH

(LADY CATHERINE and ELIZABETH enter, walking slowly, and stopping occasionally on their way.)

LADY CATHERINE: You can be at no loss, Miss Bennet, to understand the reason of my journey hither. Your own heart, your own conscience, must tell you why I come.

ELIZABETH: *(Astonished)* **Indeed, you are mistaken, madam. I have not been at all able to account for the honor of seeing you here.**

LADY CATHERINE: *(Angrily)* **Miss Bennet, you ought to know that I am not to be trifled with. But, however insincere *you* may choose to be, you shall not find *me* so. My character has ever been celebrated for its sincerity and frankness, and in a cause of such moment as this, I shall certainly not depart from it. A report of a most alarming nature reached me two days ago. I was told that not only your sister was on the point of being most advantageously married, but that you would, in all likelihood, be soon afterwards united to my own nephew, Mr. Darcy. Though I know it must be a scandalous falsehood, and though I would not injure him so much as to suppose the truth of it possible, I instantly resolved on setting off for this place, that I might make my sentiments known to you.**

ELIZABETH: *(Taken aback and speaking with astonishment and disdain)* **If you believed it impossible to be true, I wonder you took the trouble of coming so far. What could your ladyship propose by it?**

LADY CATHERINE: At once to insist upon having such a report universally contradicted.

ELIZABETH: *(Coolly)* **Your coming to Longbourn to see me and my family will be rather a confirmation of it, if, indeed, such a report is in existence.**

LADY CATHERINE: **If! Do you pretend to be ignorant of it? Has it not been industriously circulated by yourselves? Do you not know that such a report is spread abroad?**

ELIZABETH: **I never heard that it was.**

LADY CATHERINE: **And can you likewise declare that there is no foundation for it?**

ELIZABETH: **I do not pretend to possess equal frankness with your ladyship. You may ask questions which I shall not choose to answer.**

LADY CATHERINE: **That is not to be borne! Miss Bennet, I insist on being satisfied. Has my nephew made you an offer of marriage?**

ELIZABETH: **Your ladyship has declared it to be impossible.**

LADY CATHERINE: **It ought to be so. It must be so, while he retains the use of his reason. But your arts and allurements may, in a moment of infatuation, have made him forget what he owes to himself and to all his family. You may have drawn him in.**

ELIZABETH: **If I have, I shall be the last person to confess it.**

LADY CATHERINE: **Miss Bennet, do you know who I am? I have not been accustomed to such language as this. I am almost the nearest relation he has in the world, and am entitled to know all his dearest concerns.**

ELIZABETH: **But you are not entitled to know *mine*, nor will such behavior as this ever induce me to be explicit.**

LADY CATHERINE: **Let me be rightly understood. This match, to which you have the presumption to aspire, can never take place. Mr. Darcy is engaged to my daughter. Now, what have you to say?**

ELIZABETH: **Only this, that if he is so, you can have no reason to suppose he will make an offer to me.**

LADY CATHERINE: *(After a slight pause)* **The engagement between them is of a peculiar kind. From their infancy, they have been intended for each other. It was the favorite**

wish of his mother as well as of hers. While in their cradles, we planned the union, and now, at the moment when the wishes of both sisters would be accomplished in their marriage, to be prevented by a young woman of inferior birth, of no importance in the world, and wholly unallied to the family! Do you pay no regard to the wishes of his friends, to his tacit engagement with Miss de Bourgh? Are you lost to every feeling of propriety and delicacy? Have you not heard me say that from his earliest hours he was destined for his cousin?

ELIZABETH: Yes, I had heard it before, but what is that to me? If there is no other objection to my marrying your nephew, I shall certainly not be kept from it by knowing that his mother and aunt wished him to marry Miss deBourgh. You both did as much as you could in planning the marriage. Its completion depended on others. If Mr. Darcy is neither by honor nor inclination confined to his cousin, why is not he to make another choice? And if I am that choice, why may I not accept him?

LADY CATHERINE: Because honor, decorum, prudence, nay, interest, forbid it! Yes, Miss Bennet, interest, for do not expect to be noticed by his family or friends if you wilfully act against the inclinations of all. You will be censured, slighted, and despised by everyone connected with him. Your alliance will be a disgrace; your name will never even be mentioned by any of us.

ELIZABETH: These are heavy mistortunes. But the wife of Mr. Darcy must have such extraordinary sources of happiness necessarily attached to her situation, that she could, upon the whole, have no cause to repine.

LADY CATHERINE: Obstinate, headstrong girl! I am ashamed of you! Let us sit down. *(They both sit down on a bench.)* **You are to understand, Miss Bennet, that I came here with the determined resolution of carrying my purpose; nor will I**

be dissuaded from it. I have not been used to submit to any person's whims. I have not been in the habit of brooking disappointment.

ELIZABETH: That will make your ladyship's situation at present more pitiable, but it will have no effect on me.

LADY CATHERINE: I will not be interrupted! Hear me in silence. My daughter and my nephew are formed for each other. They are descended on the maternal side from the same noble line, and on the fathers' from respectable, honorable, and ancient, though untitled families. Their fortune on both sides is splendid. They are destined for each other by the voice of every member of their respective houses. If you were sensible of your own good, you would not wish to quit the sphere in which you have been brought up.

ELIZABETH: In marrying your nephew I should not consider myself as quitting that sphere. He is a gentleman; I am a gentleman's daughter. So far we are equal.

LADY CATHERINE: True, you are a gentleman's daughter. But who was your mother? Who are your uncles and aunts? Do not imagine me ignorant of their condition.

ELIZABETH: Whatever my connections may be, if your nephew does not object to them, they can be nothing to you.

LADY CATHERINE: Tell me, once for all, are you engaged to him?

ELIZABETH: *(After a pause in which she is obviously unwilling to make answer)* **I am not.**

LADY CATHERINE: Ah! And will you promise me never to enter into such an engagement?

ELIZABETH: I will make no promise of the kind.

LADY CATHERINE: Miss Bennet, I am shocked and astonished. I expected to find a more reasonable young woman. But do not deceive yourself into a belief that I will ever recede. I shall not go away till you have given me the assurance I require.

ELIZABETH: *(Rising and walking a little away from the bench)*

And I certainly never shall give it. I am not to be intimidated into anything so wholly unreasonable. Your ladyship wants Mr. Darcy to marry your daughter, but would my giving you the wished-for promise make their marriage at all more probable? Supposing him to be attached to me, would my refusing to accept his hand make him wish to bestow it on his cousin? Allow me to say, Lady Catherine, that the arguments with which you have supported this extraordinary application have been as frivolous as the application was ill-judged. You have widely mistaken my character if you think I can be worked on by such persuasions as these. How far your nephew might approve of your interference in his affairs I cannot tell; but you have certainly no right to concern yourself in *mine*. I must beg, therefore, to be importuned no farther on the subject.

LADY CATHERINE: You are, then, resolved to have him?

ELIZABETH: I have said no such thing. I am only resolved to act in that manner which will, in my own opinion, constitute my happiness, without reference to you, or to any person so wholly unconnected with me.

LADY CATHERINE: You refuse, then, to oblige me. You refuse to obey the claims of duty, honor, and gratitude. You are determined to ruin him in the opinion of all his friends, and make him the contempt of the world.

ELIZABETH: Neither duty, nor honor, nor gratitude has any possible claim on me in the present instance. No principle of either would be violated by marriage with Mr. Darcy. And with regard to the resentment of his family or the indignation of the world, if the former were excited by his marrying me, it would not give me one moment's concern, and the world in general would have too much sense to join in the scorn.

LADY CATHERINE: And this is your final resolve! Very well, I shall now know how to act. Do not imagine, Miss Bennet,

that your ambition will ever be gratified. I came to try you. I hoped to find you reasonable, but depend upon it, I will carry my point. I take no leave of you. I send no compliments to your mother. You deserve no such attention. I am most seriously displeased! *(She sweeps out. ELIZABETH watches her leave with a mixture of indignation and concern.)*

From

JANE EYRE

By Charlotte Brontë

Charlotte Brontë's beautiful romance novel, *Jane Eyre,* published in 1847, relates the story of Jane Eyre, orphaned as a young child, placed with a cruel aunt, educated at a strict school, and finally situated as a governess at Thornfield Hall. There Jane and her employer, Edward Rochester, fall in love and plan a wedding, but the ceremony is tragically interrupted by the shocking relevation that Rochester has a wife, living, but an incurable lunatic. Devastated, Jane leaves Thornfield, finds refuge with the Rivers family, and later learns that she is an heiress to her uncle's fortune. St. John Rivers wants to marry her, but Jane has never forgotten Rochester and feels compelled to return to Thornfield. Obeying an irresistible summons she cannot comprehend, she goes back, only to find the hall a charred ruin. She learns that Rochester's wife died in the fire and that he had tried to save her. He now lives at Ferndean, blind and crippled. Jane travels to Ferndean and convinces the housekeeper, Mary, to let her see Rochester. Shakily holding a tray with candles and a glass of water, she enters the room where he sits despondently before the hearth, his head bowed forward and one arm hidden inside his coat. For a moment, the sight of him, so lonely and worn, nearly overcomes her.

CHARACTERS: JANE EYRE, EDWARD ROCHESTER

ROCHESTER: *(Raises his head slightly, hearing her enter.)* **Mary? Give me the water, Mary. I am thirsty.**

JANE: *(Sets the tray on a table beside his chair and hands him the glass.)* **Here, sir.**

ROCHESTER: *(Starts, holding the glass without drinking.)* **This is you, Mary, is it not?**

JANE: *(Struggling to control her voice)* **Mary is in the kitchen.**

ROCHESTER: *(Lowers the glass to the table and reaches out with his hand, but not seeing her, cannot touch her.)* **Who is it? Who is it? Answer me! Speak again!**

JANE: Will you have a little more water, sir? I spilt half of what was in the glass.

ROCHESTER: *Who* is it? Who speaks? That voice...

JANE: Mary knows I am here. I came only this evening.

ROCHESTER: Great God! What delusion has come over me? What sweet madness has seized me? *(He continues to reach out, blindly.)*

JANE: No delusion, no madness. Your mind, sir, is too strong for delusion, your health too sound for frenzy.

ROCHESTER: Is it only a voice? I cannot see, but I must feel, or my heart will stop and my brain burst! *(He gropes in the air; she stops his wandering hand and holds it in both of hers.)* **Her fingers! Her small, slight fingers! If so, there must be more of her!** *(He frees his hand and takes her by the arm, then draws her to him.)* **Is...is it Jane?**

JANE: She is here. God bless you, sir! I am glad to be so near you again.

ROCHESTER: *(Holding her tightly to him)* **Jane Eyre! Jane Eyre!**

JANE: My dear master, I have found you. I am come back to you.

ROCHESTER: I cannot be so blest, after all my misery. It is a dream, such dreams as I have had at night when I have clasped her once more to my heart, as I do now, and kissed

her, as thus... *(Kisses her)* **...and felt that she loved me, and trusted that she would not leave me again.**

JANE: Which I never will, sir, from this day.

ROCHESTER: Never will, says the vision? But I always woke and found it an empty mockery, and I was desolate and abandoned, my life dark, lonely, hopeless, my soul athirst and forbidden to drink, my heart famished and never to be fed. Gentle, soft dream, nestling in my arms now, you will fly, too, but kiss me before you go.

JANE: *(Kissing his eyes and sweeping his unruly hair from his brow)* **There, sir!**

ROCHESTER: It *is* you! You *are* come back to me, and you do not lie dead in some ditch, under some stream? You are not a pining outcast among strangers?

JANE: No, sir. I am an independent woman now.

ROCHESTER: Independent! What do you mean, Jane?

JANE: My uncle in Madeira is dead and he left me five thousand pounds. I am quite rich, sir, and now, I will be your nurse, your companion, to read to you, to walk with you, sit with you, wait on you, to be eyes and hands to you. Cease to look so melancholy, my dear master. You shall not be left desolate so long as I live. *(She hesitates.)* **Unless...you object.**

ROCHESTER: No, no, Jane, you must stay with me. I cannot give up this joy! I have so little left in myself, I must have you. But you...you...cannot always be my nurse, Jane. You are young. You must marry some day.

JANE: I don't care about being married.

ROCHESTER: You should care. If I were what I once was, I would try to make you care, but...a sightless block! And on this arm... *(He draws his crippled arm from inside his coat.)* **...I have no hand. It is a mere stump, a ghastly sight!**

JANE: It is a pity to see it, and your eyes, and the scar of fire across your forehead. I may be in danger of loving you too well and making too much of you because of these

wounds. *(Rising, becoming cheerful)* **It is time someone undertook to rehumanize you. Have you a pocket-comb about you, sir?**

ROCHESTER: What for?

JANE: *(Looking among the articles on the table)* **Just to comb out this shaggy mane, for I see you are being metamorphosed into a lion, or something of that sort.**

ROCHESTER: Am I hideous, Jane?

JANE: *(Finding a comb and applying it to his hair)* **Very, sir. You always were, you know.**

ROCHESTER: *(Relishing her attention and the change in her manner)* **Humph! The wickedness has not been taken out of you, wherever you have sojourned.**

JANE: I have been with good people, far better than you, a hundred times better people, possessed of ideas and views you never entertained in your life, quite more refined and exalted.

ROCHESTER: *(Almost shouting)* **Who the deuce have you been with?**

JANE: If you twist in that way, you will make me pull the hair out of your head. Now then, you are redd up and made decent.

ROCHESTER: Jane! Who have you been with?

JANE: You must wait till tomorrow. To leave my tale half told will be a sort of security that I shall appear at your breakfast table to finish it. And I will bring you an egg at least, to say nothing of fried ham.

ROCHESTER: You mocking changeling, fairy-born and human-bred! You make me feel as I have not felt these twelve months. If Saul could have had you for his David, the evil spirit would have been exorcised without the aid of the harp.

JANE: Now I'll leave you. I have been traveling these last three days, and I am tired. Good night. *(She kisses him gently, grasps his hand, and slowly goes out, full of the confidence* *that she has found her happiness again.)*

ROCHESTER: Jane...good night. *(He watches after the sound of her leaving.)* **How can it be that Jane is with me, and says she loves me? Will she not depart as suddenly as she came? Tomorrow...?** *(His voice trembles with his hope and love.)* **Jane...my Jane Eyre!**

From

WUTHERING HEIGHTS

By Emily Brontë

In *Wuthering Heights*, Emily Brontë's passionate, romantic novel published in 1847, her wild and provocative heroine, Catherine Earnshaw, sets herself apart from most heroines through her unfathomable and tragic love for Heathcliff, an untamed and untaught orphan brought into the Earnshaw family by Catherine's father, and eventually forced into the role of a servant by Catherine's brother. Catherine and Heathcliff have grown up together, devotedly inseparable. In this scene, set in the kitchen of Wuthering Heights, the Earnshaw family home on the moors of England, Ellen, the housekeeper, sometimes called Nelly, is seated on a bench by the hearth, busy with handwork. Catherine, who has known her from childhood and seeks to confide in her when she pleases, now peers in from the doorway.

CHARACTERS: CATHERINE EARNSHAW, age 22, young mistress of Wuthering Heights; ELLEN DEAN, the housekeeper, sometimes called Nelly.

CATHERINE: Are you alone, Nelly?

ELLEN: Yes, Miss.

CATHERINE: *(Enters, looking disturbed and anxious. She seems about to speak, then sighs and turns away.)* **Where's Heathcliff?**

ELLEN: About his work in the stable, I suppose. He was here but a moment ago, but he has gone out. *(She glances to one side, then returns to her work.)*

CATHERINE: Oh, dear! Nelly, I'm very unhappy!

ELLEN: That's a pity. You're hard to please. So many friends and so few cares, and you can't make yourself content!

CATHERINE: *(Kneeling at her feet)* **Nelly, will you keep a secret for me?**

ELLEN: Is it worth keeping?

CATHERINE: Yes, it worries me, and I must let it out! Today, Edgar Linton has asked me to marry him, and I've given him an answer. Now, before I tell you whether it was a consent or a denial, you tell me which it ought to have been.

ELLEN: If you have accepted him, what good is it discussing the matter? You have pledged your word and you cannot retract it.

CATHERINE: But say whether I should have done so!

ELLEN: Do you love Mr. Edgar?

CATHERINE: Who can help it? Of course, I do!

ELLEN: And why do you love him?

CATHERINE: Well, because he is handsome and pleasant to be with, and he is young and cheerful, and because he loves me, and will be rich, and I shall like to be the greatest woman of the neighborhood, and I shall be proud of having such a husband.

ELLEN: Now, say *how* you love him.

CATHERINE: I love the ground under his feet, and the air over his head, and everything he touches, and every word he says. I love all his looks and all his actions and him entirely and altogether. There now!

ELLEN: There are several other handsome, rich young men in the world, handsomer, possibly, and richer than he is. What should hinder you from loving them?

CATHERINE: I've seen none like Edgar!

ELLEN: You may see some, and Edgar won't always be handsome and young, and he may not always be rich.

CATHERINE: He is now, and I have only to do with the present. Now tell me if I have done right.

ELLEN: Perfectly right, if people be right to marry only for the present. And now, let me hear what you are unhappy about. Your brother will be pleased. Mr. Edgar's parents will not object, I think, and you will escape from a disorderly, comfortless home into a wealthy, respectable one. You love Edgar and he loves you. So, what is the obstacle to your happiness?

CATHERINE: *(Striking her forehead and then her heart)* **Here and here! In whichever place the soul lives – in my soul and in my heart, I'm convinced I'm wrong!**

NELLY: That is very strange, Miss.

CATHERINE: It's my secret, but if you will not mock me, I'll give you a feeling of how I feel. *(Sits beside her, her hands clasped together.)* **Nelly, do you ever dream queer dreams?**

NELLY: Yes, now and then.

CATHERINE: So do I. I've dreamt in my life dreams that have stayed with me ever after and changed my ideas. They've gone through and through me, like wine through water, and altered the color of my mind. Oh, if I were in heaven, Nelly, I should be extremely miserable!

NELLY: Because you are not fit to go there. All sinners would be miserable in heaven.

CATHERINE: But I dreamt once that I was there and I was miserable because heaven did not seem to be my home, and I broke my heart with weeping to come back to earth, and the angels were so angry that they flung me out into the middle of the heath on the top of Wuthering Heights, where I woke sobbing for joy. Don't you see, Nelly, I've no more business to marry Edgar Linton than I have to be in heaven, and if my brother had not brought Heathcliff so low, I shouldn't have thought of it. It would degrade me to marry Heathcliff now. *(ELLEN starts, looking up suddenly as if she heard something.)*

CATHERINE: What is it?

ELLEN: I thought I heard something at the door...

CATHERINE: *(Paying her no heed)* **Heathcliff shall never know how I love him because he's more myself than I am. Whatever our souls are made of, his and mine are the same, and Linton's is as different as a moonbeam from lightning or frost from fire. But Heathcliff has no notion of these things. He does not know what being in love is.**

ELLEN: I see no reason that he should not know, as well as you, Miss. And if you are his choice, he'll be the most unfortunate creature that ever was born! As soon as you become Mrs. Linton, he loses friend and love and all! Have you considered how you'll bear the separation, and how he'll bear to be quite deserted in the world?

CATHERINE: Deserted? Separated? Who is to separate us? Every Linton on the face of the earth might melt into nothing before I could consent to forsake Heathcliff. I shouldn't be Mrs. Linton were such a price demanded! He'll be as much to me as he has been all his lifetime. Edgar must shake off his antipathy and tolerate him, at least. He will when he learns my true feelings towards him. Nelly, I see now, you think me a selfish wretch, but did it never strike you that if Heathcliff and I married, we

should be beggars? If I marry Edgar Linton, I can aid Heathcliff to rise and place him out of my brother's power.

NELLY: With your husband's money, Miss Catherine? You'll find him not so pliable as you calculate, and though I'm hardly a judge, I think that's the worst motive you've given yet for being the wife of young Linton.

CATHERINE: It is not! It is the best! My great miseries in this world have been Heathcliff's miseries, and I watched and felt each from the beginning. My great thought in living is himself. If all else perished and he remained, I should still continue to be, and if all else remained and he were annihilated, the Universe would turn to a mighty stranger. I should never seem a part of it. My love for Edgar is like the foliage in the woods. Time will change it as winter changes the trees; but my love for Heathcliff resembles the eternal rocks beneath, a source of little visible delight, but necessary. Nelly, I *am* Heathcliff! He is always – always in my mind, not as a pleasure, any more than I am always a pleasure to myself, but as my own being, so don't talk of our separation again.

ELLEN: If I can make any sense out of your nonsense, Miss, it only goes to convince me that you are ignorant of the duties you undertake in marrying, or else that you are a wicked, unprincipled girl. Trouble me with no more secrets. I'll not promise to keep them!

CATHERINE: You'll keep this one!

ELLEN: No, I'll not promise! But I will tell you, Miss, that I believe Heathcliff was there in the chimney corner a moment ago.

CATHERINE: *(Jumping to her feet)* Here? He overheard us?

ELLEN: How could he help it? It was when you said that it would degrade you to marry him that I heard a noise...

CATHERINE: Oh, Nelly! Where did he go? What did I say? I've forgotten! Was he vexed at my bad humor this afternoon?

Oh, tell me what I've said to grieve him? *(She rushes to the outside door and flings it open.)* **Heathcliff!** *(She runs out, screaming.)* **Heathcliff! Heathcliff!**

From

A MARRIAGEABLE GIRL

By Anton Chekov

Anton Chekhov is known for his stories and plays of nineteenth century Russian life, with emphasis on what he termed "life's trifles" or the everyday problems and pleasures of simple people. This story, written in 1903, a year before Chekhov's death, concerns a young woman's decision to do something meaningful in her life, regardless of the sacrifice. Nadya Shumin is twenty-three and engaged to be married, but she has doubts about her future and shares her thoughts with Sasha, an artist friend and distant relation, who is in poor health and spends his summers with Nadya, her mother, and grandmother. It is a delightful evening in May and Nadya and Sasha are drinking tea on the porch of her home in a small country town.

CHARACTERS: NADYA, the marriageable girl; SASHA, her friend, an artist.

SASHA: *(Coughs now and then, and shivers in the warm night air.)* **So, everything is fine with you, Nadya?**

NADYA: Yes. You must stay with us until September, and the wedding. *(She looks off into the house.)*

SASHA: I suppose I will. What are you looking at?

NADYA: My mother. She looks very young from where I am sitting, but I know she's not young, and she's unhappy.

SASHA: In her own way your mother is a very good and kind woman, but she never changes. Neither does your grandmother. Nothing has changed in this house in twenty years.

NADYA: You have said all this before, Sasha. Every summer you say the same thing.

SASHA: And I will say it again! Everything here is preposterous, somehow, from lack of use. Nobody does anything. Your mother, your grandmother, they do nothing all day. And your betrothed, Andre Andreich, he does nothing!

NADYA: *(Laughing lightly)* **You are boring me. Can't you think of something new to talk about? And leave Andre out of it. You don't know him.**

SASHA: I know that he has no position, no definite business, and he loves to be idle. Let me tell you how this evening will progress after we have eaten dinner. It will be as it was last night and the night before that. Andre will play his violin and your mother will accompany him on the piano, and then talk of her belief in hypnotism. Then your grandmother will fuss at the servants, and then tell me for the hundredth time that I look terrible and should eat better. Then the clock will finally strike twelve and Andre will take his leave of you in the hall, and we will all yawn for the dozenth time and go off to bed.

NADYA: *(With a sad smile)* **It will be just as you say. And after I**

have gone to bed, I will lie awake a while, listening to the servants cleaning up, and then I will fall asleep, but before dawn sleep will leave me. I will sit up in bed, feeling frightened and vague and troubled, and I will say aloud, "My God, why am I so depressed!"

SASHA: I suppose that every bride-to-be feels this way.

NADYA: I didn't used to. I was happy, but now...

SASHA: Now you are not happy. I have seen this every day. If only you would listen to me! You should go away from here – go to school! Only enlightened, educated people are interesting. Leave this miserable place, Nadya! Show your mother and grandmother and Andre that this dull, immobile life bores you and you mean to change it. Or if not for them, at least prove this to *yourself!*

NADYA: *(Rises and turns away from him.)* **I can't leave, Sasha. I'm going to be married in September.**

SASHA: Bah! Is that what you really want?

NADYA: Andre loves me. He calls me his precious, his darling, his beautiful, and tells me how lucky he is to have me.

SASHA: So what? Those words can be found in any novel. Do you love him? How can you think of living here in this town with him, forever? I can't bear it for a month! No running water, no sewers, terrible food! Your grandmother's kitchen is filthy. The servants sleep on the floor with the cockroaches. Nothing has changed in twenty years!

NADYA: *(Desperately)* **But it *will* change! I'm to have a dowry with six fur coats. Andre and I will have a good house in Moscow Street, two-storied, with a polished floor of painted parquet, and a piano, and a stand for his violin, and a dining room with a buffet, and furniture covered in bright blue material, and a bathroom with running water, and...and...oh, God! How banal! How stupid it all is! Andre has hung a painting of a female nude, in a gold frame, on the wall of the reception room!** *(She buries her face in her hands.)*

SASHA: *(Drolly)* **I can just picture it.**

NADYA: And do you know what Andre said to me just the other day, after you had scolded him for not doing anything? He said, "My darling, he's right! Sasha is absolutely right! I *don't* do anything, and I *can't* do anything. It is against my nature to think of going into service. When I see a lawyer or a teacher, or a member of the Council, I have no thoughts of ever being like them. Oh, Mother Russia! How many of us indolent and useless beings do you carry on your back?" That's what he said to me, and he sees nothing wrong in it at all.

SASHA: Face it, Nadya. He has never done anything, and he never will. It is not in him.

NADYA: Oh, Sasha, what is happening to me? I have always dreamed of marriage, and now, I...I cannot marry Andre! I don't love him! What am I going to do?

SASHA: *(Taking her hand)* **It will be all right, Nadya.**

NADYA: *(Almost in a whisper)* **When you leave here, Sasha, take me with you!**

SASHA: *(Staring at her)* **Do you mean it?**

NADYA: Yes! I don't understand, but I know I must leave here, before it's too late.

SASHA: *(Breaking into a smile)* **Wonderful! Oh, this is splendid! We'll leave tomorrow!**

NADYA: *(Stepping back)* **Tomorrow? But...how...?**

SASHA: You will come with me to the station to see me off on the train. I will take your things in my trunk. I'll get your ticket, and you will go with me as far as Moscow. From there you will travel on alone to Petersburg, and go to school, and learn everything, and meet people, and change your whole life! Do you have a passport?

NADYA: *(Breathless)* **Yes.**

SASHA: I swear that you will not be sorry. When you overturn your life, everything will change, and all you leave behind

will be unnecessary. You must never forget that.

NADYA: Something new is going to open up to me! Oh, but can I go through with it?

SASHA: Yes! You can! You must! You will! My own dear heart, there is no other way!

NADYA: And you, Sasha? You will always be my friend. I will always be so obliged to you for caring about me this way.

SASHA: We will both turn our lives over. I have you to thank for helping me to leave so soon. I am dying here! But not a word to anyone. Go and pack your things. Tomorrow – you begin a new life.

NADYA: Tomorrow. *(She grasps his hands, then runs out.)*

From

THE MOONSTONE

By Wilkie Collins

In *The Moonstone*, published in 1868, Wilkie Collins gave his readers a new, believable detective in the character of Sergeant Cuff, a man who challenges all to a battle of wits and plays fair all the way. When a priceless Indian diamond, the Moonstone, is stolen and ends up in the quiet English Verinder estate, Sergeant Cuff is called in to investigate. However, his efficiency does not make him popular with the Verinder family or its venerable steward, Gabriel Betteredge, who is both fascinated and outraged by Cuff.

CHARACTERS: SERGEANT CUFF, a London detective; GABRIEL BETTEREDGE, a house-steward.

SCENE: CUFF, calm and pleasant, and BETTEREDGE, in control but not pleased, are on the veranda of the house.

CUFF: I have been through your rose garden, Mr. Betteredge. It has the right exposure here to the south and southwest. *(Obviously pleased)* **It is the right shape for a rosery. Nothing like a circle set in a square. Yes, yes, with walks between all the beds. But they oughtn't to be gravel walks. Grass walks are needed between your roses, sir. Gravel is too hard for them. That's a sweet bed of white and blush roses along the wall. They always mix well together, don't they?**

BETTEREDGE: *(Dryly)* **You seem to be fond of roses, Sergeant?**

CUFF: I haven't much time to be fond of anything, but when I have a moment's fondness to bestow, the roses get it. I began my life among them in my father's nursery garden, and I shall end my life among them, if I can. Yes, one of these days, please God, I shall retire from catching thieves and try my hand at growing roses. And there will be *grass* walks between *my* beds.

BETTEREDGE: It seems an odd taste, sir, for a man in your line of work.

CUFF: If you will look about you, which most people won't do, you will see that the nature of a man's taste is, most times, as opposite as possible to the nature of a man's business. Show me any two things more opposite from the other than a rose and a thief, and I'll correct my tastes accordingly.

BETTEREDGE: If you'll pardon me, sir, with regard to the missing diamond, as things are now, if I was in your place, I should be at my wit's end.

CUFF: If you were in my place, you would have formed an

opinion, and as things are now, any doubt you might previously have felt about your own conclusions would be completely set at rest. I haven't brought you out here to draw me like a badger. I have brought you out here to give you some information. I might have given it in the house, but doors and listeners have a knack of getting together, and in my line of life, we cultivate a healthy taste for the open air.

BETTEREDGE: Tell me the truth, sergeant. What do you suspect?

CUFF: I don't suspect. I know.

BETTEREDGE: You know? What?

CUFF: You will not like to hear this, Mr. Betteredge, but you asked for the truth. Your young lady, Miss Rachel Verinder, has stolen her own diamond.

BETTEREDGE: What!

CUFF: She has been in secret possession of the Moonstone from first to last, and she has taken the housemaid, Rosanna Spearman, into her confidence, because she has calculated on my suspecting Rosanna of the theft. There is the whole case in a nutshell.

BETTEREDGE: *(Angrily seizes CUFF by the collar.)* **Do you not know, Sergeant, that I have served this family for fifty years! Miss Rachel has climbed on my knees and pulled my whiskers, many and many a time when she was a child. Miss Rachel, with all her little faults, is the dearest and prettiest and best young mistress that ever an old servant waited on and loved!**

CUFF: *(Quietly)* **Then why does she hinder my work by not allowing me to search her room, when she knows I have searched all other rooms in the house? And why has she suddenly resolved to leave here and visit her aunt in Frizinghall, when I specifically told her that such an action would considerably obstruct my investigation?**

BETTEREDGE: I don't know! I don't understand her at all at the

moment! *(He releases CUFF.)* **Oh, sir, I beg your pardon. This whole business about the Moonstone has completely undone me.**

CUFF: *(Kindly)* **Don't distress yourself, Mr. Betteredge. In my line of life, if we were quick at taking offense, we shouldn't be worth salt to our porridge. If it's any comfort to you, collar me again. You don't in the least know how to do it, but I'll overlook your awkwardness in consideration of your feelings.**

BETTEREDGE: Sergeant Cuff, I stand firm to my belief in Miss Rachel. If you were Solomon in all his glory, and as wise as he was, and you told me that my young lady had mixed herself up in a mean and guilty plot, I should have but one thing to say to you: "You don't know her, and I do." And as for poor Rosanna Spearman, that unfortunate girl is a good girl, and I pity her heartily, and I hope you don't think she is concerned in the loss of the diamond.

CUFF: Rosanna Spearman is not in the slightest danger of getting into trouble. She is simply an instrument and will be held harmless for...for another person's sake.

BETTEREDGE: You mean my young lady! Oh, I wish to God the Moonstone had never found its way into this house!

CUFF: *(Gravely)* **So do I. But at the moment, your young lady is leaving this house, and she has got a traveling companion in her carriage. The name of that traveling companion is the Moonstone!**

BETTEREDGE: The Moonstone! I saw it when my young lady received it yesterday for her birthday. It is nearly as large as a plover's egg – and worth well more than twenty thousand pounds! The light that streamed from it was like the light of the harvest moon. When you looked down into the stone, you looked into a yellow deep that drew your eyes into it so that they saw nothing else! We set it in the sun and then shut the light out of the room, and it shone

awfully out of the depths of its own brightness. Miss Rachel was fascinated.

CUFF: And well she might be. I have learned something of its history – a famous gem in the native annals of India, said to have been set in the forehead of the four-handed Indian god who typifies the moon. Legend has it that Vishnu the Preserver breathed the breath of divinity on the diamond in the forehead of the moon-god, and commanded that it always be watched by three priests, night and day, to the end of the generations of man. The deity predicted certain disaster to the presumptuous mortal who laid hands on the sacred gem, and to all of his house and name who received it after him.

BETTEREDGE: *(Shuddering)* **It is a frightful legend, sir. How my young lady's wicked uncle came to be in possession of it, we do not know. Nor why he insisted on bequeathing it to her.**

CUFF: Why do you call Colonel Herncastle wicked?

BETTEREDGE: Because I know he was one of the greatest blackguards that ever lived! The man's character closed all the family doors against him, and I have heard it said that he got possession of the Moonstone by means he didn't dare acknowledge. There are three questions, Sergeant, that we must find answers for. Is the diamond the object of a conspiracy in India? If so, has that conspiracy followed the diamond from India to England? And if it has, did Colonel Herncastle purposely leave a legacy of trouble and danger to his family through the innocent medium of his niece, my young lady? All I know, sir, is that our quiet English house has been invaded and upset by this devilish Indian diamond, and now it is gone! And why my young lady should be accused of stealing it is more than I can understand! Why she should even want to possess it at all is more than I can fathom!

CUFF: This is a miserable world, Mr. Betteredge. Human life is

a sort of target. Misfortune is always firing at it and always hitting the mark. Collar me again, if it's any vent to your feelings, but understand me. I will do my duty and the Moonstone will be recovered and returned to its rightful owner and place. Now, I'd like to walk among your roses again. Your white musk roses, in particular. There it is, our old English rose holding up its head along with the best and newest of them! And you have so many of them. *(He wanders off.)*

BETTEREDGE: Roses! My young lady's reputation is at stake – and all he can think of is roses! *(He stalks out after CUFF.)*

From

THE GLORIOUS ADVENTURES OF TYL ULENSPIEGL

By Charles de Coster

Belgian author Charles de Coster published his epic novel, *The Glorious Adventures of Tyl Ulenspiegl*, in 1869. Set in the sixteenth century, the book traces the history of the Low Country people in their revolution against the religious persecution of King Philip II of Spain. Tyl Ulenspiegl, born in Flanders (today's Belgium), is not only a prankster and a wit, but a popular Flemish hero in his country's fight for liberation. While in his teens, Tyl is condemned to make a pilgrimage to Rome to seek ablution from the Pope for making a joke at the expense of the priests in his native village. On his journey to Rome, he must use his wits to earn his bread.

CHARACTERS: TYL ULENSPIEGL, HOSTESS OF AN INN.

TYL: *(TYL enters, poorly dressed, carrying a bag over his shoulder and using a stout walking stick.)* **How cold it is! How hungry and thirsty I am! And how empty my pockets are! Not a florin to my name.** *(Looking up)* **That wicked cloud has the look of a large watering pot, but it will not rain coins upon me. Nor that great idle horse-chestnut tree, living without doing anything! Why are there not florin trees? They would be lovely and quite useful to a poor fellow like me.** *(He suddenly ducks and dodges about, trying to shield his head with his bag.)* **Ouch! Hail! Ouch! Ouch! It's not my fault that I have no palace nor yet a tent to shelter my poor thin body! Ouch! Oh, the nasty hailstones! They're hard as bullets! No, it's not my fault if I am forced to drag my tatters about the world. Ouch! These hailstones are trying to force their way into my ears, like bad words. And my poor nose will soon be pierced through and can serve as a pepper-shaker! Oh, I am hungry! Empty belly, do not complain so loud! Oh, fortune, where are you hiding?** *(Looks up.)* **The hail stops! And here is the sun again. Good day to you, sun, my only friend, coming to dry me. And look here – an inn!** *(He stops as the HOSTESS bustles in with a small table and bench which she sets to one side.)* **And a hostess, smiling and charming to look at.** *(With a bow)* **Good morning, goodwife!**

HOSTESS: Good morning, young master. Do you wish to eat for your money?

TYL: Eat for my money? Yes! But for what sum can I eat here?

HOSTESS: You may eat at the baron's table for six florins *(She gestures to the table)* **or** *(Pointing off)* **the burgher's table for four, or the family table for two.**

TYL: The more money the better for me. *(He sits at the table.)* **The baron's table it is!**

HOSTESS: A wise choice, young master. *(She exits and returns immediately with a plate of food and a tankard of wine.)* **Enjoy your dinner.** *(She lingers.)* **Who are you, handsome young master? Where do you come from?**

TYL: *(Eating with great relish)* **I am a pilgrim from Flanders, a land where they sow the seed of illusions, wild hopes, and airy promises.**

HOSTESS: And where do you go, hungry pilgrim from Flanders?

TYL: To Rome, to speak to the Pope.

HOSTESS: La! The Pope! How brave you must be!

TYL: Not at all. I simply must ask him for remission of my so-called sins.

HOSTESS: How do you know the Pope will even see you?

TYL: I shall worry about that when I get to Rome. For now I see *you*, charming hostess of amber skin and eyes that glisten like pearls. Your hair is burnished gold and your cheeks like the choicest apples!

HOSTESS: *(Flattered, but not taken in)* **Your tongue is bold, young master. Eat well, and be silent!**

TYL: Oh, I shall eat very well for my money, just as you invited me. You can give me the six florins now.

HOSTESS: *(With a laugh)* **Are you mocking me? *You* will pay *me* six florins, and at once!**

TYL: *(Continuing to eat)* **My dear charming hostess, you don't have the face of a bad debtor. On the contrary, I see in your lovely face such good faith and so much love for your neighbor, that you would sooner pay me eighteen florins than refuse me the six that you owe me. Such lovely eyes! They are like the sun shining on me, causing my amorous yearnings to rise higher than weeds in a neglected garden.**

HOSTESS: *(Still cheerful)* **Your madness and your weeds have nothing to do with me. Pay me at once and then you must go.**

TYL: Go? If I go, I'll never see you again. Come, my dear, pay me now, for I've earned the six florins well by the hard labor

of my jawbones. And when you give me the coins, I will give you a kiss in return. *(He tries to snatch her hand.)*

HOSTESS: *(Dodging away)* **Oh, you nasty villain!** *(Laughs.)* **Be happy that I fed you and asked for nothing more. Go, before my husband wakes up!**

TYL: *(Chasing her around the table)* **A husband, have you? Then I will be a gentle creditor. Only give me *one* florin that I may ease my future hunger and thirst.**

HOSTESS: *(Tossing him a coin)* **Oh, here, you bad boy! Now, will you kindly go?**

TYL: To go kindly would be to go *toward* you, my dear. To leave your fairy face and your shining eyes would be to go *unkindly*. If you'll let me stay here with you, I'll eat for no more than a florin a day.

HOSTESS: *(Exasperated)* **Must I take a stick to you?**

TYL: Oh, take mine! *(Offers her his stick.)*

HOSTESS: *(Taking the stick)* **Gladly, if it will help you on your way.** *(Still laughing, she swings at him, chasing him off. Their laughter is heard offstage, then TYL returns, with his stick, and picks up his bag.)* **Such a delightful hostess! To her health and good nature!** *(Drains the tankard dry.)* **I have eaten well. I have a florin in my pocket. My wits have saved me for another day, and I thank God I still have them. On to Rome, Ulenspiegl! The Pope awaits.** *(Looking up)* **And the sun is still shining!** *(He strides off.)*

From

NICHOLAS NICKLEBY

By Charles Dickens

In Charles Dickens' novel, *Nicholas Nickleby*, the young man, Nicholas, often has some strange, but humorous conversations with his mother, a goodhearted, chatty woman who concerns herself with everything about her. In this scene, a rather remarkable occurrence leads Mrs. Nickleby to call her son to tea for his counsel and advice.

CHARACTERS: NICHOLAS NICKLEBY, a young man; MRS. NICKLEBY, his mother.

SCENE: The parlor of the Nickleby cottage at Bow. MRS. NICKLEBY is seated near a window, looking expectantly out. Beside her on a small table is a tea tray with a plate of cakes. NICHOLAS enters, kisses her on the cheek, and sits opposite her.

NICHOLAS: Mother, you haven't had your tea.

MRS. NICKLEBY: Oh, Nicholas, my dear, I am extremely anxious about something and it's very consoling to have a grown up son to put confidence in. Indeed, I don't know any use there would be in having sons at all, unless people could put confidence in them.

NICHOLAS: *(Pouring her tea)* **I am entirely at your service, Mother.**

MRS. NICKLEBY: Thank you, my dear. There was a lady in our neighborhood – speaking of sons puts me in mind of her - a lady in our neighborhood when we lived near Dawlish – I think her name was Rogers...if it wasn't Murphy...or was it Riffin?

NICHOLAS: Is it about her that you wish to speak to me?

MRS. NICKLEBY: About her? Good gracious, Nicholas, my dear, how can you be so ridiculous? But that was always the way with your poor dear papa. Always wandering, never able to fix his thoughts on any one subject for two minutes altogether. I can see him now, looking at me while I was talking to him, just as if his ideas were in a state of perfect conglomeration! Anybody who had come in upon us suddenly would have supposed I was confusing and distracting him instead of making things plainer.

NICHOLAS: I'm sorry, Mother, if I have inherited this unfortunate slowness of apprehension, but I'll do my best to understand you if you'll only go straight on.

MRS. NICKLEBY: Your poor papa! However, he has nothing

whatever to do with the gentleman in the next house, my dear.

NICHOLAS: I should suppose that the gentleman in the next house has as little to do with us, Mother.

MRS. NICKLEBY: There can be no doubt that he is a gentleman. He has the manners and the appearance of a gentleman, although he does wear smalls and gray worsted stockings. Of course, he may be proud of his legs. Indeed, I don't see why he shouldn't be. The Prince Regent was proud of his legs.

NICHOLAS: *(Calmly)* What about him?

MRS. NICKLEBY: Who? Oh, the gentleman in the next house! Well, the bottom of his garden joins the bottom of ours, and I have several times seen him sitting among his scarlet beans, or working in his hot beds. I used to think he stared rather, but I didn't take any particular notice of that, as we were newcomers and he might be curious to see what we were like. *(With a sigh)* But when he began to throw his cucumbers over our wall...

NICHOLAS: Throw his cucumbers over our wall!

MRS. NICKLEBY: *(Mildly)* Yes, my dear, his cucumbers, and other vegetables, likewise.

NICHOLAS: *(Not amused)* Confound his impudence! What does he mean by that?

MRS. NICKLEBY: *(Smiling, looking out the window)* I don't think he means it impertinently, my dear.

NICHOLAS: What? Vegetables flying at the heads of the family as they walk in their own garden, and not meant impertinently?

MRS. NICKLEBY: He must be a very foolish and inconsiderate man; at least, I suppose other people would think so. Still, his attentions are, to a certain extent, a flattering sort of thing, and although I should never dream of marrying again with a dear girl like your sister Kate still unsettled in life...

NICHOLAS: Surely, Mother, such an idea never entered your brain for an instant!

MRS. NICKLEBY: *(Somewhat peevishly)* **Bless my heart, my dear, isn't that precisely what I am saying, if you will only let me speak? Of course, I never gave it a second thought, and I am surprised and astonished that you should suppose me capable of such a thing! All I ask of you, Nicholas, my dear, is what step should I take to reject these advances, civilly and delicately, without hurting his feelings too much and driving him to despair? Suppose he was to do something rash to himself? Could I ever be happy again?**

NICHOLAS: *(Smiling to himself)* **Do you think, mother, that such a result would be likely to ensue from even the most cruel repulse?**

MRS. NICKLEBY: My dear, I don't know. I am sure there was a case in yesterday's paper about a French journeyman shoemaker who was jealous of a young girl who loved somebody else, and went and hid himself in a wood with a sharp-pointed knife! And when the girl was passing by that wood with a few friends, he rushed out at them and killed himself first and then killed all the friends and then her. no, no, he killed all the friends first, then her, and then himself, which is quite frightful to think of! Somehow or other there are always journeymen shoemakers who do these things in France. I don't know how it is. Something in the leather, I suppose.

NICHOLAS: But we are in England, mother, and the gentleman in the next house is not a shoemaker. What has he done? What has he said? You know there is no language of vegetables which converts a cucumber into a formal declaration of attachment.

MRS. NICKLEBY: Oh, my dear, he has done and said all sorts of things.

NICHOLAS: Are you sure there is no mistake on your part?

MRS. NICKLEBY: Mistake? My dear, do you suppose I don't know when a man is in earnest? Everytime he sees me at this window, he kisses one hand and lays the other upon his heart. Of course, it's very foolish of him to do so, and I dare say you'll say it's very wrong. But he does it very respectfully and very tenderly. Extremely tenderly! And then there are all those lovely presents which come pouring over the wall every day. We had one of the cucumbers at dinner yesterday, and I think of pickling the rest for next winter.

NICHOLAS: Mother...

MRS. NICKLEBY: And last evening, Nicholas, as I was walking in the garden, he called gently to me over the wall, in a voice as clear and musical as a bell, and proposed marriage and an elopement! So the question is, my dear, what am I to do?

NICHOLAS: My dear Mother, do what your better sense and feeling and respect for my father's memory would prompt. There are a thousand ways in which you can show your dislike of these preposterous attentions.

MRS. NICKLEBY: But, my dear, I don't . . .

NICHOLAS: Simply recall your age and condition in life, and your children, and you will see clearly that the gentleman is totally unworthy of serious thought. *(Glaring out the window)* **Absurd old idiot!**

MRS. NICKLEBY: *(Rising, patting her hair)* **Do you know, my dear, that an old and very dear friend of mine once predicted that when you were one and twenty, you would have more the appearance of my brother than my son?**

NICHLOLAS: Mother!

MRS. NICKLEBY: *(Suddenly peering out window)* **Why, bless my heart! It is nearly dusk, and a bad light to distinguish things in, and my eyes are not very good, but...upon my word! Nicholas, my dear, do look!**

NICHOLAS: *(Looking out)* **What, Mother?**

MRS. NICKLEBY: There! I believe I see another large cucumber at the foot of the garden wall! How can you possibly have any doubt of his earnest intentions? Just look! Another cucumber! *(NICHOLAS stares out the window in astonishment, then at his mother with an amused, hopeless expression.)*

From

OLIVER TWIST

By Charles Dickens

In Charles Dickens' novel, *Oliver Twist,* the young orphan, Oliver, becomes an unwilling member of a gang of pickpockets and thieves, headed by an old rascal called Fagin. One of the older members of his gang, a goodhearted girl called Nancy, sympathizes with Oliver. When the boy is rescued by a gentleman, Mr. Brownlow, who wishes to befriend him and help him, Fagin forces Nancy to kidnap Oliver to prevent him from telling about the gang. With Oliver back in Fagin's clutches, and apparently destined to become a thief and beggar, Nancy regrets her action and takes a dangerous step on his behalf. She goes to Brownlow's home where she meets Rose Maylie, Mr. Brownlow's ward, and tells her a startling story.

CHARACTERS: NANCY, a girl of the streets; ROSE MAYLIE, a young lady.

SCENE: The parlor of the Brownlow home. NANCY, dirty, carelessly dressed, and obviously very nervous, paces anxiously until ROSE enters. The contrast in appearance and manners of the two is striking.

NANCY: *(Tossing her head, carelessly)* **It's a hard matter to get to see you, lady. If I had taken offense and gone away, you'd have been sorry for it one day.**

ROSE: *(Gently)* **I am very sorry if anyone has behaved harshly to you. I am Rose Maylie. Please tell me why you wished to see me.**

NANCY: Oh, lady, if there were more like you, there would be fewer like me! There would!

ROSE: Please, sit down. If you are in any trouble, I shall be glad to help you if I can.

NANCY: Let me stand, and do not speak to me so kindly till you know me better...is that door shut?

ROSE: *(Backing away a step)* **Yes. Why?**

NANCY: Because I am about to put my life and the lives of others in your hands.

ROSE: *(Sitting down, alarmed)* **What do you mean?**

NANCY: I am the girl that dragged Oliver back to old Fagin on the night he went out with the books.

ROSE: You!

NANCY: Yes. I am the infamous creature you have heard of, that lives among thieves, and that never from the first moment I opened my eyes on London streets have known any better life or kinder words than they have given me!

ROSE: What dreadful things do you tell me?

NANCY: Thank heaven on your knees, dear lady, that you had friends to care for and keep you in your childhood, and

that you were never in the midst of cold and hunger and riot and drunkenness! The alley and the gutter were my cradle and they shall be my deathbed. But let me come to my business. I have stolen away from those who would surely murder me if they knew I was here, to tell you what I've overheard. *(She looks around furtively.)* **Do you know a man named Monks?**

ROSE: No.

NANCY: He knows you. Some time ago I overheard a conversation between him and Fagin. Monks had seen Oliver accidentally with two of our boys and recognized him to be the child he was looking for. He struck a bargain with Fagin, that if he could make Oliver a thief, he'd be paid a good sum of money.

ROSE: Make Oliver a thief! For what possible reason?

NANCY: He caught sight of my shadow on the wall as I listened in hope of finding out, and I had to get away quickly. But Monks came again last night and I listened again at the door. The first words I heard Monks say were these: "The only proofs of the boy's identity lie at the bottom of the river, and the old hag that received them from his mother lies rotting in her coffin."

ROSE: How strange!

NANCY: They laughed, and talked of his success in doing this. Then Monks went on to say that if he could gratify his hatred by taking the boy's life without bringing his own neck in danger, he would, but as he couldn't, he'd be on the watch for him, and if he ever took advantage of his birth and history, he might harm him yet. "In short, Fagin," he said, "you never laid such snares as I'll contrive for my young brother Oliver!"

ROSE: His brother!

NANCY: Those were his words. And more. When he spoke of you and said it seemed contrived by heaven against him that

Oliver should come into your hands, he laughed. Then he said there was some comfort in that, for what would you not give to know who Oliver really is!

ROSE: Who Oliver really is? What can this mean?

NANCY: I cannot say, lady. It is growing late and I have to reach home without being suspected of being on such an errand as this.

ROSE: *(Standing)* **But what can I do? To what use can I turn this message without you? Why do you wish to return to companions you paint in such terrible colors? If you repeat this information to a gentleman in the next room, you can be taken to some place of safety without half an hour's delay.**

NANCY: No, I must go back because...oh, how can I tell such things to an innocent lady like you? *(She hesitates.)* **I must go back because there is a man, the most desperate of them all, that I cannot leave.**

ROSE: But you have interfered in Oliver's behalf and come here at so great a risk! Surely, you might yet be saved from the misery you tell me of.

NANCY: *(Tearfully)* **No, lady, it is too late for me. I cannot leave him, I tell you. I cannot bring about his death.**

ROSE: Why should you do that?

NANCY: If I told others what I have told you, and it led to him being taken by the police, he would be sure to die. He is the boldest and has been so cruel!

ROSE: Is it possible that for such a man as this you can resign every future hope and the certainty of immediate rescue? It is madness!

NANCY: I don't know what it is. I only know it is so. I must go back, for I am drawn to him through every suffering and ill-usage. I should be this way even if I knew I would die by his hand at last.

ROSE: I should not let you go away like this.

NANCY: You should, and I know you will, lady. I have trusted in your goodness and forced no promise from you, as I might have done.

ROSE: But this mystery must be investigated, or how will its disclosure to me benefit Oliver?

NANCY: You surely have some kind gentleman about you that will hear it as a secret and advise you what to do.

ROSE: Yes. Mr. Brownlow. But where can I find you again?

NANCY: Will you promise to keep my secret strictly and come alone, or with the only other person that knows it, and will you promise that I shall not be watched or followed?

ROSE: I promise you, solemnly.

NANCY: Every Sunday night, from eleven until the clock strikes twelve, I will walk on London Bridge, if I am alive. *(She moves toward door.)*

ROSE: Please, stay another moment. Think once again. Will you return to this gang of thieves and to this man, when a word can save you? What fascination is it that draws you back?

NANCY: When such as I who have no certain roof but the coffin lid, set my rotten heart on any man and let him fill the place that has been a blank through all my wretched life, who can hope to cure me?

ROSE: Oh, do not close your heart against all my efforts to help you! I wish to serve you in some way.

NANCY: You would serve me best, if you could take my life at once. I have felt more grief to think of what I am tonight, than I ever did before. God bless you, sweet lady, and send as much happiness on your head as I have brought shame on mine! *(She rushes out.)*

ROSE : *(Looking after her)* **Poor Oliver! If anyone can save him, she can...and I know she will! I must tell Mr. Brownlow - and then we must wait until Sunday – and hope.** *(She exits.)*

From

A TALE OF TWO CITIES

By Charles Dickens

In Charles Dickens' novel, *A Tale of Two Cities,* the sinister Madame Defarge is remembered for her place in front of the guillotine where she sits watching and knitting as the executions are carried out. In this scene, Madame Defarge meets her match in the loyal English maidservant, Miss Pross, whose mistress, Lucie Manette, and her family, have just escaped Paris and the guillotine by the narrowest margin. Miss Pross is packing her bags and preparing to follow them to safety. Unknown to her, the evil Madame Defarge, is on her way to the house, unaware of the family's escape and intent upon condemning them. A unique request of the audience is to consider that while Madame Defarge actually speaks in English, one must imagine that she is speaking in French, and that neither Madame nor Miss Pross understands what the other is saying.

CHARACTERS: MISS PROSS, an English maidservant; MADAME DEFARGE, a French revolutionary.

MISS PROSS: *(Hastily throwing things into a bag)* **Here is everything ready at last. But stop! What am I doing? If I am seen going along the streets with a valise, will it not be the worst thing I could do to arouse suspicion? I should be stopped and questioned immediately.** *(She tosses the bag aside.)* **Oh, I haven't my wits about me, I am so worried, so frightened for my dear Lucie, my dear Ladybird, and her poor father, and her husband, and little Lucie! Oh, I am so frightened for all of them! If I ever get out of this cursed Paris, this cursed France, I shall never return! Never!** *(As she paces about the room, wringing her hands, MADAME DEFARGE enters quietly and stands watching her intently.)* **I must try to think clearly. There must be a way to...** *(Turning, she sees MADAME DEFARGE, and screams.)* **What's this? I didn't hear you knock, madam! Indeed, I'm sure you didn't knock, but brought yourself in here with no intention of knocking!**

MADAME DEFARGE: *(Sharply)* **The wife of Evremonde! Where is she? I must see her!**

MISS PROSS: **I don't understand your words, but I think I understand your meaning. You shall not see the people you have come to see if I can help it!**

MADAME: *(Measures MISS PROSS for a moment with her eyes and sees that she is quite determined.)* **I ask you again, woman, where is Madame Evremonde?**

MISS PROSS: **You might, from your appearance, be the wife of the devil. Indeed, you are closer to the devil than you may think! You shall not get the better of me! I am an Englishwoman!**

MADAME: *(Changing her tactics by softening her tone of voice)* **On my way to the executions where they reserve my chair and my knitting for me, I thought I would make my compli-**

ments to Madame Evremonde in passing. I wish to see her.

MISS PROSS: Don't lower your voice to me! I know your intentions are evil. You are my family's worst enemy! You would see them all killed by that dreadful guillotine! But I am their most devoted friend and servant, and you may depend upon it, I'll hold my own against you for their sakes!

MADAME: *(Impatiently)* **Come, come! It will do her no good to keep herself concealed from me. Good patriots will know what that means. If she mourns for her husband, if she sympathizes with him as he goes to the guillotine, then she is guilty and she will follow him there! Now let me see her!**

MISS PROSS: If those eyes of yours were windlasses, and I were an English four-poster, they shouldn't loose a splinter of me! No, you wicked woman, I am your match!

MADAME: *(Angrily)* **Stupid woman! Either tell her that I demand to see her, or stand out of the way and let me go to her!** *(She shakes her fist at MISS PROSS.)*

MISS PROSS: I little thought I should ever want to understand your nonsensical language, but I would give all I have, except the clothes that I wear, to know whether you suspect the truth. Do you know that they have escaped? Eh? Do you know that my ladybird's dear husband has been smuggled out of prison and is now in a coach with his family racing for the border? Eh? No, I don't think you do. And as long as you do not know it, the farther away they will be! *(As MADAME moves toward her, she stiffens and runs to a door at the side and stands in front of it.)* **I am a Briton! I am desperate! I don't care an English twopence for myself. I know that the longer I keep you here, the greater hope there is for my loved ones. My Lucie! Have I not brought her up from the time she was ten years old? Is she not the dearest one in the world to me? I'll not leave a handful of that hair upon your head if you lay a finger on me!** *(She is so agitated that she suddenly bursts into a sob.)*

MADAME: *(Takes this as a sign of weakness.)* **Ha! You poor wretch! What are you worth? A common, stupid servant! I will address myself to someone else.** *(Calling)* **Doctor Manette! Wife of Evremonde! Child of Evremonde! Any person but this miserable fool answer the Citizeness Defarge!** *(There is no answer. She listens, then, growing suspicious, runs about the room, throwing various doors open and looking in.)* **These rooms are empty! They are in disorder...there has been packing!** *(Facing MISS PROSS who stands firmly in front of her door)* **Let me look in that room behind you!**

MISS PROSS: You'll never get by me! Never! *(She spreads her arms wide in front of the door.)*

MADAME: If they are not in that room, they are gone, but they can be pursued and brought back. Let me look!

MISS PROSS: As long as you don't know if they are here or not, you are uncertain what to do, and you shall not know it if I can prevent you. You shall not leave here while I can hold you!

MADAME: I have been in the streets from my childhood. Nothing has ever stopped me, and you will not stop me! If I have to, I will tear you to pieces to get you away from that door! *(She moves toward MISS PROSS threateningly.)*

MISS PROSS: We are alone at the top of a high house in a solitary courtyard. We are not likely to be heard by anyone, and I pray for bodily strength to keep you here. Every moment you are here is another moment of safety for my Lucie! *(MADAME lunges at MISS PROSS, who immediately seizes her around the waist and holds her tightly. They struggle fiercely, neither getting the advantage. Suddenly, MADAME reaches into the front of her dress.)* **Now what are you doing? What! A pistol! No!** *(As MADAME pulls out the pistol, MISS PROSS frees one hand to strike at it. The pistol discharges with a deafening sound. MADAME screams, drops the pistol, then sinks to the floor. MISS PROSS lets her fall,* *staring down at her in horror. As MADAME does not move, MISS PROSS backs away from her.)* **It was your own fault, you wicked woman! It was all your doing!** *(She suddenly puts her hands to her ears.)* **What...what is the matter with me? I...I can't hear myself. I know I am talking, but I can't hear myself! Heaven help me! The pistol discharged so close to my ear. Have I gone deaf in a moment?** *(She hastily grabs up her cloak and bonnet.)* **But what does it matter if my darling and her dear ones are safe! And soon I will be with them. My dear Lucie! I am coming – and this wicked, wicked woman will never harm any of us again!** *(She rushes out of the room.)*

From

A TALE OF TWO CITIES

By Charles Dickens

In a time of terror and treason, when a starving and downtrodden people rise up against a decadent regime of oppression, certain innocent people go about their lives and create unforgettable stories of their own. In *A Tale of Two Cities*, Charles Dickens' historical novel set against the French Revolution, two of these quiet characters emerge in Sydney Carton, a drunken lawyer's clerk, and the beautiful Lucie Manette. Although his life has been degraded and purposeless, Carton loves Lucie passionately and hopelessly. One summer afternoon, he summons his nerve, resolves on a course of action, and calls on her at her home.

CHARACTERS: LUCIE MANETTE, SYDNEY CARTON.

SCENE: LUCIE is seated by a small table, busy with needlework. She has never been perfectly at ease in CARTON's presence. CARTON sits moodily in a chair nearby.

LUCIE: *(Watching him closely.)* **I fear you are not well, Mr. Carton.**

CARTON: No, but the life I lead, Miss Manette, is not conducive to health. What is to be expected of, or by, such profligates?

LUCIE: Is it not – forgive me, I have begun the question on my lips – a pity to live no better life?

CARTON: God knows it is a shame!

LUCIE: *(Looking gently at him)* **Then why not change it?**

CARTON: *(He turns away briefly, tears in his eyes and in his voice.)* **It is too late for that. I shall never be better than I am. I shall sink lower and be worse.** *(He leans on the table, covering his eyes with his hand.)* **Pray forgive me, Miss Manette. I break down before the knowledge of what I want to say to you. Will you hear me?**

LUCIE: If it will do you any good, Mr. Carton, if it would make you happier, it would make me very glad!

CARTON: God bless you for your sweet compassion! *(He looks up and speaks steadily.)* **Don't be afraid to hear me. Don't shrink from anything I say. I am like one who died young. All my life might have been.**

LUCIE: I am sure that the best part of it might still be. I am sure that you might be much, much worthier of yourself.

CARTON: Although in the mystery of my own wretched heart I know better, I shall never forget your words! If it had been possible, Miss Manette, that you could have returned the love of the man you see before you – self-flung away, wasted, drunken, poor creature of misuse as you know him to be – he would have been conscious this day and hour, in spite of his happiness, that he would

bring you to misery, bring you to sorrow and repentance, blight you, disgrace you, pull you down with him. I know very well that you can have no tenderness for me; I ask for none. I am even thankful that it cannot be.

LUCIE: Can I not save you, Mr. Carton? Can I in no way repay your confidence? I know you would say this to no one else. Can I turn it to no good account for yourself?

CARTON: To none. If you will hear me through a very little more, all you can ever do for me is done. *(She nods gently.)* **I wish you to know that you have been the last dream of my soul. In my degradation I have not been so degraded but that the sight of you with your father, and of this home made such a home by you, has stirred old shadows that I thought had died out of me. Since I knew you, I have been troubled by a remorse that I thought would never reproach me again, and have heard whispers from old voices impelling me upward, that I thought were silent forever. I have had unformed ideas of striving afresh, beginning anew, shaking off sloth and sensuality, and fighting out the abandoned fight. It is a dream that ends in nothing, but I wish you to know that you inspired it.**

LUCIE: Will nothing of it remain? O, Mr. Carton, think again! Try again!

CARTON: No, Miss Manette; all through it, I have known myself to be quite undeserving. And yet I have had the weakness to wish you to know with what a sudden mastery you kindled me, heap of ashes that I am, into fire – a fire, however, inseparable in its nature from myself, quickening nothing, lighting nothing, doing no service, idly burning away.

LUCIE: Since it is my misfortune to have made you more unhappy than you were before you knew me —

CARTON: Don't say that, for you would have reclaimed me, if

anything could. You will not be the cause of my becoming worse.

LUCIE: Can I use no influence to serve you? Have I no power for good with you at all?

CARTON: The utmost good that I am capable of now, I have come here to realize. Let me carry through the rest of my misdirected life the remembrance that I opened my heart to you, last of all the world; and that there was something left in me at this time which you could deplore and pity.

LUCIE: Which I entreated you to believe again and again, most fervently, with all my heart, was capable of better things, Mr. Carton! *(She is near tears.)*

CARTON: Entreat me to believe it no more, Miss Manette. I have proved myself, and I know better. I distress you; I draw fast to an end. Will you let me believe, when I recall this day, that the last confidence of my life was reposed in your pure and innocent breast, and that it lies there alone and will be shared by no one?

LUCIE: If that will be a consolation to you, yes.

CARTON: Not even by the dearest one ever to be known to you?

LUCIE: The secret is yours, not mine; and I promise to respect it.

CARTON: Thank you. And again, God bless you! *(He takes her hand to his lips, rises, and moves slightly away.)* **Be under no apprehension of my ever resuming this conversation by so much as a passing word. I will never refer to it again. In the hour of my death, I shall hold sacred the one good remembrance – and shall thank and bless you for it – that my last avowal of myself was made to you and that my name, and faults and miseries were gently carried in your heart. May it otherwise be light and happy!** *(Seeing that she weeps for him)* **Be comforted! I am not worth such feeling. An hour or two hence, and the low companions and low habits that I scorn but yield to, will render me less worth such tears as those, than any wretch who creeps long the streets. Be**

comforted! But within myself, I shall always be, towards you, what I am now, though outwardly I shall be what you have heretofore seen me. The last supplication but one I make to you is that you will believe this of me.

LUCIE: I will, Mr. Carton.

CARTON: My last supplication of all is this. It is useless to say it, I know, but it rises out of my soul. For you, and for any dear to you, I would do anything. If my career were of that better kind that there was any opportunity or capacity of sacrifice in it, I would embrace any sacrifice for you and for those dear to you. Try to hold me in your mind, at some quiet times, as ardent and sincere in this one thing. The time will not be long in coming, when new ties will be formed about you – ties that will bind you yet more tenderly and strongly to the home you so adorn – the dearest ties that will ever grace and gladden you. O Miss Manette, when the little picture of a happy father's face looks up in yours, when you see your own bright beauty springing up anew at your feet, think now and then that there is a man who would give his life to keep a life you love beside you! Farewell! God bless you! *(He leaves.)*

From

THE HISTORY OF TOM JONES, A FOUNDLING

By Henry Fielding

Henry Fielding was dubbed the "Father of the English novel" by Sir Walter Scott, and when *The History of Tom Jones, a Foundling* was published in 1749, it was essentially the first real comic novel of manners of his time. The story encompasses the mystery of Tom Jones' birth and his love of Sophia Western, a neighboring squire's daughter of good birth, beauty, and fortune. When Tom rescues Sophia from certain disaster on an unruly horse, he breaks his arm and is taken to the Western house to be cared for. Sophia learns of his interest in her from her maid, Mrs. Honour, for in those times a young lady's maid was often her only spy and confidant.

CHARACTERS: SOPHIA WESTERN, a young lady; MRS. HONOUR, her maid.

SCENE: SOPHIA's room where she is seated at a dressing table. MRS. HONOUR is combing and arranging her hair, while she holds a mirror.

SOPHIA: How does Mr. Jones do, Honour? My father gave orders that he was to be given every possible attention.

MRS. HONOUR: Oh, ma'am, to be sure he is, and such magnanimity I never saw before in such a pretty, charming creature! To have risked his life and limb in so bold and brave a manner, and he so handsome and young and heedless of his own self, ma'am!

SOPHIA: *(Smiling)* **Then you must certainly be in love with this young fellow, Honour.**

HONOUR: I, in love, ma'am? Upon my word, I assure you, I am not!

SOPHIA: But if you were, I see no reason that you should be ashamed of it. He is certainly a pretty fellow and of goodly speech, too, for when I thanked him for rescuing me and taking such good care of me, he answered: "If I have preserved you, madam, I am sufficiently repaid, for I promise you, I would have secured you from the least harm at the expense of a much greater misfortune to myself than I have suffered on this occasion." His misfortune, of course, was the breaking of his arm, poor creature!

HONOUR: *(Seeing how impressed with him her mistress is)* **Yes, ma'am, he is certainly well spoken and the most handsomest man I ever saw in my life. And as your ladyship says, I don't know why I should be ashamed of loving him, though he is my betters. To be sure, gentlefolks are but flesh and blood no more than us servants. And, as for Mr. Tom Jones, as your ladyship well knows, though Squire**

Allworthy has took him in and made a gentleman of him, he was not so good as myself at birth, for though I am a poor body, I am an honest person's child, and my father and mother were married, which is more than some people can say, as high as they hold their heads!

SOPHIA: With regard to the young gentleman's birth, those who can say nothing more to his disadvantage may as well be silent on that head, as I desire you will be for the future!

HONOUR: Oh, I'm sorry if I have offended your ladyship, but as for abusing Mr. Jones, I can call all of the servants in the house to witness that I have always taken his part. "For which of you," says I to the footmen, "would not be a bastard, if he could, to be made a gentleman of?" And, says I, "I am sure Mr. Jones is a very fine gentleman with the whitest hands, and is one of the sweetest temperdest, best naturedest men in the world!" And to be sure, I could tell your ladyship something else, but I am afraid it would offend you.

SOPHIA: I'm sure it would not. What could you tell me, Honour?

HONOUR: Nay, ma'am, to be sure, he meant nothing by it. Therefore, I would not have your ladyship be offended for the world!

SOPHIA: Tell me, Honour! I will know it this instant!

HONOUR: Why, ma'am, before this accident with the horse, he came into the room one day when I was at work, and there lay your ladyship's muff on a chair, and he put his hands into it! "La," says I, "Mr. Jones, you will stretch my lady's muff and spoil it!" But he still kept his hands in it and then he kissed it! To be sure, I hardly ever saw such a kiss in my life as he gave it!

SOPHIA: *(Hiding her delight by turning her face away from HONOUR)* **I suppose he did not know it was mine.**

HONOUR: Oh, he kissed it again and again and said it was the prettiest muff in the world. "La, sir," says I, "but you have

seen it a hundred times." "Yes, Mrs. Honour," cries he, "but who can see anything beautiful in the presence of your lady but herself?"

SOPHIA: Oh! He certainly did not know what he was saying!

HONOUR: And that's not all! But I do hope your ladyship won't be offended, for, to be sure, he meant nothing. *(She pauses, combing briskly.)*

SOPHIA: *(Impatiently)* **Well?**

HONOUR: Well, one day, as your ladyship was playing on the harpsichord, Mr. Jones was sitting in the next room, and methought he looked melancholy. "La," says I, "Mr. Jones, what's the matter? A penny for your thoughts," says I. "Why," says he, starting up as from a dream, "what can I be thinking of when that angel, your mistress, is playing?" And then he squeezed me by the hand. "Oh, Mrs. Honour," says he, "how happy will that man be!" And then he sighed, and his breath was as sweet as a nosegay! But, to be sure, he meant no harm by it! So I beg your ladyship will not mention a word, for he gave me a crown never to mention it, and made me swear upon a book, but I believe it was not the Bible.

SOPHIA: *(Flustered)* **Honour, I...I...if you will not mention this anymore to me, nor to anybody else, I will not betray you. I mean, I will not be angry, but I am afraid of your tongue. Why, my girl, will you give it such liberties?**

HONOUR: Nay, ma'am, I would sooner cut out my tongue than offend your ladyship! To be sure, I shall never mention a word to anybody!

SOPHIA: You must not, for it may come to my father's ears, and he would be angry with Mr. Jones, though I really believe, as you say, that he meant nothing. Indeed, I should be very angry myself if I imagined that he...for one moment... that he...

HONOUR: Nay, ma'am, I protest, I believe he meant nothing at

all. I thought he talked as if he was out of his senses!

SOPHIA: Well then, go on. You may mention anything you have not told me before.

HONOUR: Well, ma'am, you will pardon me if what I say now offends your ladyship, but you have asked for it. "Yes, Mrs. Honour," says Mr. Jones, " I am neither such a coxcomb, nor such a villain, as to think of her – that is you he is speaking of, ma'am – in any other delight but as my goddess. As such I will always worship and adore her while I have breath." Well, ma'am, I was in a passion with him myself, till I found he meant no harm. And, to be sure, I would sooner cut out my tongue than offend your ladyship!

SOPHIA: I am not offended, Honour. I'm sure he meant no harm. Not in the least. You may leave me now.

HONOUR: *(With a curtsy)* **I'll just see how the young gentleman is doing, ma'am, and if you should wish to know anything else, ma'am, just ring the bell.** *(She exits, with a knowing glance back at her mistress.)*

SOPHIA: *(Twirling a finger in her curls and smiling into the mirror)* **"My goddess!" says he. "And I will always worship and adore her while I have breath!"** *(She sighs and breaks into a smile of complete delight.)*

From

DIALOG BETWEEN FRANKLIN AND THE GOUT

By Benjamin Franklin

During his years in France (1776-1785), where he served as an agent for the new United States, Benjamin Franklin, always a prolific writer, created humorous little pieces for the entertainment of his friends. In this one, dated 1780, he makes himself a major character, suffering from gout and taking himself to task for getting too little exercise and enjoying too much food and drink.

CHARACTERS: BENJAMIN FRANKLIN, MADAM GOUT.

SCENE: FRANKLIN is seated in a chair with one leg propped on a stool. MADAM GOUT, representing his affliction, sits on the floor at his feet.

FRANKLIN: *(Groaning)* **Oh! Oh-h! What have I done to merit these cruel sufferings?**

MADAM GOUT: Many things. You eat and drink too freely! You indulge your legs in too much indolence.

FRANKLIN: *(Looking around for the source of the voice)* **Who is it that accuses me?**

MADAM GOUT: It is I, the Gout!

FRANKLIN: What! My enemy, in person?

MADAM GOUT: No, not your enemy.

FRANKLIN: But you are my enemy! You not only torment my body to death, you ruin my good name! You reproach me as a glutton and a tippler, but all the world that knows me will allow that I am neither the one or the other!

MADAM GOUT: The world may think as it pleases, but I very well know that the quantity of meat and drink proper for a man who takes a reasonable degree of exercise would be too much for another who never takes any!

FRANKLIN: Oh! I take as much exercise as I can, Madam Gout. You know my sedentary state, and on that account you might spare me a little, seeing it is not altogether my fault.

MADAM GOUT: Not a jot! If your situation in life is a sedentary one, your amusements and recreations should be active. Instead of gaining an appetite for breakfast by salutary exercise, you amuse yourself with books, pamphlets, or newspapers, which commonly are not worth reading. Yet you eat for breakfast four dishes of tea with cream, and one or two buttered toasts, with slices of salted beef, which are not things the most easily digested. Immediately after-

ward, you sit down to write at your desk, or converse with persons who apply to you on business. Thus the time passes till one, without any kind of bodily exercise. And what is your practice after dinner? You sit down to play chess for two or three hours! Wrapt in the speculations of this wretched game, you destroy your constitution! What can be expected from such a course of living, but a body replete with stagnant humors, ready to fall prey to all kinds of dangerous maladies, if I, the Gout, did not occasionally bring you relief by agitating those humors, and so purifying or dissipating them? So take that twinge! *(She makes a pass with her hands over his foot.)* **And that!**

FRANKLIN: Oh! Oh-h-h! Pray, Madam, a truce!

MADAM GOUT: No, sir! I will not abate a particle!

FRANKLIN: But it is not fair to say I take no exercise, when I do very often, going out to dine and returning in my carriage.

MADAM GOUT: That, of all imaginable exercises, is the most slight and insignificant, if you allude to a carriage suspended on springs. Providence has appointed few to roll in carriages, while he has given to all a pair of legs, which are machines infinitely more commodious and serviceable. Be grateful then and make a proper use of yours!

FRANKLIN: You grow tiresome!

MADAM GOUT: Oh, then I will be silent and continue my business. Take that! *(She makes more passes over his foot.)* **And that! And that!**

FRANKLIN: Oh-h-h! Oh-h-h! Very well! Talk on! Talk on!

MADAM GOUT: No, no, I have a good number of twinges for you tonight, and you may be sure of some more tomorrow.

FRANKLIN: I shall go distracted! How can you torment me so?

MADAM GOUT: I am your physician.

FRANKLIN: Oh-h-h! What a devil of a physician!

MADAM GOUT: How ungrateful you are to say so! Have I not saved you from palsy, dropsy, and apoplexy? One or the

other would have done for you long ago but for me.

FRANKLIN: I submit, and thank you for the past, but I entreat the discontinuance of your visits for the future. In my mind, one had better die than be cured so dolefully. Permit me to hint that I have not been unfriendly to you. I never call in physician or quack of any kind to attempt to cure you.

MADAM GOUT: As to quacks, I despise them! They may kill you, but cannot injure me. And, as to regular physicians, they are convinced that the Gout, in such a subject as you are, is no disease but a remedy. And why cure a remedy? Therefore, to business! *(Making another pass over his foot)* **Take that!**

FRANKLIN: Oh! Oh! Oh! For Heaven's sake, leave me! I promise never more to play at chess, but to take exercise daily and live temperately.

MADAM GOUT: I know you too well. You promise fair, but after a few months of good health, you will return to your old habits. Your fine promises will be forgotten like the forms of last year's clouds. But I will go, and leave you with the assurance of visiting you again at a proper time and place, for my object is your good, and I believe you are sensible now that I am your real friend.

FRANKLIN: Oh-h-h! I'm grateful I have no other friends like you!

From

THE SCARLET LETTER

By Nathaniel Hawthorne

Nathaniel Hawthorne's masterpiece, *The Scarlet Letter,* written in 1850, tells the story of Hester Prynne, a woman in the colony of Massachusetts in the 1640s, who, by an old colony law, is condemned to wear the letter A sewed onto her dress in token of having committed adultery and borne a child while in prison. She refuses to name the child's father or reveal that she has a husband she believes has deserted her. Hawthorne, in his own words, hoped to "achieve a novel that should evoke some deep lesson and should possess physical substance enough to stand alone." The story begins when Hester and her infant daughter are put on public display, that her shame, in the form of the scarlet letter A on her dress, may be an example to everyone in the town, a living sermon against sin. She bears the insults and humiliation alone. When she is returned to prison, she is exhausted and ill. A physician, Roger Chillingworth, who in reality is her long-lost husband, is admitted to the cell to attend her.

CHARACTERS: HESTER PRYNNE, a young woman; ROGER CHILLINGWORTH, an old man.

SCENE: HESTER lies on a pallet in her cell, her baby beside her. CHILLINGWORTH enters, speaking to the unseen jailor.

CHILLINGWORTH: Prithee, friend, leave me alone with my patient. Trust me, good jailer, you shall briefly have peace in your house, and I promise you, Mistress Prynne shall hereafter be more amenable to just authority than you may have found her heretofore. *(He turns to HESTER who watches him, breathing heavily.)* **My old studies in alchemy and my sojourn, for above a year past, among a people well versed in the kindly properties of simples, have made a better physician of me than many that claim the medical degree.** *(He mixes a powder with water in a cup and hands it to HESTER.)* **I have learned many new secrets in the wilderness, and here is one of them, a recipe that an Indian taught me. Drink it! It may be less soothing than a sinless conscience. That I cannot give thee. But it will calm the swell and heaving of thy passion, like oil thrown on the waves of a tempestuous sea.**

HESTER: *(Slowly takes the cup, watching him earnestly.)* **I have thought of death, have wished for it, would even have prayed for it, were it fit that such as I should pray for anything. Yet, if death be in this cup, I bid thee think again, ere thou beholdest me quaff it. See! It is even now at my lips.**

CHILLINGWORTH: Drink, then. Does thou know me so little, Hester Prynne? Are my purposes wont to be so shallow? Even if I imagine a scheme of vengeance, what could I do better for my object than to let thee live, than to give thee medicines against all harm and peril of life, so that this burning shame may still blaze upon thy bosom? *(He touches the scarlet letter A on her dress; she draws back.)* **If**

thee would but speak the man's name, that, and thy repentance, might avail to take the scarlet letter off thy breast.

HESTER: Never! It is too deeply branded. Ye cannot take it off. And would that I might endure his agony, as well as mine!

CHILLINGWORTH: Then thy child is not to have a father?

HESTER: My child must seek a heavenly Father; she shall never know an earthly one.

CHILLINGWORTH: Live, therefore, and bear about thy doom with thee, in the eyes of men and women, in the eyes of him whom thou didst call thy husband, in the eyes of yonder child! *(HESTER drinks, and seems the better for it. She hands the cup back to him. He sits in a chair beside her bed.)* **Hester, I ask not wherefore, nor how, thou hast fallen in the pit, or say, rather, thou hast ascended to the pedestal of infamy on which I found thee. The reason is not far to seek. It was my folly, and thy weakness. I, a man of thought, the bookworm of great libraries, a man already in decay, having given my best years to feed the hungry dream of knowledge, what had I to do with youth and beauty like thine own? Misshapen from my birth hour, how could I delude myself with the idea that intellectual gifts might veil physical deformity in a young girl's fantasy! Men call me wise. If sages were ever wise in their own behoof, I might have foreseen all this. I might have known that, as I came out of the vast and dismal forest, and entered this settlement of Christian men, the very first object to meet my eyes would be thyself, Hester Prynne, standing up, a statue of ignominy, before the people. Nay, from the moment when we came down the old church steps together, a married pair, I might have beheld the bale-fire of that scarlet letter blazing at the end of our path!**

HESTER: Thou knowest that I was frank with thee. I felt no love, nor feigned any.

CHILLINGWORTH: True, it was my folly! But up to that epoch

of my life, I had lived in vain. The world had been so cheerless! My heart was a habitation large enough for many guests, but lonely and chill, and without a household fire. I longed to kindle one! It seemed not so wild a dream, old as I was, and sombre as I was, and misshapen as I was, that the simple bliss, which is scattered far and wide for all mankind to gather up, might yet be mine. And so, Hester, I drew thee into my heart, into its innermost chamber, and sought to warm thee by the warmth which thy presence made there!

HESTER: *(Quietly)* I have greatly wronged thee. But thou didst send me here to Boston ahead of thee, and in these two years since, I have not seen thee nor had tidings of thee until now.

CHILLINGWORTH: We have wronged each other. Mine was the first wrong, when I betrayed thy budding youth into a false and unnatural relation with my decay. Therefore, as a man who has not thought and philosophized in vain, I seek no vengeance, plot no evil against thee. Between thee and me, the scale hangs fairly balanced. But, Hester, the man lives who has wronged us both! Who is he?

HESTER: Ask me not! *(Firmly)* Thou shalt never know!

CHILLINGWORTH: Never? Never know him? Believe me, Hester, there are few things, whether in the outward world, or to a certain depth, in the invisible sphere of thought, few things hidden from the man who devotes himself earnestly and unreservedly to the solution of a mystery. Thou mayest cover up thy secret from the prying multitude. Thou mayest conceal it, too, from the ministers and magistrates, even as thou didst this day, when they sought to wrench the name out of thy heart and give thee a partner on thy pedestal. But, as for me, I come to the inquest with other senses than they possess. I shall seek this man, as I have sought truth in books; as I have sought gold in alchemy.

There is a sympathy that will make me conscious of him. I shall see him tremble. I shall feel myself shudder, suddenly and unawares. Sooner or later, he must needs be mine! Thou wilt not reveal his name? Not the less he is mine. He bears no letter of infamy wrought into his garment, as thou dost; but I shall read it on his heart. Yet fear not for him! Think not that I shall interfere with Heaven's own method of retribution, or, to my own loss, betray him to the gripe of human law. Neither do thou imagine that I shall contrive aught against his life; no, nor against his fame, if, as I judge, he be a man of fair repute. Let him live! Let him hide himself in outward honor, if he may! Not the less, he shall be mine!

HESTER: *(Bewildered and frightened)* **Thy acts are like mercy, but thy words interpret thee as a terror!**

CHILLINGWORTH: One thing, thou that wast my wife, I would enjoin upon thee. Thou has kept the secret of thy paramour. Keep, likewise, my secret. There are none in this land that know me. Breathe not, to any human soul, that thou didst ever call me husband! Here, on this wild outskirt of the earth, I shall pitch my tent. I find here a woman, a man, a child, amongst whom and myself there exists the closest ligaments. No matter whether of love or hate; no matter whether of right or wrong! Thou and thine, Hester Prynne, belong to me. My home is where thou art, and where he is. But betray me not!

HESTER: Wherefore doest thou desire it? Why not announce thyself openly and cast me off at once?

CHILLINGWORTH: It may be because I will not encounter the dishonor that besmirches the husband of a faithless woman. It may be for other reasons. Enough, it is my purpose to live and die unknown. Let, therefore, thy husband be to the world as one already dead, and of whom no tidings shall ever come. Recognize me not, by word, by

sign, by look! Breathe not the secret, above all, to the man. Shouldst thou fail me in this, beware! His fame, his position, his life, will be in my hands. Beware!

HESTER: I will keep thy secret, as I have his.

CHILLINGWORTH: Swear it!

HESTER: I swear!

CHILLINGWORTH: And now, Mistress Prynne, I leave thee alone with thy infant and the scarlet letter. *(He rises, with a strange smile.)* **How is it, Hester? Doth thy sentence bind thee to wear the token in thy sleep? Art thou not afraid of nightmares and hideous dreams?**

HESTER: Why dost thou smile so at me? Art thou like the Black Man that haunts the forest round about us? Hast thou enticed me into a bond that will prove the ruin of my soul?

CHILLINGWORTH: Not thy soul. No, not thine! *(He leaves her.)*

From

TREASURE ISLAND

By Robert Louis Stevenson

In Robert Louis Stevenson's famous pirate tale, *Treasure Island,* young Jim Hawkins sails in search of buried treasure along with his friends Squire Trelawney, Dr. Livesey, and Captain Smollett. Also on board the ship are an unsavory group of sailors who turn out to be pirates, with the sea cook, Long John Silver, as their leader, also intent upon securing the treasure. Once ashore on the treasure island, a battle of wits and arms ensues between Jim and his friends, and the pirates, over who will get to the treasure first. One night young Jim returns late to the stockade he believes his friends are holding, and suddenly finds himself a prisoner at the mercy of the infamous Long John and the pirates.

CHARACTERS: LONG JOHN SILVER, a pirate; JIM HAWKINS, a boy of 16.

LONG JOHN: *(To JIM, who stands against the wall, held at sword point)* **So, here's Jim Hawkins, shiver my timbers! dropped in, like, eh? Well, come, I take that friendly.** *(He watches JIM for a moment, slowly shaking his head.)* **Now, I see you were smart when first I set my eyes on you, but this here gets away from me clean, it do.** *(JIM watches him closely, saying nothing.)* **Now, I've always liked you for a lad of spirit, and the picter of my own self when I was young and handsome. I always wanted you to jine with me and take your share, and die a gentleman, and now, my cock, you've got to. Cap'n Smollett's a fine seaman, as I'll own up to any day, but stiff on discipline. "Dooty is dooty" says he, and right he is. Just you keep clear of the cap'n and jine with me, lad. Your friend, the doctor himself is gone dead again' you – "ungrateful scamp" was what he said; and the short and long of the whole story is about here: you can't go back to your own lot, for they won't have you; and, without you start a third ship's company all by yourself, which might be lonely, you'll *have* to jine with Cap'n Silver.**

I don't say nothing as to your being in our hands. I'm all for argyment; I never seen good come out o' threatening. If you like the service, well, you'll jine; and if you don't, Jim, why, you're free to answer no – free and welcome, shipmate; and if fairer can be said by mortal seaman, shiver my sides!

JIM: *(In a trembling voice, feeling the threat of death all around him)* **Am I to answer then?**

LONG JOHN: **Lad, no one's a-pressing you. Take your bearings. None of us won't hurry you, mate; time goes so pleasant in your company, you see.**

JIM: *(Growing bolder)* **Well, if I'm to choose, I declare I have a**

right to know what's what, and why you're here in this stockade, and where my friends are.

LONG JOHN: Well, yesterday morning, Mr. Hawkins, in the dog-watch, down came Doctor Livesey with a flag of truce. Says he, "Cap'n Silver, you're sold out. Ship's gone." Well, maybe we'd been taking a glass and a song to help it round. I won't say no. Leastways, none of us had looked out. We looked out, and by thunder! the old ship was gone. I never seen a pack o' fools look fishier; and you may lay to that, if I tells you that looked the fishiest. "Well," says the doctor, "let's bargain." We bargained, him and I, and here we are: stores, brandy, block-house, the firewood you was thoughtful enough to cut, and, in a manner of speaking, the whole blessed boat, from cross-trees to kelson. As for them, they've tramped; I don't know where's they are. And lest you should take it into that head of yours that you was included in the treaty, here's the last word that he said: "As for that boy, I don't know where is he, confound him, nor I don't much care. We're about sick of him." These was his last words.

JIM: Is that all?

LONG JOHN: Well, it's all that you're to hear, my son.

JIM: And now am I to choose?

LONG JOHN: And now you are to choose, and you may lay to that.

JIM: Well, I am not such a fool but I know pretty well what I have to look for. Let the worst come to the worst, it's little I care. I've seen too many die since I fell in with you. But there's a thing or two I have to tell you. *(Growing more excited)* **The first is this: here you are, in a bad way, ship lost, treasure lost, men lost; your whole business gone to wreck; and if you want to know who did it – it was I! I was in the apple barrel the night we sighted land, and I heard every word of your plan to take our map and get the treasure and kill us all. And so I warned my friends and when**

we got ashore, we were ready for you. And as for the schooner, it was I who cut her cable, and it was I that killed the men you had aboard of her, and it was I who brought her where you'll never see her more, not one of you.

The laugh's on my side; I've had the top of this business from the first; I no more fear you than I fear a fly. Kill me, if you please, or spare me. But one thing I'll say, and no more: if you spare me, bygones are bygones, and when you fellows are in court for piracy, I'll save you all I can. It is for *you* to choose. Kill another and do yourselves no good, or spare me and keep a witness to save you from the gallows. *(He looks around, as if many threatening eyes are upon him.)* **And now, Mr. Silver, I believe you're the best man here, and if things go to the worst, I'll take it kind of you to let the doctor know the way I took it.**

LONG JOHN: *(Staring, obviously amazed at what he has just heard)* **I'll bear it in mind.**

From

ANNA KARENINA

By Leo Tolstoy

Set in nineteenth-century Russia, Leo Tolstoy's powerful novel, *Anna Karenina*, presents a realistic picture of Russian society and how it restricts and influences a beautiful woman who loves a man who is not her husband. Anna Karenina, whose husband is a successful but dispassionate, no-nonsense public official, is pursued by the handsome Count Vronsky who fell in love with her the first time he saw her. Anna tries to resist him, but cannot, and when she returns his love, she finds genuine happiness for the first time in her life. At the same time, guilt and hopelessness overwhelm her.

CHARACTERS: ANNA KARENINA, COUNT VRONSKY.

SCENE: VRONSKY has come to see ANNA at a time when he knows her husband is away. He finds her on the garden terrace and stands for a moment, watching her and loving her in silence. Suddenly, she turns to him with a sick and anxious look on her face.

VRONSKY: *(Going to her and taking her hands)* **What's the matter, Anna? Are you ill?**

ANNA: No, I am well. I...I did not expect you.

VRONSKY: What cold hands!

ANNA: You startled me, Aleksey. I am here alone. My little son has gone for his walk and I am waiting for him to return. *(She seems ready to cry at any moment.)*

VRONSKY: Forgive me for coming, but I couldn't pass the day without seeing you. I am racing this afternoon – and I wanted to see you before I —

ANNA: Forgive you? Aleksey, I am so glad to see you!

VRONSKY: But you are ill...or worried. What were you thinking of just now?

ANNA: *(With a gentle smile)* **Always the same thing – my happiness...and...** *(Almost a whisper as she turns away from him)* **...my unhappiness.**

VRONSKY: *(Leading her to a seat)* **I can see that something has happened.** *(He sits near her.)* **I cannot be at peace knowing you have a trouble I am not sharing. Please, tell me.**

ANNA: *(Searches his face for a moment.)* **Shall I really tell you? You...must realize how...how serious...**

VRONSKY: Yes, yes...tell me!

ANNA: *(Grasping his hands)* **I'm pregnant.**

VRONSKY: *(He starts, then bows his head, allowing her hands to drop from his.)* **The turning point has come. Yes, neither you nor I have looked on our relations as a passing amuse-**

ment – it was so much more than that. And now our fate is sealed. It is absolutely necessary to put an end to the deception in which we are living.

ANNA: *(Calmer)* **Put an end? How put an end, Aleksey?**

VRONSKY: You must leave your husband and make our life one.

ANNA: It is one as it is.

VRONSKY: Yes, but altogether. Altogether, Anna!

ANNA: But how? Is there any way out of our position? Am I not the wife of my husband?

VRONSKY: There is a way out of every situation. We must make a decision. Anything is better than the situation in which you're living now. Of course, I see how you torture yourself over everything – the world, your son, your husband.

ANNA: *(Quickly)* **Not my husband! I don't think of him. He doesn't exist for me.**

VRONSKY: You are not speaking sincerely. I know you, Anna. You worry about him, too.

ANNA: Oh, he doesn't even know about us, although I believe he suspects. *(She turns away, ashamed.)* **Let's not talk of him.**

VRONSKY: Whether he knows or not, that's nothing to do with us. We cannot continue like this, especially now, after what you have told me.

ANNA: Then what's to be done?

VRONSKY: You must tell him everything, and then leave him.

ANNA: And suppose I do that? Do you know what the result would be? I can tell you beforehand. *(She rises and mimics her husband's awkward walk and sneering tone.)* **"Oh, you love another man, and have entered into a *criminal* liaison with him? I warned you of the consequences from the religious, the civil, and the domestic points of view. You have not listened to me. Now I cannot let you disgrace my name!"** *(In her own voice)* **In general terms, he'll say in his official manner, and with all distinctness and precision, that he cannot let me go, but will take all measures in his power to**

prevent scandal. And he will calmly and punctually act in accordance with his words. Oh, Aleksey, he's not a man, he's a machine, and a very spiteful machine when he's angry.

VRONSKY: *(Gently)* **But, Anna, we must tell him and then be guided by the line he takes.**

ANNA: You mean run away?

VRONSKY: Why not? I don't see how we can keep on like this.

ANNA: I must run away...and become your mistress?

VRONSKY: Anna...

ANNA: Yes, become your mistress and complete the ruin of... *(Almost a whisper)* **...my son. Oh, I beg you, Aleksey, I entreat you, never speak of this to me again.**

VRONSKY: But, Anna...

ANNA: Never! Leave things to me. I know all the baseness and horror of my position, but it's not so easy to arrange as you think. Leave it to me and do as I say. Never speak to me of it. Promise me!

VRONSKY: I promise, but after what you have told me today, I can't be at peace when you are not at peace.

ANNA: I? Oh, yes, I am worried sometimes, but that will pass. It only worries me when you talk about it.

VRONSKY: I don't understand. How can you endure this state of deceit and not desire to get out of it?

ANNA: I know how hard it is for your truthful nature to lie, and I grieve for you. I often think you have ruined your whole life for me.

VRONSKY: I was just thinking the same thing, how could you sacrifice everything for my sake? I can't forgive myself for making you so unhappy.

ANNA: Unhappy? *(With all her love in her voice)* **I am like a hungry man who has been given food. I may be cold and dressed in rags, and deeply ashamed, but not unhappy. No, Aleksey, you are my happiness. Don't you understand that from the day I loved you, everything has changed for me?**

For me there is one thing, and one thing only – your love. If that is mine, I feel so exalted, so strong...

VRONSKY: And yet, you will not leave your husband?

ANNA: He will never let me go. He will save his reputation at any price. But I can no longer be his wife. You are everything to me now.

VRONSKY: And you to me, no matter that we both shall suffer for it. *(He kisses her.)* **Anna... you are my life!**

ANNA: *(Suddenly breaking away)* **I hear my son's voice. He is returning with the servant.**

VRONSKY: We can never be truly alone!

ANNA: *(Takes his face in her hands and kisses both his eyes, then his mouth.)* **I will come see you in the race today. Now you must go.**

VRONSKY: I must see you after the race. I'll send a message. *(He releases her, reluctantly, and goes.)*

From

THE ADVENTURES OF HUCKLEBERRY FINN

By Mark Twain

Of the many river characters that Huck Finn and Jim meet up with on their raft journey down the Mississippi River, the two rascals known as The Duke and The King are the most shrewd and conniving. Running from an angry mob in a small river town, they take refuge on Huck and Jim's raft and find temporary safety on the river. They quickly make themselves at home on the crowded raft, and even though they are strangers to each other, they waste no time in sounding each other out and making plans for the future.

CHARACTERS: THE DUKE, an old rascal of 70; THE KING, a younger rascal, about 30.

KING: What got you into trouble back there?

DUKE: Well, I'd been selling an article to take the tartar off the teeth – and it does take it off, too, and generally the enamel along with it – but I stayed about one night longer than I ought to, and was just in the act of sliding out when I ran across you on the trail.

KING: Well, I'd been a-runnin' a little temperance revival thar 'bout a week, and was the pet of the womenfolks, and takin' as much as five or six dollars a night. Business was a-growin' all the time, when a little report got around last night that I had a way of puttin' in my time with a private jug on the sly. I heard this mornin' that the people was getherin' on the quiet with their dogs and horses, and they'd be along pretty soon and give me 'bout half an hour's start, and then run me down if they could, and if they got me, they'd tar and feather me and ride me on a rail, sure. I didn't wait for no breakfast. I warn't hungry.

DUKE: Old man, I reckon we might double team it together. What do you think?

KING: I ain't undisposed. What's your line, mainly?

DUKE: Printer by trade; do a little in patent medicines; theater actor – tragedy, you know; take a turn to mesmerism and phrenology when there's a chance; teach singing-geography school for a change; sling a lecture sometimes – oh, I do lots of things – most anything that comes handy, so it ain't work. What's your lay?

KING: I've done considerable in the doctoring way in my time. Layin' on of hands is my best holt – for cancer and paralysis, and sich things; and I can tell a fortune pretty good when I've got somebody along to find out the facts for me. Preachin's my line, too, and workin' camp meetin's, and

missionaryin' around.

DUKE: *(Suddenly strikes a despondent pose and heaves a deep sigh.)* **Alas!**

KING: What're you alassin' about?

DUKE: To think I should have lived to be leading such a life, and be degraded down into such company! *(He pulls out a dirty bandana and wipes imaginary tears from his eyes.)*

KING: Dern your skin, ain't the company good enough for you?

DUKE: Yes, it's as good as I deserve; for who fetched me so low when I was so high? I did myself. Let the cold world do its worst; one thing I know, there's a grave somewhere for me. The world may go on just as it's always done, and take everything from me – loved ones, property, everything; but it can't take that. Someday I'll lie down in it and forget it all, and my poor broken heart will be at rest. *(He sobs loudly.)*

KING: Drat your pore broken heart! I ain't done nothing!

DUKE: No, I know you haven't. I ain't blaming you. I brought myself down.

KING: Whar was you brought down from?

DUKE: Ah, you would not believe me! The secret of my birth . . .

KING: The secret of your birth!

DUKE: I will reveal it to you, for I feel I may have confidence in you. *(Takes a deep breath.)* **By rights I am a duke!**

KING: No! You can't mean it!

DUKE: Yes. My great-grandfather, eldest son of the Duke of Bridgewater, fled to this country to breathe the pure air of freedom; married here, and died, leaving a son. The second son of the late duke seized the titles and estates – the infant real duke was ignored. I am the lineal descendant of that infant – I am the rightful Duke of Bridgewater, and here am I, forlorn, torn from my high estate, hunted of men, despised by the cold world, ragged, worn, heartbroken, and degraded to the companionship of felons on a raft! *(He sobs harder.)*

KING: *(After a moment, watching him slyly)* **Looky here, Bilgewater, I'm nation sorry for you, but you ain't the only person that's had troubles like that.**

DUKE: No?

KING: You ain't the only person that's been snaked down wrongfully out'n a high place.

DUKE: Alas!

KING: You ain't the only person that's had a secret of his birth. *(He begins to cry.)*

DUKE: Hold! What do you mean?

KING: *(Seizing his hand)* **Bilgewater, can I trust you?**

DUKE: To the bitter death! That secret of your being – speak!

KING: Bilgewater, I am the late Dauphin!

DUKE: *(Dropping his hand)* **You are what?**

KING: Yes, my friend, your eyes is lookin' at the pore disappeared Dauphin, Looy the Seventeen, son of Looy the Sixteen and Marry Antonette.

DUKE: You mean you're the late Charlemagne? You must be six or seven hundred years old, at the very least.

KING: Trouble has done it, Bilgewater. Trouble has brung these gray hairs and this premature balditude. Yes, you see before you, in blue jeans and misery, the wanderin', exiled, trampled-on, and sufferin' rightful King of France! *(He bawls piteously for a moment, then notices the DUKE looking sourly at him.)* **Now looky here, like as not, we got to be together a blamed long time on this here raft, Bilgewater.**

DUKE: Bridgewater!

KING: So what's the use of your bein' sour? It'll only make things oncomfortable. It ain't my fault I warn't born a duke, it ain't your fault you warn't born a king, so what's the use to worry? Make the best of things the way you find 'em, says I, that's my motto. This ain't no bad thing that we've struck here – plenty of grub and an easy life – come, give us your hand, duke, and let's be friends.

DUKE: *(After a moment, he reluctantly shakes the King's hand.)* **Well, I suppose we better lay out a campaign. Have you ever trod the boards, Royalty?**

KING: No.

DUKE: You shall, then, before you're three days older, Fallen Grandeur. The first good town we come to we'll hire a hall and do the sword fight in Richard III and the balcony scene in Romeo and Juliet. How does that strike you?

KING: I'm in, up to the hub, for anything that will pay, Bilgewater, but you see, I don't know nothing about play-actin', and hain't ever seen much of it. I was too small when pap used to have 'em at the palace. Do you reckon you can learn me?

DUKE: Easy!

KING: All right. I'm just a-freezin' for something fresh. Let's commence right away.

DUKE: For encores I'll do the Highland fling and you can do Hamlet's soliloquy!

KING: Hamlet's which?

DUKE: Hamlet's soliloquy, you know, the most celebrated thing in Shakespeare. Ah, it's sublime, sublime! Always fetches the house. I'll just walk up and down a minute, and see if I can call it back from recollection's vaults. *(He stomps about, frowning, mumbling, then strikes a noble attitude and recites with great energy and dramatic gestures.)*

"To be, or not to be; that is the bare bodkin that makes calamity of so long life; for who would fardels bear, til Birnam Wood do come to Dunsinane, but that the fear of something after death murders the innocent sleep, great nature's second course, and makes us rather sling the arrows of outrageous fortune than fly to others that we know not of. Wake Duncan with thy knocking! I would thou couldst; for who would bear the whips and scorns of time, in the dead waste and middle of the night, when

churchyards yawn in customary suits of solemn black, and all the clouds that lowered o'er our housetops lose the name of action. 'Tis a consummation devoutly to be wished. But soft you, the fair Ophelia; ope not thy ponderous and marble jaws, but get thee to a nunnery - go!" *(The KING is speechless with awe; the DUKE exhausted, but triumphant.)*

From

A CONNECTICUT YANKEE IN KING ARTHUR'S COURT

By Mark Twain

Mark Twain's satirical venture into the sixth century with a nineteenth century hero was published in 1889. Hank Morgan, a self-styled "Yankee of the Yankees," who works in an arms factory in Hartford, Connecticut, in 1879, is knocked unconscious by a blow on the head with a crowbar during a fight. When he comes to his senses again, he discovers that he is in Camelot, the residence of the legendary King Arthur. He is taken prisoner and despite his efforts to explain who he is, he is judged to be a wicked magician, condemned to death, stripped to his underwear, and thrown into a dungeon to await his fate. His only friend is Clarence, a young page boy of gentle and innocent disposition.

CHARACTERS: HANK MORGAN, the Yankee; CLARENCE, a page in King Arthur's Court.

SCENE: A dungeon cell furnished with a rough cot and a stool. HANK lies on the cot, wearing only his longjohns, and shackled to the floor with chains. CLARENCE, in the colorful dress of a court page, sits on the stool, waiting for him to awaken.

HANK: *(Stirs, yawns, stretches, with eyes half open.)* **I must have been asleep for hours! And what an astonishing dream I've had! I reckon I've waked only just in time to keep from being hanged or drowned or burned or something. Well, I'll just nap some more until the noon whistle blows and then I'll go down to the arms factory and have it out with...** *(As he turns on his side, he sees CLARENCE smiling cheerfully at him.)* **What? You still here?** *(He sits up.)* **Go along with the rest of the dream! Scatter!**

CLARENCE: *(Laughing)* **What dream?**

HANK: Why, the dream that I am in King Arthur's court, a person who never existed, and that I'm talking to you who are nothing but a work of my imagination!

CLARENCE: Indeed! And is it a dream that you're to be burned at the stake tomorrow?

HANK: What! Now I know some dreams can have a very lifelike intensity, but being burned to death, even in a dream, is far from being a joke and definitely to be avoided. Clarence, my boy, you're the only friend I've got here. *(He hesitates.)* **You *are* my friend, aren't you?**

CLARENCE: *(Beaming)* **Can you doubt it?**

HANK: Then help me to devise some way of escaping from this place.

CLARENCE: Escape? Why, the corridors are in guard and keep of men-at-arms.

HANK: No doubt, but how many, Clarence? Not many, I hope?

CLARENCE: Full a score. One may not hope to escape. *(Hesitating)* **And there may be other reasons to prevent escape...*weightier* reasons.**

HANK: What *weightier* reasons?

CLARENCE: Well, they say...oh, I dare not speak of it!

HANK: Why, poor lad, what's the matter? You're trembling.

CLARENCE: Oh, I *do* want to tell you, but...

HANK: Come, come, be brave! Be a man! Speak out!

CLARENCE: *(Obviously frightened, he creeps to the door, looks out, listens, then returns to HANK and speaks fearfully, close to his ear.)* **Merlin, the great magician, in his malice, has woven a spell about this dungeon, and no man in all the kingdom would dare cross its lines! Oh! I have told it! Be kind to me, be merciful to a poor boy who means you well! If you betray me, I am lost!**

HANK: *(With a hearty laugh)* **Merlin has woven a spell? That cheap old humbug? That maundering old ass? Bosh! Pure bosh!** *(CLARENCE reacts with horror.)* **If Merlin isn't the most childish, idiotic, chuckleheaded, chicken-livered, superstitious old fraud... oh, damn Merlin!**

CLARENCE: *(On his knees, petrified)* **Oh, beware! These are awful words. Any moment these walls may crumble upon us. Oh, call back your words before it's too late!**

HANK: Why, Clarence, here, sit down, my boy. Is everybody here so sincerely afraid of Merlin's pretended magic?

CLARENCE: Pretended? Oh, take back that word! Take it back! *(He looks around wildly, expecting the walls to fall in at any moment.)*

HANK: Well now, certainly a superior man like me ought to be shrewd enough to contrive some way to take advantage of such a superstitious and ignorant state of things. *(He thinks. CLARENCE trembles and moans.)* **Hah! I've got just the thing! Get up, my lad, pull yourself together. Here, look me in the eye. Do you know why I laughed at Merlin?**

CLARENCE: No, and I beg of you, pray don't do it ever again!

HANK: I laughed because I'm a magician myself.

CLARENCE: *(Recoiling)* **You?**

HANK: I've known Merlin for seven hundred years.

CLARENCE: *(Incredulous)* **Seven hundred...**

HANK: Don't interrupt. He has died and come alive again thirteen times and traveled under a new name each time – Smith – Jones – Robinson – Merlin. I knew him in Egypt three hundred years ago. I knew him in India five hundred years ago. He is always blethering around in my way, everywhere I go. He makes me tired. He don't amount to shucks as a magician. Oh, he knows some of the old common tricks and he is good enough for the provinces, one-night stands, and that sort of thing. But he oughtn't to set up for an expert when there's a *real* artist, like me, around. Now look here, Clarence, I'll be your friend and you must be mine. *(CLARENCE nods vigorously.)* **I want you to get word to the King that I am a magician, the Supreme Grand High Muckamuck and head of the tribe. And you tell him that I will quietly arrange a little calamity that will make the fur fly in these realms if any harm comes to me. Do you understand?**

CLARENCE: *(His knees knocking)* **Yes, yes, only pray do not cast any evil enchantments upon me!**

HANK: I do not cast evil enchantments upon my friends, my boy.

CLARENCE: But what shall I tell our liege the King you will do? What calamity must I describe to him?

HANK: How long have I been shut up in this hole?

CLARENCE: Since last night. It is now nine in the morning.

HANK: This is the twentieth?

CLARENCE: The twentieth, yes.

HANK: Of June?

CLARENCE: Of June.

HANK: And you swore to me awhile ago that this was the year 528?

CLARENCE: 528.

HANK: And I am to be burned alive *(Shuddering)* **...when?**

CLARENCE: *(Shuddering)* **Tomorrow.**

HANK: At what hour?

CLARENCE: At high noon.

HANK: Good! Now, I'll tell you what to say to the King. *(He paces, collecting his thoughts, while CLARENCE cowers at his feet. Then, with a deep voice charged with doom and growing more and more dramatic...)* **Tell the King that at high noon tomorrow I will smother the whole world in the dead blackness of midnight! I will blot out the sun and it will never shine again!** *(CLARENCE falls on his face in terror.)* **The fruits of the earth shall rot for lack of light and warmth! The peoples of the earth shall famish and die to the last man!** *(Pulls CLARENCE to his feet and guides him to the door.)* **Go! Tell him!** *(CLARENCE, wobbling, gives him a pleading glance.)* **Go!** *(CLARENCE tumbles out the door.)*

HANK: I just may carry this off. Luckily, I happen to know that the only total eclipse of the sun in the first half of the sixth century occurred on the twenty-first of June, A.D. 528 and began at three minutes after twelve noon. I also know that no total eclipse of the sun is due in 1879, where I was when I took that crusher to the head back at the arms factory in Hartford. So, being a practical Connecticut man, I'll wait to see if my memory and history will save me. If it really is the sixth century, as everybody I've met here insists, then the eclipse will save me and I'll be boss of this whole country inside of three months! I judge I have the start on the best educated man in the kingdom by thirteen hundred years! *(He pauses and heaves a great sigh.)* **Now, if that eclipse just comes in on schedule!**

From

BEN-HUR

By Lew Wallace

Ben-Hur, A tale of the Christ, written by the American Civil War General Lew Wallace, was published in 1880, and told the story of Judah Ben-Hur as the head of his household in Rome who was cruelly wronged by his boyhood friend, Messala, cast into slavery, rescued, and finally restored to honor and destined to know the man called Jesus Christ. In this scene, set on a galley ship at sea, Judah is among the slaves who work the oars. In charge of the ship is the Roman tribune, Quintus Arrius, who has noticed that Judah is not the usual type of galley slave. He sends for him in order to know more about him, and quickly learns how his terrible misfortune began.

CHARACTERS: JUDAH BEN-HUR, QUINTUS ARRIUS.

SCENE: ARRIUS, dressed as befits a Roman tribune, is seated on a bench. JUDAH, in the dirty rags of a slave, approaches him respectfully.

JUDAH: *(Bowing)* **The chief called you the noble Arrius and said it was your will that I come to you.**

ARRIUS: *(Looking him over carefully)* **I am told that you are the best rower on this ship. I have seen you at your labor. Have you seen much service?**

JUDAH: About three years.

ARRIUS: At the oars?

JUDAH: I cannot recall a day of rest away from them.

ARRIUS: The labor is hard. Few men bear it a year without breaking. You are hardly more than a boy.

JUDAH: The noble Arrius forgets that the spirit has much to do with endurance. By its help the weak sometimes thrive when the strong perish.

ARRIUS: From your speech I note that you are a Jew.

JUDAH: *(Standing erect)* **My ancestors, further back than the first Roman, were Hebrews.**

ARRIUS: The stubborn pride of your race is not lost in you.

JUDAH: Pride is never so loud as when in chains.

ARRIUS: What cause have you for pride?

JUDAH: I am a Jew!

ARRIUS: *(With a smile)* **I have not been to Jerusalem, but I have heard of its princes. I knew one of them – a merchant who sailed the seas. He was fit to have been a king. Of what degree are you?**

JUDAH: I must answer from the bench of a galley. I am of the degree of slaves. But my father was a prince of Jerusalem and was a merchant who sailed the seas.

ARRIUS: His name?

JUDAH: Ithamar, of the house of Hur.

ARRIUS: *(Astonished)* **You are a son of Hur? What brought you here?**

JUDAH: *(Lowers his head, struggling to control his feelings.)* **I was accused of attempting to assassinate Valerius Gratus, the procurator.**

ARRIUS: You! You that assassin? All Rome rang with that story. I thought the family of Hur had been blotted from the earth.

JUDAH: *(Unable to contain himself any longer)* **My mother! My mother and my little sister, Tirzah! Where are they? O noble tribune, if you know anything of them, tell me!** *(He falls to his knees.)* **Tell me if they are living, and if so, where are they and in what condition? I pray you, tell me!** *(He realizes he must control himself; rises, remembering with pain.)* **The horrible day is three years gone, and every hour a whole lifetime of misery with not a word from anyone – not a whisper! Oh, if in being forgotten, we could only forget! If only I could hide from that scene! My sister torn from me, my mother's last look! And mine was the hand that laid them low.**

ARRIUS: *(Sternly)* **Do you admit your guilt?**

JUDAH: *(Suddenly enraged, he clenches his fists.)* **You have heard of the God of my fathers, the infinite Jehovah. By his truth and almightiness and by the love with which He has followed Israel from the beginning, I swear I am innocent! O noble Roman, give me a little faith! Into my darkness, deeper darkening every day, send a light!**

ARRIUS: *(Obviously moved, he rises and paces slowly.)* **Did you not have a trial?**

JUDAH: No!

ARRIUS: *(Surprised)* **No trial? No witnesses? Who passed judgment on you?**

JUDAH: I appealed to the man who had been the friend of my

youth – *(With hatred)* **Messala! We had recently quarreled, but for the love of my mother and sister, I forgot that quarrel. "Help them, Messala! Remember our childhood and help them! I, Judah, pray you!" I begged him to intervene. But he affected not to hear. He turned away and gave his brutal orders. The soldiers bound me with cords and dragged me to a vault in the tower. I saw no one. No one spoke to me. The next day soldiers took me to the seaside. I have been a galley slave ever since.**

ARRIUS: If there had been a trial, what could you have proved?

JUDAH: I was a boy, too young to be a conspirator. Gratus was a stranger to me. If I had meant to kill him, that was not the time or the place. He was riding in the midst of a legion and it was broad day. I was of a class most friendly to Rome. My father had been distinguished for his services to the emperor. We had a great estate to lose. Ruin was certain to myself, my mother and my sister. I had no cause for malice, while every consideration, property, family, life, conscience, the Law – to a son of Israel as the breath of his nostrils – would have stayed my hand though the foul intent had been ever so strong. I was not mad. Death was preferable to shame, and believe me, I pray, it is so yet.

ARRIUS: Who was with you when the blow was struck?

JUDAH: I was on my father's housetop. Tirzah was with me. Together we leaned over the parapet to see the legion pass. A tile gave way under my hand and fell upon Gratus. *(With a shudder)* **I thought I had killed him.**

ARRIUS: Where was your mother?

JUDAH: In her chamber below.

ARRIUS: What became of her?

JUDAH: I do not know! I saw them drag her away. Out of the house they drove every living thing - the servants, even the cattle, and they sealed the gates so that no one should ever

enter them again. Oh, for one word! My mother, at least, was innocent!

ARRIUS: *(To himself)* **A whole family blotted out to atone an accident?** *(After a moment, turns to JUDAH.)* **Enough. Go back to your place at the oars.**

JUDAH: *(Bows, starts to go, then turns back.)* **If you ever think of me again, noble tribune, let it not be lost in your mind that I asked only for word of my people, my mother, and my sister.**

ARRIUS: *(Turning aside)* **With teaching, what a man for the arena! What an arm for the sword!** *(To JUDAH)* **Stay! If you were free, what would you do?**

JUDAH: The noble Arrius mocks me.

ARRIUS: No! By the gods, I do not.

JUDAH: I would know no rest until my mother and Tirzah were restored to home. I would give every hour and day to their happiness.

ARRIUS: I spoke of your ambition. If your mother and sister were dead, or not to be found, what would you do?

JUDAH: *(Again struggling to control himself)* **Only the night before the dreadful day of which I have spoken, I obtained permission to be a soldier.**

ARRIUS: Go now, and do not build on what has passed between us. Perhaps I do but play with you. Or, if you do think of this with any hope, choose between the renown of a gladiator and the service of a soldier. The former may come by the favor of the emperor. There is no reward for you in the latter. You are not a Roman. *(He leaves.)*

JUDAH: *(Looking after him)* **Noble tribune, you have given me bread upon which I will feed my hungry spirit. Surely something good will come of this!** *(He looks upward with clasped hands.)* **O God! I am a true son of the Israel You have so loved! Help me, I pray you! And in the hour of your vengenace, O Lord, let it be my hand to put it upon Messala!**

From

THE PICTURE OF DORIAN GRAY

By Oscar Wilde

Famous for his witty observations on British life in the late nineteenth century, Oscar Wilde wrote a number of plays which remain popular to this day. His one side trip, so to speak, into a more serious subject, was the novel, *The Picture of Dorian Gray,* where mystery and the supernatural are revealed in a strange story of power, greed, and cruelty, centering around a single portrait. Wilde's notable wit, however, is found in the character of Lord Henry Wotten, who opens the story with his remarks on art.

CHARACTERS: LORD HENRY WOTTEN; BASIL HALLWARD, an artist.

SCENE: LORD HENRY WOTTEN reclines on a sofa, idly watching BASIL HALLWARD who is standing before a large portait of a young man on an easel. BASIL smiles in a pleased way, then suddenly turns away, the smile fading.

LORD HENRY: It is your best work, Basil, the best thing you have ever done. You must certainly send it next year to the Grosvenor. The Academy is too large and too vulgar. Whenever I have gone there, there have either been so many people that I have not been able to see the pictures, which was dreadful, or so many pictures that I have not been able to see the people, which was worse. The Grosvenor is really the only place.

BASIL: I don't think I shall send it anywhere.

LORD HENRY: Not send it anywhere? My dear fellow, why? What odd chaps you painters are! You do anything in the world to gain a reputation. As soon as you have one, you seem to want to throw it away. It is silly of you, for there is only one thing in the world worse than being talked about, and that is *not* being talked about. A portrait like this would set you far above all the young men in England, and make the old men quite jealous, if old men are ever capable of any emotion at all.

BASIL: I know you will laugh at me, but I really can't exhibit it. I have put too much of myself into it.

LORD HENRY: *(Laughing)* **Too much of yourself in it! Upon my word, Basil, I didn't know you were so vain. I really can't see any resemblance between you and this young Adonis. He is a Narcissus, and you – well, of course, you have an intellectual expression and all that. But beauty, real beauty, ends where an intellectual expression begins.**

Intellect is in itself a mode of exaggeration, and destroys the harmony of any face. The moment one sits down to think, one becomes all nose, or all forehead, or something horrid. Your mysterious young friend, whose name you have never told me, but whose picture really fascinates me, never thinks. I feel quite sure of that. He is some brainless, beautiful creature who should always be here in winter when we have no flowers to look at, and always here in summer when we want something to chill our intelligence. Don't flatter yourself, Basil; you are not in the least like him.

BASIL: You don't understand me, Harry. Of course I am not like him. Indeed, I should be sorry to look like him. There is a fatality about all physical and intellectual distinction, the sort of fatality that seems to dog through history the faltering steps of kings. It is better not to be different from one's fellows. The ugly and stupid have the best of it in this world. If they know nothing of victory, they are at least spared the knowledge of defeat. They neither bring ruin upon others, nor ever receive it from alien hands. Your rank and wealth, Harry, my brains, such as they are, my art, whatever it may be worth – Dorian Gray's good looks – we should all suffer for what the gods have given us. Suffer terribly!

LORD HENRY: Dorian Gray? Is that his name?

BASIL: Yes. I didn't intend to tell it to you.

LORD HENRY: Why not?

BASIL: I can't explain. When I like people immensely, I never tell their names to anyone. It is like surrendering a part of them. I have grown to love secrecy. The commonest thing is delightful if one only hides it. When I leave town now, I never tell anyone where I am going. If I did, I would lose all my pleasure. I suppose you think me foolish.

LORD HENRY: Not at all. You seem to forget that I am married and the one charm of marriage is that it makes a life of

deception absolutely necessary for both parties. I never know where my wife is, and my wife never knows what I am doing. When we meet, we tell each other the most absurd stories with the most serious faces. My wife is very good at it, much better than I am. She never gets confused over dates and I always do. But when she does find me out, she makes no row about it. I sometimes wish she would, but she merely laughs at me.

BASIL: Harry, I believe you are really a very good husband, but you are thoroughly ashamed of your own virtues. You are an extraordinary fellow. You never say a moral thing, and you never do a wrong thing. Your cynicism is simply a pose.

LORD HENRY: *(Laughing)* **Being natural is simple a pose and the most irritating pose I know.** *(Pulls out his pocket watch.)* **I am afraid I must be going, Basil, but I insist on your telling me why you won't exhibit Dorian Gray's picture. I want the real reason.**

BASIL: I told you the real reason.

LORD HENRY: No, you did not. Too much of yourself in it! That is childish!

BASIL: Harry, every portrait that is painted with feeling is a portrait of the artist, not of the sitter. The sitter is merely the occasion. It is not he who is revealed by the painter; it is rather the painter who, on the colored canvas, reveals himself. The reason I will not exhibit this picture is that I am afraid I have shown in it the secret of my own soul!

LORD HENRY: And what is that?

BASIL: *(After a moment)* **I will tell you. When I saw Dorian Gray for the first time, a curious sensation of terror came over me. I knew that I had come face to face with someone whose mere personality was so fascinating, that if I allowed it to do so, it would absorb my whole nature, my whole soul, my very art itself. You know, Harry, how independent I am by nature. I have always been my own**

master, had at least always been so until I met Dorian Gray. Then something seemed to tell me that I was on the verge of a terrible crisis in my life. Lady Brandon introduced me to him, and now he is all my art to me. The work I have done since I met Dorian Gray is the best work of my life. His personality has suggested to me an entirely new manner in art, an entirely new mode of style. I see things differently. I can now recreate life in a way that was hidden from me before.

LORD HENRY: This is extraordinary! I must see Dorian Gray.

BASIL: I don't want you to see him.

LORD HENRY: Why not?

BASIL: Dorian Gray is my dearest friend. He has a simple and beautiful nature. I don't want you to try to influence him. Your influence would be bad. The world is wide and has many marvelous people in it. Don't take away from me the one person who gives to my art whatever charm it possesses. My life as an artist depends on him.

LORD HENRY: What nonsense you talk! Perhaps you will tire of him sooner than you think. It is a sad thing to think of, but there is no doubt that Genius lasts longer than Beauty. That accounts for the fact that we all take such pains to over educate ourselves. In the wild struggle for existence, we want to have something that endures. But someday you will look at Dorian Gray and he will seem to you to be a little out of drawing, or you won't like his tone of color, or something. You will bitterly reproach him in your own heart.

BASIL: Don't talk like that! As long as I live, the personality of Dorian Gray will dominate me. I know it. The portrait is *his*.

LORD HENRY: Then he is a very lucky fellow.

BASIL: *(Looking steadily at the picture)* **Lucky?** *(He shudders.)* **I wonder.**

Scenes for Three Performers

From

SENSE AND SENSIBILITY

By Jane Austen

Two sisters of opposite temperaments and outlooks are eligible for marriage, and the matter of a choosing a prospective husband consumes every waking hour in Jane Austen's enduring novel, *Sense and Sensibility*, published in 1813. The elder sister, Elinor Dashwood is practical and conventional, representing "sense," and her sister Marianne, who is sentimental and emotional, is the embodiment of "sensibility." The sisters are devoted to each other and to securing each other's happiness, but the choice of a husband requires careful and thorough consideration. In this scene, adapted freely from different parts of the novel, the two girls and their mother discuss the merits and defects of two gentlemen, Edward Ferrars and Colonel Brandon.

CHARACTERS: MRS. DASHWOOD; ELINOR, her eldest daughter; MARIANNE, her middle daughter.

SCENE: MRS. DASHWOOD, ELINOR and MARIANNE are seated in their parlor. They occupy themselves with handwork which does not in any way detract from their conversation.

ELINOR: I think you will like Edward, Mother, when you know more of him.

MRS. DASHWOOD: Like him? If he is such a contrast to his detestable sister, I can feel no sentiment of approbation inferior to love. He is very quiet and unobtrusive, and that is very much in his favor.

ELINOR: You may esteem him.

MRS. DASHWOOD: My dear Elinor, I have never yet known what it was to separate esteem and love. He holds you in the highest regard, my dear. Indeed, his warm heart and affectionate temper increase my interest in him daily. And, *(Turning to MARIANNE)* **in a few months, my dear Marianne, Elinor will in all probability be settled for life. We shall miss her, but *she* will be happy.**

MARIANNE: Oh, Mama, how shall we do without her?

ELINOR: Mother, what are you saying?

MRS. DASHWOOD: My love, it will scarcely be a separation. We shall live within a few miles of each other and shall meet every day of our lives. You will gain a brother, a real, affectionate brother, for I have the highest opinion in the world of Edward's heart. But you look grave, Marianne. Do you disapprove your sister's choice?

ELINOR: Mother, Edward Ferrars is not to be regarded as my choice. I have scarcely met him, and while I —

MARIANNE: *(Ignoring the interruption)* **Perhaps I may consider it with some surprise. Edward is very amiable, and I love him tenderly, yet, he is not the kind of young man I should**

expect who could seriously attach my sister.

ELINOR: Marianne, whatever do you mean?

MARIANNE: His eyes want all that spirit, that fire, which at once announce virtue and intelligence. And I am afraid he has no real taste. Music seems scarcely to attract him, and though he admires your drawings very much, it is not the admiration of a person who can understand their worth. And how spiritless, how tame was his manner in reading to us last night! I felt for you, Elinor, most severely. Yet you bore it with so much composure, you seemed scarcely to notice it. I could hardly keep my seat. To hear those beautiful lines which have frequently almost driven me wild, pronounced with such impenetrable calmness, such dreadful indifference!

MRS. DASHWOOD: He would certainly have done more justice to simple and elegant prose. But you *would* give him Cowper!

MARIANNE: But we must allow for difference of taste. Elinor has not my feelings, and therefore she may overlook it and be happy with him. But it would have broke my heart had I loved him to hear him read with so little sensibility. Mama, the more I know of the world, the more am I convinced that I shall never see a man whom I can really love. I require so much! He must have all Edward's virtues, and his person and manners must ornament his goodness with every possible charm.

MRS. DASHWOOD: Remember, my love, you are not yet seventeen. It is yet too early in life to despair of such a happiness.

MARIANNE: Oh, but what a pity it is, Elinor, that Edward should have no taste for drawing.

ELINOR: No taste for drawing? Why should you think that? He does not draw himself, but he has great pleasure in seeing the performances of other people, and I assure you he is by no means deficient in natural taste.

MARIANNE: Do not be offended, Elinor, if my praise of him is

not in everything equal to your sense of his merits. I have not had so many opportunities of estimating the minuter propensities of his mind, his inclinations, and tastes, as you have; but I have the highest opinion in the world of his goodness and sense. I think him everything that is worthy and amiable.

ELINOR: *(With a smile)* **I am sure that his dearest friends could not be dissatisfied with such commendation as that. The excellence of his understanding and his principles can be concealed only by that shyness which too often keeps him silent. I have seen a great deal of him, have studied his sentiments and heard his opinion on subjects of literature and taste, and upon the whole, I venture to pronounce that his mind is well-informed, his enjoyment of books exceedingly great, his imagination lively, his observation just and correct, and his taste delicate and pure. His abilities in every respect improve as much upon acquaintance as his manners and person. At first sight his address is certainly not striking, and his person can hardly be called handsome till the expression of his eyes, which are uncommonly good, and the general sweetness of his countenance, is perceived. At present I know him so well that I think him really handsome, or, at least, almost so. What say you, Marianne?**

MARIANNE: I shall very soon think him handsome, Elinor, if I do not now. When you tell me to love him as a brother, I shall no more see imperfection in his face than I now do in his heart.

ELINOR: *(Hastily)* **Marianne, I do not attempt to deny that I think very highly of him, that I greatly esteem, that I like him.**

MARIANNE: *(Indignantly)* **Esteem him! Like him! Cold-hearted, Elinor! Oh! worse than cold-hearted! Use those words again and I will leave the room this moment!**

ELINOR: *(Laughing)* **Excuse me, and be assured that I meant no**

offence to you by speaking in so quiet a way of my own feelings. Believe them to be stronger than I have declared; believe them, in short, to be such as his merit and the suspicion, the hope of his affection for me may warrant without imprudence or folly. But further than this you must not believe. I am by no means assured of his regard for me. In my heart I feel little, scarcely any doubt of his preference. But there are other points to be considered besides his inclination. He is very far from being independent.

MARIANNE: *(Exchanging an anxious look with her mother, then to ELINOR)* **And you really are not engaged to him?**

ELINOR: Certainly not.

MARIANNE: Yet it certainly soon will happen. But two advantages will proceed from this delay. I shall not lose you so soon, and Edward will have greater opportunity of improving that natural taste for your favorite pursuit which must be so indispensably necessary to your future felicity. Oh, if he should be so far stimulated by your genius as to learn to draw himself, how delightful it would be!

ELINOR: Enough of me, my dear sister. What have you to say concerning the delightful Colonel Brandon, who I have heard from Mrs. Jennings is very much in love with you.

MARIANNE: Whatever are you saying, Elinor? How absurd! The colonel's advanced years and his forlorn condition as an old bachelor make him quite unacceptable as a suitor.

MRS. DASHWOOD: Advanced years! He is but five and thirty!

MARIANNE: Mama, *you* cannot deny the absurdity of the accusation, though you may not think it intentionally ill-natured. Colonel Brandon is certainly younger than Mrs. Jennings, but he is old enough to be *my* father, and if he were ever animated enough to be in love, must have long outlived every sensation of the kind. It is too ridiculous! When is a man to be safe from such wit if age and infirmity will not protect him?

ELINOR: Infirmity? Do you call Colonel Brandon infirm? I can easily suppose that his age may appear much greater to you than to my mother, but you can hardly deceive yourself as to his having the use of his limbs!

MARIANNE: Did not you hear him complain of the rheumatism? And is not that the commonest infirmity of declining life?

MRS. DASHWOOD: My dearest child, at this rate you must be in continual terror of *my* decay. And it must seem to you a miracle that my life has been extended to the advanced age of forty!

MARIANNE: Mama, you are not doing me justice. I know very well that Colonel Brandon is not old enough to make his friends yet apprehensive of losing him in the course of nature. He may live twenty years longer. But thirty-five has nothing to do with matrimony.

ELINOR: Perhaps thirty-five and seventeen had better not have anything to do with matrimony together. But if there should by any chance happen to be a woman who is single at seven and twenty, I should not think Colonel Brandon's being thirty-five any objection to his marrying *her*.

MARIANNE: A woman of seven and twenty can never hope to feel or inspire affection again, and if her home be uncomfortable, or her fortune small, I can suppose that she might bring herself to submit to the offices of a nurse for the sake of the provision and security of a wife. In his marrying such a woman there would be nothing unsuitable. It would be a compact of convenience, and the world would be satisfied. In my eyes it would be no marriage at all, but a commercial exchange in which each wished to be benefited at the expense of the other.

ELINOR: It would be impossible, I know, to convince you that a woman of seven and twenty could feel for a man of thirty-five anything near enough to love to make him a desirable

companion to her. But I must object to your dooming Colonel Brandon and his wife to the constant confinement of a sick chamber merely because he chanced to complain yesterday, a very cold, damp day, of a slight rheumatic feel in one of his shoulders.

MARIANNE: But he talked of flannel waistcoats, and with me a flannel waistcoat is invariably connected with aches, cramps, rheumatisms, and every species of ailment that can afflict the old and the feeble.

ELINOR: Had he been only in a violent fever, I'm sure you would not have despised him half so much. Confess, Marianne, is not there something interesting to you in the flushed cheek, hollow eye, and quick pulse of a fever, even in a man of five and thirty?

MARIANNE: Oh, Elinor, how can you be so ridiculous? Really, I shall have to leave the room and find someone else to talk to! *(She puts down her work and hurries out, leaving her mother and ELINOR laughing gently.)*

From

JANE EYRE

By Charlotte Brontë

In Charlotte Brontë's novel, *Jane Eyre*, Jane as a child is sent by her aunt to Lowood School, where she and a number of other girls are forced to obey strict rules and teachers and lead a very regimented way of life. Having an independent spirit, Jane finds it hard to adapt to the place but sincerely tries to do her best. However, trouble seems to stalk her. In this scene, after she has been unjustly humiliated in front of her class, she sits alone, crying. Her one close friend in the school, an older girl named Helen Burns, tries to comfort her.

CHARACTERS: JANE EYRE, age 10; HELEN BURNS, age 14; MISS TEMPLE, a teacher.

SCENE: JANE sits on a bench, wiping her eyes. HELEN enters with a cup of water and a piece of bread.

HELEN: *(Gently)* **Jane, I've brought your supper. You must eat something.**

JANE: I'm not hungry.

HELEN: *(Sits beside her.)* **Perhaps later then.**

JANE: *(After a moment)* **Helen, why do you sit here with a girl whom everybody believes to be a liar?**

HELEN: Everybody? Why, there are only eighty people who have heard you called so, and the world contains hundreds of millions.

JANE: But what have I to do with them? The eighty I know despise me.

HELEN: No, Jane, you are mistaken. Probably not one in the school despises or dislikes you. Many, I am sure, pity you very much.

JANE: How can they pity me after Mr. Brocklehurst sat me up on that high stool in front of the whole school and called me a liar?

HELEN: Mr. Brocklehurst is not a god. He is not even a great or admired man. He is little liked here. Had he treated you as a favorite, you would find enemies all around you. As it is, the greater number of girls would offer you sympathy if they dared.

JANE: *(Surprised)* **Would they?**

HELEN: I'm sure of it. Both teachers and pupils may look coldly on you for a day or two, but friendly feelings are concealed in their hearts.

JANE: If only I could be sure! *(She moves closer and puts her hand in HELEN's.)*

HELEN: *(Clasping her hand)* **What does it matter, Jane, if all the world hates you and believes you wicked? If your own conscience absolves you from guilt, you will not be without friends.**

JANE: *(With a sigh)* **I know I should think well of myself, but that is not enough if others don't love me. I cannot bear to be alone and hated, Helen.**

HELEN: Yet it is your duty to bear whatever you cannot avoid. It is weak and silly to say you cannot bear what you must.

JANE: But you must suffer so much, Helen. That teacher, Miss Scatcherd, is so cruel to you. She flogged you for nothing!

HELEN: Cruel? Not at all. She is severe. She dislikes my faults and never punishes me for no reason.

JANE: If I were in your place, I should dislike her. I should resist her if she struck me with that rod!

HELEN: It is far better to endure patiently a smart which nobody feels but yourself than to commit a hasty action whose evil consequences will extend to all connected with you.

JANE: But it seems disgraceful to be flogged! How can you have faults? To me you seem very good.

HELEN: Then learn from me not to judge by appearances. I am, as Miss Scatcherd said, slatternly. I seldom put and never keep things in order. I am careless. I forget rules. I read when I should learn my lessons. This is all very provoking to Miss Scatcherd, who is naturally neat, punctual, and particular.

JANE: And cross and cruel! If only more of our teachers were like Miss Temple!

HELEN: *(Smiling)* **Miss Temple is full of goodness. It pains her to be severe to anyone. She sees my errors and tells me of them gently, and if I do anything worthy of praise, she gives me my portion of it liberally.**

JANE: She is always kind to me. Only this morning she told me she was pleased with my progress, and she promised to

teach me drawing and French. Just when I was doing so well in my lessons, Mr. Brocklehurst has ruined me! Now, everything is lost!

HELEN: You must not think this, Jane. I know you are innocent of this charge which Mr. Brocklehurst has pompously made, repeated secondhand from your aunt. You see, I read a sincere nature in your eyes. And I'm certain Miss Temple does not believe it either.

MISS TEMPLE: *(Enters.)* I have come on purpose to find you, Jane Eyre.

JANE: *(Jumps up, hastily wiping her eyes.)* Miss Temple.

HELEN: *(Rising)* Miss Temple.

MISS TEMPLE: Sit down, Helen. You look very tired. *(As HELEN sits down, MISS TEMPLE sits beside JANE.)* Is it all over, Jane? Have you cried your grief away?

JANE: I'm afraid I shall never do that.

MISS TEMPLE: Why?

JANE: Because I have been wrongly accused, and you, ma'am, and everybody else will now think me wicked.

MISS TEMPLE: We shall think of you what you prove yourself to be, Jane. Continue to act as a good girl and you will satisfy me.

JANE: *(Hopefully)* Shall I, Miss Temple?

MISS TEMPLE: Yes. And now, tell me, who is the lady whom Mr. Brocklehurst called your benefactress?

JANE: She is not my benefactress! Mrs. Reed is my uncle's wife. When my father died, I was sent to live with my uncle and aunt. And when my uncle died, he left me to Mrs. Reed's care.

MISS TEMPLE: Did she not adopt you of her own accord?

JANE: No, ma'am. She was sorry to keep me, but my uncle made her promise that she would before he died.

MISS TEMPLE: Well, Jane, surely you know that when a criminal is accused, he is always allowed to speak in his own

defense. You have been charged with lying. Now you must defend yourself to me as well as you can.

JANE: *(Breathlessly)* **You will really listen to me?**

MISS TEMPLE: Yes, Jane.

JANE: I was never happy at Gateshead with Mrs. Reed. However carefully I obliged, however hard I tried to please her, she always treated me with miserable cruelty. The worst thing she ever did was to shut me up in the Red Room!

MISS TEMPLE: And what is the Red Room?

JANE: A horrible place! There was a ghost in it, the ghost of my uncle, for he died in that room and was laid out there. No one would go into it at night if they could help it, but Mrs. Reed shut me up in there alone, without a candle! I cried and begged her to let me out, but she wouldn't! I was so frightened! I was suffocating!

MISS TEMPLE: Why did Mrs. Reed do this?

JANE: Because her wicked son, John Reed, threw a book at me which cut my head, and when I screamed, he rushed at me and began to beat me with his fists, and I tried to defend myself and pushed him down. And then his sisters, Eliza and Georgiana, flew at me and called me a rat and a murderer, and said I deserved everything I got because I was less than a servant and would always be poor. And they could treat me as cruelly as they liked because I was an orphan and had no money and must depend on them for my living. And Mrs. Reed blamed me for hurting John and locked me up in the Red Room to punish me. Oh, I hated that place! I wished to go away from it. I told Mr. Lloyd so, and he said he would help me come away to school.

MISS TEMPLE: Who is Mr. Lloyd?

JANE: The good apothecary who came to see me when I was ill. For I was very ill after that night in the Red Room.

MISS TEMPLE: *(Gently)* **That's enough for now, Jane. I will write to Mr. Lloyd. If his reply agrees with what you have just told**

me, you shall be publicly cleared of every accusation before the entire school. To me, Jane, you are clear now.

JANE: Oh, thank you, Miss Temple!

MISS TEMPLE: Now you must come with me to my room. We'll have tea together. And since Helen Burns is here with you, she may come, too.

HELEN: Thank you, Miss Temple.

MISS TEMPLE: *(With concern)* **How are you tonight, Helen? Have you coughed much today?**

HELEN: Not quite so much as usual, I think, ma'am.

MISS TEMPLE: And the pain in your chest?

HELEN: It is a little better.

MISS TEMPLE: I hope so. Come with me now, both of you. You will be my special guests tonight. *(Rises and starts out.)* **I have a little seed cake that we all can share with our tea. I've been saving it for a special occasion.** *(She exits.)*

HELEN: You see, Jane, you are not without friends as long as you have me and Miss Temple. It is an honor to be invited to tea with her.

JANE: I think I am hungry now, after all. Oh, Helen, how good she is to believe my story! *(She takes HELEN's hand and they follow MISS TEMPLE off.)*

A Dramatic Reading of

FATHER WILLIAM

By Lewis Carroll

Lewis Carroll (1832-1898) is a pseudonym for Charles Lutridge Dodgson. Though he is popularly known as a writer of books for children, he was a mathematician of distinction. His books and pamphlets on principles of mathematics were widely used in academic settings. He was a skilled writer of humorous verse and had contributed his verse to *The Comic Times* in 1855, *The Train* in 1856 and later to *Punch* and *College Rhymes*. His inspiration failed him in middle life and toward the end he became somewhat of a recluse and eccentric.

CHARACTERS: NARRATOR, FATHER WILLIAM, THE YOUNG MAN.

SCENE: This humorous poem by Lewis Carroll may be performed by FATHER WILLIAM seated in a chair, the YOUNG MAN seated on a stool at his feet, and the NARRATOR standing at one side. The lines should flow smoothly from one speaker to the next. Actions such as standing on one's head, turning a back somersault, or producing the ointment box are optional.

YOUNG MAN: You are old, Father William,
NARRATOR: The young man said,
YOUNG MAN: And your hair has become very white.
And yet you incessantly stand on your head –
Do you think, at your age, it is right?
FATHER WILLIAM: In my youth,
NARRATOR: Father William replied to his son,
FATHER WILLIAM: I feared it might injure the brain;
But now that I'm perfectly sure I have none,
Why, I do it again and again.
YOUNG MAN: You are old,
NARRATOR: Said the youth,
YOUNG MAN: As I mentioned before,
And have grown most uncommonly fat;
Yet you turned a back somersault in at the door –
Pray, what is the reason for that?
FATHER WILLIAM: In my youth,
NARRATOR: Said the sage, as he shook his gray locks,
FATHER WILLIAM: I kept all my limbs very supple
By the use of this ointment – one shilling the box –
Allow me to sell you a couple?
YOUNG MAN: You are old,
NARRATOR: Said the youth,
YOUNG MAN: And your jaws are too weak
For anything tougher than suet;

Yet you finished the goose, with the bones and the beak;
Pray how did you manage to do it?

FATHER WILLIAM: In my youth,

NARRATOR: Said his father,

FATHER WILLIAM: I took to the law,
And argued each case with my wife.
And the muscular strength which it gave to my jaw
Has lasted the rest of my life.

YOUNG MAN: You are old,

NARRATOR: Said the youth,

YOUNG MAN: One would hardly suppose
That your eye was as steady as ever;
Yet you balanced an eel on the end of your nose –
What made you so awfully clever?

FATHER WILLIAM: I have answered three questions, and that is enough,

NARRATOR: Said his father,

FATHER WILLIAM: Don't give yourself airs!
So you think I can listen all day to such stuff?
Be off, or I'll kick you downstairs!

(The YOUNG MAN makes a hurried exit.)

From

THROUGH THE LOOKING GLASS

By Lewis Carroll

The delightful nonsense of Lewis Carroll lives on today in his novel for all ages, *Through the Looking Glass.* Published in 1871, this book continues the adventures of Alice in a topsy-turvy world where she meets unpredictable and exasparating characters such as the White Queen and the Red Queen in a windy woods.

CHARACTERS: ALICE, THE WHITE QUEEN, THE RED QUEEN.

ALICE: *(Enters, carrying a shawl.)* **Here's somebody's shawl that's blown away. It seems there's quite a hurricane here in this wood. I wonder who this shawl belongs to?**

WHITE QUEEN: *(Enters, running, with a helpless, frightened look, her clothes awry and her hair tumbled with a brush caught in it. She mutters to herself as she runs here and there with both arms outstretched as if she were flying.)* **Bread and butter... bread and butter...bread and butter...**

ALICE: It's the White Queen, and this shawl must be hers. I'm very glad I happened to be in the way to find it. *(She catches up with the WHITE QUEEN and tries to help her adjust the shawl around her. To herself)* **How dreadfully untidy she is! Every single thing is crooked and she's all over pins.** *(To the WHITE QUEEN)* **May I put your shawl straight for you?**

WHITE QUEEN: *(In a melancholy tone)* **I don't know what's the matter with it. It's out of temper, I think. I've pinned it here, and I've pinned it there, but there's no pleasing it.**

ALICE: It *can't* go straight, you know, if you pin it all on one side. And dear me, what a state your hair is in!

WHITE QUEEN: The brush has got entangled in it. *(Sighs.)* **And I lost the comb yesterday.**

ALICE: Let me help you. *(She releases the brush and tries to put the WHITE QUEEN's hair in order.)* **I'll do my best, and I'm sure you'll look rather better in a moment. But really, you should have a lady's maid.**

WHITE QUEEN: I'll take *you* with pleasure! Twopence a week and jam every other day.

ALICE: *(Laughing)* **I don't want you to hire *me*, and I don't care for jam.**

WHITE QUEEN: It's very good jam.

ALICE: Well, I don't want any today.

WHITE QUEEN: You couldn't have it today if you *did* want it.

The rule is, jam tomorrow and jam yesterday, but never jam *today*.

ALICE: But it must come sometimes to jam today.

WHITE QUEEN: No, it can't. It's jam every *other* day. Today isn't any *other* day, you know.

ALICE: I don't understand. It's dreadfully confusing.

WHITE QUEEN: *(Kindly)* **That's the effect of living backwards. It always makes me a little giddy at first.**

ALICE: Living backwards! I never heard of such a thing.

WHITE QUEEN: There's one great advantage in it. One's memory works both ways.

ALICE: I'm sure *mine* only works one way. I can't remember things before they happen.

WHITE QUEEN: It's a poor sort of memory that only works backwards.

ALICE: What sort of things do *you* remember best?

WHITE QUEEN: Oh, things that happened the week after next. *(Shrieks suddenly.)* **Oh! Oh! Oh! My finger's bleeding! Oh! Oh!**

ALICE: What's the matter? Have you pricked your finger?

WHITE QUEEN: I haven't pricked it yet, but I soon shall. Oh! Oh!

ALICE: *(Trying not to laugh)* **And when do you expect to do it?**

WHITE QUEEN: When I fasten my shawl again. The pin will come undone directly. Oh! Oh! *(She fumbles with the pin that holds her shawl closed.)*

ALICE: Take care! You're holding it all crooked!

WHITE QUEEN: Oh! Oh! There! You see? I've pricked my finger! That accounts for the bleeding, you know. Now you understand the way things happen here.

ALICE: But why don't you scream now?

WHITE QUEEN: Why, I've done all the screaming already. What would be the good of having it all over again? *(The shawl falls to the ground.)* **Oh, there goes the shawl again.** *(She stoops to pick it up and bumps into the RED QUEEN who enters. Both bow to each other, then sit down on a log, one on* *either side of ALICE.)*

ALICE: *(Looking at both QUEENS, curiously)* **Well, this is grand! It's almost as if I were a Queen, too, and queens have to be dignified, you know. Those crowns look heavy.** *(Timidly, to the RED QUEEN)* **Please, would you tell me —**

RED QUEEN: *(Sharply)* **Speak when you're spoken to!**

ALICE: But if everybody obeyed that rule, and if you only spoke when you were spoken to, and the other person always waited for *you* to begin, nobody would ever say anything.

RED QUEEN: Ridiculous! Did I hear you say you wanted to be a queen?

ALICE: Well, I thought it might be –

RED QUEEN: You can't be a queen, you know, til you've passed the proper examination.

ALICE: Oh, I'm sure I didn't mean –

RED QUEEN: You *should* have meant! What is the use of a child without any meaning? Even a joke should have some meaning and a child's more important than a joke, I hope. You couldn't deny that, even if you tried with both hands.

ALICE: I don't deny things with my hands.

RED QUEEN: Nobody said you did!

WHITE QUEEN: *(Wearily)* **She's in that state of mind that she wants to deny *something,* only she doesn't know what to deny.**

RED QUEEN: *(After a pause)* **I invite you to Alice's dinner party this afternoon.**

WHITE QUEEN: *(Feebly)* **And I invite *you*.**

ALICE: I didn't know I was to have a party at all, but if there *is* to be one, I think I ought to invite the guests.

RED QUEEN: We gave you the opportunity of doing it, but I daresay you've not had many lessons in manners.

ALICE: Manners are not taught in lessons. Lessons teach you to do sums and things of that sort.

WHITE QUEEN: Can you do addition? What's one and one and

one and one and one and one and one and one and one and one?

ALICE: I don't know. I lost count.

RED QUEEN: She can't do addition. Can you do subtraction? Take nine from eight.

ALICE: I can't take nine from eight, you know.

WHITE QUEEN: She can't do subtraction. Can you do division? Divide a loaf by a knife. What's the answer to that?

ALICE: I suppose –

RED QUEEN: Bread and butter, of course!

RED QUEEN & WHITE QUEEN: She can't do sums a bit!

RED QUEEN: Can you answer useful questions? How is bread made?

ALICE: Oh, I know that. You take some flour –

WHITE QUEEN: Where do you pick the flower? In a garden or in the hedges?

ALICE: It isn't picked at all. It's ground.

WHITE QUEEN: How many acres of ground?

RED QUEEN: Never mind! Do you know languages? What's the French for fiddle-de-dee?

ALICE: Fiddle-de-dee isn't English.

RED QUEEN: Whoever said it was?

ALICE: If you'll tell me what language fiddle-de-dee is, I'll tell you the French for it.

RED QUEEN: *(Drawing herself up, stiffly)* **Queens never make bargains!**

ALICE: *(With a loud sigh)* **I wish queens never asked questions!**

WHITE QUEEN: *(Anxiously)* **Don't let us quarrel. What is the cause of lightning?**

ALICE: The cause of lightning is the thunder. No, no, I meant the other way.

RED QUEEN: Too late! Once you've said a thing, that fixes it, and you must take the consequences.

WHITE QUEEN: *(Yawning)* **Oh, I am suddenly so sleepy.** *(Leans* *her head on ALICE's shoulder.)*

RED QUEEN: She's tired, poor thing! Smooth her hair, lend her your nightcap, and sing her a soothing lullaby.

ALICE: I haven't got a nightcap with me, and I don't know any soothing lullabies.

RED QUEEN: I must do it myself, then. *(Sings.)* **"Hushaby lady, in Alice's lap; till the feast's ready, we've time for a nap. When the feast's over, we'll go to the ball, Red Queen and White Queen, and Alice and all!" And now you know the words, just sing it through to me.** *(Lays her head on ALICE's other shoulder.)* **I'm getting sleepy, too.** *(Both QUEENS fall asleep.)*

ALICE: Now what am I to do? I don't think it ever happened before that anyone had to take care of two queens asleep at once! No, not in all the history of England! Oh, do wake up, you heavy things! *(Sighs.)* **Well, if they are sleeping, I may as well sleep, too.** *(She yawns.)* **Everything is so very strange here. Perhaps when I wake up, things will make more sense.** *(She yawns again, then falls sleep between the two sleeping QUEENS.)*

From

DON QUIXOTE

By Miguel de Cervantes

First published in 1604, Miguel de Cervantes' bold and whimsical adventures of Don Quixote have delighted readers of all ages. In his novel, Cervantes attacks and ridicules the romance of chivalry and extravagant adventure so popular in the Spanish literature of his time through his self-made knight, Don Quixote. This colorful character, obsessed to the point of absurdity with knight errantry from his vast reading of romantic literature, leaves his home in the company of his squire, a country laborer named Sancho Panza, determined to right wrongs, rescue damsels in distress, and ever display himself as the supreme example of chivalrous knighthood. His lady is an imaginary virtuous and beautiful vision called Dulcinea del Toboso. He rides a bony steed named Rocinante. His squire straddles a gray ass named Dapple, and together they have numerous disastrous adventures wherein they suffer bodily injury and mental frustration.

CHARACTERS: DON QUIXOTE, a Spanish Knight; SANCHO PANZA, his squire; A PEASANT GIRL.

SCENE: DON QUIXOTE and SANCHO, continuing their search for the Lady Dulcinea, come to the city of El Toboso where the knight is convinced she resides. It is very late at night.

(DON QUIXOTE and SANCHO enter, very dusty, weary, and disheveled from their long day's ride.)

DON QUIXOTE: Sancho, my son, lead on to the palace of Dulcinea. It may be that we shall find her awake.

SANCHO: Great heavens! Is this a likely hour to find the gate open? And would it be right for us to start knocking till they hear us and open for us, and put all the people into uproar and confusion? Besides, how are we to recognize our lady's house in the dark, even though you must have seen it thousands of times?

DON QUIXOTE: You will drive me to despair, Sancho. Have I not told you a thousand times that I have never seen the peerless Dulcinea in all the days of my life, nor ever crossed the threshold of her palace, and that I am only enamoured of her by hearsay and because of the great reputation she bears for beauty and wisdom?

SANCHO: Well, sir, day's coming on apace. It'll be better for your worship to hide in some bushes somewhere near. I will then come and not leave a corner of this whole place unsearched for the house, castle, or palace of my lady. And when I find it, I will speak to her Grace and tell her where and how your worship is waiting and expecting her to give you orders and instructions how you may see her without damage to her honor and reputation.

DON QUIXOTE: Sancho, I welcome this advice and accept it with very good will. I will hide myself, then you go, and do not be confused when you find yourself before the light of

the sun of beauty you are going to seek. *(They move to one side.)* **How much more fortunate you are than all other squires in the world! Bear in your mind, and let it not escape you, the manner of your reception; whether she changes color whilst you are delivering her my message; whether she is stirred or troubled on hearing my name; whether she shifts from her cushion, should you, by chance, find her seated on the rich dais of her authority. If she is standing, watch whether she rests first on one foot and then on the other; whether she repeats her reply to you two or three times; whether she changes from mild to harsh, from cruel to amorous; whether she raises her hand to her hair to smooth it, although it is not untidy. In fact, my son, watch all her actions and movements, because if you relate them to me as they were, I shall deduce what she keeps concealed in the secret places of her heart as far as concerns the matter of my love. For you must know, Sancho, that between lovers the outward actions and movements they reveal when their loves are under discussion are most certain messengers, bearing news of what is going on in their innermost souls. Go, friend, and may better fortune than mine guide you and send you better success than I expect, waiting between fear and hope in this bitter solitude where you leave me.**

SANCHO: I'll go and come back quickly. Cheer up that little heart of yours, dear master, for it must be no bigger now than a hazel nut. Remember the saying that a stout heart breaks bad luck, and where there are no flitches there are no hooks, and they say, too, where you least expect it, out jumps the hare.

DON QUIXOTE: Indeed, Sancho, you always bring in your proverbs very much to the purpose of our business. May God give me as good luck in my ventures as you have in your sayings. *(He crouches down at one side with his back to SANCHO, looking very anxious and sad.)*

SANCHO: *(Sees that his master is settled, then goes off a little way to commune with himself.)* **Now, brother Sancho, where are you going? What are you going to look for? I am going to look for a Princess, and in her the sun of beauty and all heaven besides. And where do you expect to find this thing you speak of, Sancho? In the great city of El Toboso. Very well, and on whose behalf are you going to see her? On behalf of the famous knight Don Quixote de la Mancha, who rights wrongs, gives meat to the thirsty, and drink to the hungry. All this is right enough. Now, do you know her house? My master says it will be some royal palace or proud castle. And have you by any chance ever seen her? No, neither I nor my master have ever seen her. And, if the people of El Toboso know that you are here for the purpose of enticing away their Princesses and disturbing their ladies, do you think it would be right and proper for them to come and give you such a basting as would grind your ribs to powder and not leave you a whole bone in your body? Yes, they would be absolutely in the right.** *(He shudders and begins to pace about.)*

Well now, I have seen from countless signs that this master of mine is a raving lunatic who ought to be tied up, and me, I can't be much better, for since I follow him and serve him, I'm more of a fool than he – if the proverb is true that says, tell me what company you keep and I will tell you what you are. Well, he's mad, and it's the kind of madness that generally mistakes one thing for another, and thinks white black and black white, as was clear when he said that the windmills were giants, and the friar's mules dromedaries, and the flocks of sheep hostile armies, and many other things to this tune. So it won't be very difficult to make him believe that the first peasant girl I run across is the lady Dulcinea. If he doesn't believe it, I'll swear and if he swears, I'll outswear him, and if he

sticks to it, I shall stick to it harder, so that, come what may, my word shall always stand up to his. Perhaps if I hold out, I shall put an end to his sending me on any more of these errands. Or perhaps he'll think, as I fancy he will, that one of those wicked enchanters who, he says, have a grudge against him, has changed her shape to vex and spite him.

(A very plain, coarse-looking PEASANT GIRL wanders in. She is dirty, dressed in rags, and wears a stupid, surly expression. She carries an armful of sticks, which she suddenly drops, and stoops to pick up.)

SANCHO: *(With a chuckle)* **Now here is the answer to my dilemma! This village girl will pass for the Lady Dulcinea with a little help from me.** *(He rushes to DON QUIXOTE.)* **Master, you have nothing more to do than to come into the open to see the Lady Dulcinea del Toboso who has come to meet your worship.** *(He helps him up.)*

DON QUIXOTE: What is that you say, Sancho, my friend? See that you do not deceive me, or seek to cheer my real sadness with false joys.

SANCHO: What could I gain by deceiving your worship? Come and see your Princess, our mistress, dressed and adorned as befits her, to dazzle the senses. *(Trying not to smile, he leads him to where the GIRL is squatting in the road, picking up and dropping her sticks.)*

DON QUIXOTE: *(Staring)* **What is this, Sancho? I see nothing but a very dirty village girl.**

SANCHO: God deliver me from the Devil! Wipe your eyes, sir, and look again!

DON QUIXOTE: My eyes see only a very awkward and ugly village girl on her hands and knees in the road.

SANCHO: Oh, sir, come and do homage to the mistress of your thoughts who is here before you, awaiting your greeting. *(To the GIRL, with a comical bow)* **Queen and Princess and Duchess of beauty, may your Highness and Mightiness**

deign to receive into your grace and good liking your captive knight, who stands here, turned to marble stone, all troubled and unnerved at finding himself in your magnificent presence. I am Sancho Panza, his squire, and he is the travel-weary knight, Don Quixote de la Mancha, called also by the name of the Knight of the Sad Countenance.

GIRL: *(Rises, staring at SANCHO in amazement and then at DON QUIXOTE who stares at her in turn, wiping his eyes in disbelief. Harshly)* **Get out of the road, confound you, and leave me in peace!**

SANCHO: *(On his knees)* **O Princess and world-famous Lady of El Toboso! How is it that your magnanimous heart is not softened when you see the column and prop of knight errantry kneeling before your sublimated presence?**

GIRL: *(Threatening SANCHO with a stick)* **Wait till I get my hand on you, you great ass! Who are you petty gentry to come and make fun of a village girl, as if I couldn't give you as good as you bring! Get on your way and leave me alone!**

DON QUIXOTE: Rise, Sancho, for I see that Fortune, unsatisfied with the ill already done me, has closed all roads by which any comfort may come to this wretched soul I bear in my body. *(Moves closer to the GIRL with arms outstretched.)* **And you, O perfection of all desire! Pinnacle of human gentleness! Sole remedy of this afflicted heart that adores you! Now that the malignant enchanter persecutes me and has put clouds and cataracts into my eyes, and has changed and transformed the peerless beauty of your countenance into the semblance of a poor peasant girl, if he has not at the same time turned mine into the appearance of some spectre to make it abominable to your sight, do not refuse to look at me softly and amorously, perceiving in this submission and prostration, which I make before your deformed beauty, the humility with which my soul adores you.** *(He kneels.)*

GIRL: **Tell that to my grandmother! Do you think I want to listen to this nonsense? Get out of the way and leave me alone, I tell you!** *(She spits at him, picks up her bundle of sticks, and runs off, threatening them both with upraised stick.)*

DON QUIXOTE: **Oh, do you see now what a spite the enchanters have against me, Sancho? See to what extremes the malice and hatred they bear me extend, for they have sought to deprive me of the happiness I should have enjoyed in seeing my mistress in her true person.** *(He struggles to get up, and Sancho helps him to his feet.)* **In truth, I was born a very pattern for the unfortunate, and to be a target and mark for the arrows of adversity. You must observe also, Sancho, that these traitors were not satisfied with changing and transforming my Dulcinea into a figure as low and ugly as that peasant girl's. They have also deprived her of something most proper to great ladies, which is the sweet smell they have from always moving among ambergris and flowers. I tell you, Sancho, that I got such a whiff of raw garlic from her as stank me out and poisoned me to the heart.**

SANCHO: *(Stamping about with clenched fists)* **Oh, the curs! Oh, wretched and spiteful enchanters! I should like to see you strung up by the gills like pilchards on a reed! Wise you are and powerful, and much evil you do! It should be enough for you, ruffians, to have changed the pearls of my lady's eyes into corktree galls, and her hair of purest gold into red oxtail bristles, and all her features, in fact, from good to bad, without meddling with her smell!**

DON QUIXOTE: *(Sadly, moving slowly away)* **I say once more, Sancho, and I will repeat it a thousand times – I am the most unfortunate of men!**

SANCHO: *(Going after him)* **Oh, come, pull yourself together, your worship. Cheer up and show that gay spirit knights errant should have. What despondency is this? Let all the**

Dulcineas in the world go to Old Nick! The well-being of a single knight errant is worth more than all the enchantments and transformations on earth. Come, sir, the road lies open before us! *(He leads his master off, but unable to resist one glance back at the way the GIRL went, he cannot squelch a hearty laugh poorly disguised as a cough.)*

From

THE RED BADGE OF COURAGE

By Stephen Crane

Stephen Crane, who never experienced actual combat, published his compellingly realistic war novel, *The Red Badge of Courage, An Episode of the American Civil War,* in 1895. Through the character of Henry Fleming, Crane reveals a young soldier's thoughts and feelings as he faces the challenge of going into battle.

CHARACTERS: Three young privates in the Union Army: HENRY FLEMING, JIM CONKLIN, WILSON.

SCENE: An army camp along a riverbank. HENRY FLEMING, who has not yet known battle, sits beside a campfire. A comrade, WILSON, lies near him, dozing in the sun. JIM CONKLIN, another comrade, suddenly dashes in, breathless with excitement.

JIM: We're goin' to move tomorrah, sure, Henry! We're goin' 'way up the river, out across, and come around in behind 'em!

HENRY: Honest, Jim? How do you know?

JIM: Didn't I hear it from a reliable friend, who heard it from a cavalryman who heard it from his own brother, one of the orderlies at division headquarters?

WILSON: *(Sitting up, irritably)* **It's a lie! A thunderin' lie! I don't believe the derned old army's ever goin' to move. I've got ready to move eight times in the last two weeks, and we ain't moved yet!**

JIM: Well, you can b'lieve me or not, jest as you like, Wilson. I don't care a hang! I tell you what I know, and you can take it or leave it. It don't make no difference to me. But pretty soon you'll find out I was right. *(He grabs his haversack and begins to arrange the articles in it with great care.)*

WILSON: Huh! You don't know everything in the world, do you?

JIM: Didn't say I knew everything in the world!

WILSON: *(Lies down again.)* **Huh!**

HENRY: *(After a thoughtful pause)* **Is there goin' to be a battle, *sure*, Jim?**

JIM: Of course there is, Henry. Of course there is! You jest wait till tomorrow and you'll see one of the biggest battles ever was!

HENRY: Thunder!

JIM: Oh, you'll see fightin' this time, my boy, what'll be regular

out-and-out fighting.

WILSON: Huh! Like as not, this story'll turn out jest like them others did.

JIM: Not much it won't! Didn't the cavalry all start this morning? They say there ain't hardly any cavalry left in camp. They're going to Richmond, or some place, while we fight all the Johnnies. It's some dodge like that. The regiment's got orders, too, and they're raising blazes all over camp. Anybody can see that!

WILSON: Shucks!

HENRY: *(After a moment)* **Jim?**

JIM: What?

HENRY: How do you think the regiment'll do?

JIM: Oh, they'll fight all right, I guess, after they once get into it. There's been heaps of fun poked at 'em because they're new, of course, but they'll fight all right, I guess.

HENRY: Think any of the boys'll run?

JIM: Oh, there may be a few of 'em run, but there's them kind in every regiment, 'specially when they first goes under fire. Of course, it might happen that the whole kit-and-kaboodle might start and run, if some big fighting come first off, and then again, they might stay and fight like fun. But you can't bet on nothing. Of course, we ain't never been under fire yet, and it ain't likely we'll lick the whole rebel army all-to-oncet the first time. But I think we'll fight better than some, if worse than others. That's the way I figger. They call the regiment "fresh fish" and everything, but the boys come of good stock, and most of 'em'll fight like sin after they once get shootin'.

WILSON *(With great scorn)* **Oh, you think you know all about it!**

HENRY: Did you ever think you might run, Jim? *(He laughs nervously.)*

WILSON: Hah!

JIM: *(With a glare at WILSON, then a thoughtful look at HENRY)* **Well, I've thought it might get too hot for Jim Conklin in some of them scrimmages, and if a whole lot of boys started and run, why, I s'pose I'd start and run. And if I once started to run, I'd run like the devil, and no mistake! But if everybody was a-standin' and a-fightin', why, I'd stand and fight! By jiminey, I would. I'll bet on it!** *(Looking off)* **There's the lieutenant. He might have some more news.** *(He drops his haversack and runs out.)*

WILSON: Huh!

HENRY: *(Ignoring WILSON, he rises and paces about the camp-fire, murmuring to himself.)* **So we're goin' to fight at last! Tomorrow, there's goin' to be a battle, and we'll be in it. Lord, we been waitin' for months. Why, the only enemy we've seen is some pickets long the river bank, and they shot at us, of course, but it didn't mean nothin'. One feller swore that the guns had exploded without their permission.** *(He laughs shortly, then sobers.)* **And them vet'rans always tellin' us tales of smoke and fire and blood, tryin' to scare us; sayin' the Johnnies'll sweep down on us like the Huns, chargin' through hell's fire and brimstone just to get a hold on a haversack, and how we won't have the stomach to resist!** *(Fiercely)* **Well, them derned ol' vet'rans ain't to be trusted, I say! But, seems like all we been doin' since we enlisted is drill and review and drill and review, and march here and there, over and over again, and now...**

WILSON: *(Abruptly, sitting up)* **Well, I don't mind marchin' if there's goin' to be fightin' at the end of it. What I hate is gettin' moved here and there with no good comin' of it exceptin' sore feet and short rations.**

HENRY: Well, there'll be plenty of fightin' this time. Jim says so!

WILSON: Well, *if* there is, then we'll thump 'em, certain sure! *(He rises and stretches.)* **If the truth was known, they've**

licked us about every clip up to now, but this time, *if* there's a fight, we'll lick 'em good!

HENRY: Oh, and if there's a fight, you're goin' to do great things, I s'pose, Wilson?

WILSON: *(Suddenly thoughtful)* **Oh, I don't know. I s'pose I'll do as well as the rest.**

HENRY: How do you know you won't run when the time comes?

WILSON: Run? Me? Of course not! *(Laughs.)*

HENRY: Well, lots of good-a-'nough men have thought they was going to do great things before the fight, but when the time come, they skedaddled.

WILSON: Well, that's all true, I s'pose, but *I'm* not going to skedaddle. The man that bets on my running will lose his money, that's all.

HENRY: Oh, shucks! You ain't the bravest man in the world, are you?

WILSON: *(Indignant)* **No, I ain't, and I didn't say I was the bravest man in the world, neither. I said I was going to do my share of fighting, that's what I said. And I am, too. Who are you, anyhow? You talk as if you thought you was Napoleon Bonaparte.** *(He stalks off.)*

HENRY: Well, you needn't git mad about it! *(He looks after WILSON a moment, then throws himself down on his blanket.)* **Good Lord, what's the matter with me? I wish I was home again! I never should've left Ma there alone on the farm. I wish I was makin' the rounds from the house to the barn, and from the barn to the fields and back again. I wish I could see that old brindle cow again and milk her and curse her and throw the milkin' stool at her!** *(He sits up anxiously.)* **I ain't formed for a soldier! I ain't like Jim Conklin and Wilson, so sure of themselves! I don't know if I'll stand and fight, or...or if I'll run.** *(He scrambles to his feet, a frightened look on his face, glancing around him.)* **I must be the only man in camp who feels**

this way. As far as this derned ol' war is concerned, I don't know nothin' about myself! Nothin'! And I won't know nothin' until a real fight comes. A real fight. Maybe tomorrow. *(He looks off across the river.)* **Maybe tomorrow.**

From

GREAT EXPECTATIONS

By Charles Dickens

Charles Dickens' novel, *Great Expectations,* published in 1861, may be remembered for three of its outstanding characters: Pip, the boy who grew up in a blacksmith's home but was destined to have great expectations; the haughty and beautiful Estella, brought up to be an instrument of revenge by Miss Havisham, the bitter old woman whose intended husband failed to appear on her wedding day. Pip falls in love with Estella, just as Miss Havisham hopes he will, and Estella offers him no encouragement, again as Miss Havisham intends. Years after both were children in Miss Havisham's house, and now in their late teens, Pip and Estella meet once again.

CHARACTERS: PIP, ESTELLA, MISS HAVISHAM.

SCENE: A room in MISS HAVISHAM's house. She is seated in a chair by the hearth, wearing the faded and tattered wedding dress she has worn for years, and leaning on a cane. ESTELLA, elegantly dressed, sits beside her. PIP enters.

MISS HAVISHAM: Come in, Pip. Come in. How do you do, Pip? *(PIP approaches and kisses her hand.)* **So you kiss my hand as if I were a queen, eh?**

PIP: I heard, Miss Havisham, that you were so kind as to wish me to come see you.

MISS HAVISHAM: Well? *(She turns to look adoringly at ESTELLA.)* **Do you see her?**

PIP: *(He takes the hand ESTELLA offers him.)* **Estella. It is a pleasure to see you again. I've looked forward to it for a long time.**

MISS HAVISHAM: Do you find her much changed, Pip? *(She strikes her cane on a chair, gesturing for him to sit down.)*

PIP: *(He sits beside her.)* **When I came in, I thought there was nothing of Estella in the face or figure, but now it all settles down so curiously into the old –**

MISS HAVISHAM: What? You are not going to say into the old Estella! She was proud and insulting, and you wanted to go away from her. Don't you remember?

PIP: That was long ago, Miss Havisham. I knew no better then.

ESTELLA: *(Smiling)* **I'm sure I must have been very disagreeable.**

MISS HAVISHAM: *(To ESTELLA)* **Is *he* changed?**

ESTELLA: Very much.

MISS HAVISHAM: Less coarse and common?

ESTELLA: A little. Yet I'm sure he has not missed me an hour since I have been to France and he to London. *(Rising)* **Come, Pip, walk with me to the window.** *(They cross to one side, looking out the window. MISS HAVISHAM watches them,* *devouring them both with her eyes.)* **There is the garden we knew so well as children, where I watched you fighting with Herbert Pocket. I must have been a singular little creature to hide and watch that day, but I did, and I enjoyed it very much.**

PIP: Herbert and I are great friends now. We share lodgings in London.

ESTELLA: You had no idea, I suppose, of your impending good fortune in those times when we were children here?

PIP: Not the least. *(Pointing off)* **See how the garden has grown up there by the brewery yard. There is where I first saw you, walking on the casks.**

ESTELLA: *(Coldly)* **Did I?**

PIP: Yes. Don't you remember when you came out of the house and brought me my meat and drink?

ESTELLA: No, I don't remember.

PIP: You don't remember that you were so scornful, you made me cry?

ESTELLA: You must know that I have no heart, if that has anything to do with my memory.

PIP: I cannot believe that.

ESTELLA: Oh, I have a heart to be stabbed in or shot in, and, of course, if it ceased to beat, I should cease to be. But I have no softness there, no sympathy, no sentiment.

PIP: Estella...

ESTELLA: I am serious. If we are to be thrown much together, you had better believe it at once. I have not bestowed any tenderness anywhere. I have never had any such thing. Now what's the matter? Are you scared again, as you were when a boy?

PIP: I should be, if I believed what you said just now.

ESTELLA: Then you don't? Very well, it is said, at any rate. You shall not shed tears for my cruelty today. *(She turns away and sits in a chair away from Miss HAVISHAM.)*

MISS HAVISHAM: *(Beckoning to PIP)* **Pip!** *(He goes to her.)* **Is she beautiful, Pip? Graceful? Well-grown? Do you admire her?**

PIP: Everybody must who sees her, Miss Havisham.

MISS HAVISHAM: *(Drawing him closer)* **Love her, Pip. Love her! If she favors you, love her. If she wounds you, love her. If she tears your heart to pieces, love her, love her, love her. Hear me, Pip! I adopted her to be loved. I bred her and educated her to be loved. I developed her into what she is, that she might be loved. Love her! I'll tell you what real love is. It is blind devotion, unquestioning self-humiliation, utter submission, trust and belief against yourself and against the whole world, giving up your whole heart and soul to the smiter – as I did!** *(She rises up, striking out with her cane. PIP eases her back into her seat, where she calms herself and looks dazedly down into her lap. ESTELLA beckons PIP to come to her.)*

ESTELLA: I am going to Richmond in Surrey soon. I am to have a carriage and you are to take me. Miss Havisham has given me a purse and you are to pay my charges out of it. We have no choice, you and I, but to obey our instructions. We are not free to follow our own devices.

PIP: Where are you going to at Richmond?

ESTELLA: I am going to live at a great expense with a lady there who has the power of taking me about and introducing me, and showing people to me and showing me to people.

PIP: I suppose you will be glad of variety and admiration?

ESTELLA: *(Carelessly)* **Yes, I suppose so.**

PIP: I wonder that Miss Havisham can part with you again so soon.

ESTELLA: It is her plan for me, Pip. There is nothing else to be done.

MISS HAVISHAM: Estella! Come sit here beside me.

ESTELLA: I am comfortable where I am.

MISS HAVISHAM: *(Flaring)* **What! Are you tired of me?**

ESTELLA: Only a little tired of myself.

MISS HAVISHAM: *(Furious)* **Speak the truth, you ingrate!** *(Strikes her cane against the floor.)* **You are tired of *me*!** *(ESTELLA looks at her calmly.)* **You stock and stone! You cold, cold heart!**

ESTELLA: *(Indifferently)* **Do you reproach me for being cold? *You?***

MISS HAVISHAM: Are you not?

ESTELLA: You should know. I am what you have made me. Take all the praise; take all the blame; the success, the failure. In short, take me.

MISS HAVISHAM: *(Bitterly)* **Oh, look at her, Pip! Look at her! So hard and thankless, on the hearth where she was reared; where I took her into this wretched breast when it was first bleeding from its stabs, and where I have lavished years of tenderness upon her!**

ESTELLA: You have been very good to me, and I owe everything to you. What would you have of me?

MISS HAVISHAM: Love.

ESTELLA: You have it.

MISS HAVISHAM: I have not.

ESTELLA: *(Still calm)* **Mother by adoption, all I possess is freely yours. All that you have given me is yours to have again. Beyond that I have nothing. And if you ask me to give you what you never gave me, my gratitude and duty cannot do the impossible.**

MISS HAVISHAM: *(Wildly, turning to PIP)* **Did I never give her love? A burning love, inseparable from jealousy and sharp pain, and she speaks thus to me! Let her call me mad!**

ESTELLA: Why should I call you mad? I, of all people? Does anyone know what set purposes you have, half as well as I do? I, who have sat on this hearth, learning your lessons and looking into your face?

MISS HAVISHAM: *(Moaning)* **Soon forgotten! Times soon forgotten!**

ESTELLA: No, not forgotten, but treasured up in my memory. When have you found me false to your teaching? Or unmindful of your lessons? Be just to me.

MISS HAVISHAM: So proud! So proud!

ESTELLA: Who taught me to be proud? Who praised me when I learnt my lesson?

MISS HAVISHAM: So hard, so hard!

ESTELLA: Who taught me to be hard and praised me when I learnt my lesson?

MISS HAVISHAM: But to be proud and hard to *me*! *(Reaching out)* **Estella, to be proud and hard to *me*?**

ESTELLA: *(Perfectly composed; after a moment)* **I cannot think why you should be so unreasonable when I have never forgotten your wrongs and their causes. I have never been unfaithful to you or your schooling. I have never shown any weakness that I can charge myself with.**

MISS HAVISHAM: Would it be weakness to return my love? Yes, yes, you would call it so. *(She moans and turns her head away.)*

ESTELLA: I must be taken as I have been made. The success is not mine, the failure is not mine, but the two together make me. I cannot love anyone or anything.

PIP: *(Unable to control himself any longer)* **Estella, you know I love *you*! You know I have loved you long and dearly, ever since I first saw you in this house, when Miss Havisham brought me here and commanded us to play together for her amusement.**

ESTELLA: When you say you love me, you address nothing in my breast. You touch nothing there. I have tried to warn you of this, have I not?

PIP: *(Miserably)* **Yes.**

ESTELLA: But you will not be warned. You think I don't mean it.

PIP: I hope you do not. Surely, it is not in nature.

ESTELLA: It is in *my* nature – the nature formed within me. You must put me out of your thoughts.

PIP: *(In a burst of passion)* **Out of my thoughts! You are part of my existence, part of myself, since the day I first came here, the rough, common boy, whose poor heart you wounded even then! You have been in every prospect I have ever seen since – on the river, on the sails of ships, on the marshes, in the clouds, in the light, in the darkness, in the wind, the woods, the sea, the streets. You have been the embodiment of every graceful fancy that my mind has ever become acquainted with. The stones of which the strongest London buildings are made are not more real, or more impossible to be displaced by your hands, than your presence and influence have been to me, there and everywhere, and will be. Estella, to the last hour of my life, you cannot choose but remain part of my character, part of the little good in me, part of the evil. I associate you only with the good, and I will faithfully hold you to that always, for you must have done me far more good than harm, let me feel now what sharp distress I may. If you say you can never love me, only keep it in your heart that I will always love you! God bless you! God forgive you!** *(He rushes out of the room. ESTELLA looks after him incredulously. MISS HAVISHAM suddenly puts her hand to her heart, the anger gone out of her, and a look of great sorrow and remorse on her face.)*

From

HANS BRINKER

By Mary Mapes Dodge

Mary Mapes Dodge wrote *Hans Brinker* or *The Silver Skates* in 1865. Her story of a Dutch family quickly became a favorite around the world. In her preface to the book, she wrote: "This little work aims to combine the instructive features of a book of travels with the interest of a domestic tale. Many of its incidents are drawn from life, and the story of Raff Brinker is founded strictly on fact." The Brinker family includes the mother, son, daughter, and father who fell from the dikes and injured his head. He has not been himself since the accident, and his family lives in poverty as he lies helplessly in bed from day to day. However, the family strives to keep their spirits up and earn their meager living. As this scene begins, it is the eve of the Festival of St. Nicholas. In their poor cottage, Dame Brinker has put on a special costume for the festival, much to the delight of her children.

CHARACTERS: HANS BRINKER; GRETEL BRINKER, his sister; DAME BRINKER, their mother.

GRETEL: Oh, Mother, Mother, Mother, how pretty you are! Look, Hans! Isn't it just a picture?

HANS: *(Cheerfully)* **Just like a picture, only I don't like those stocking things on the hands.**

GRETEL: Not like the mitts, brother Hans? Why, they're very important. See, they cover up all the red. Oh, Mother, how white your arm is where the mitt leaves off, and I declare, the bodice is tight for you. You're growing!

DAME BRINKER: *(Laughing)* **This was made long ago, lovey, when I wasn't much thicker about the waist than a churn-dasher. And how do you like the cap?**

GRETAL: Oh, ever so much, Mother. It's beautiful! See, the father is looking!

DAME BRINKER: *(Turns hopefully.)* **Is he?** *(Her smile quickly fades.)* **No, no, he sees nothing. Come, Hans, don't stand gaping at me all day, and the new skates waiting for you at Amsterdam.**

HANS: Ah, Mother, you need many things. Why should I buy the skates?

DAME BRINKER: Nonsense, child. The money was given to you on purpose, or the work was by Hilda van Gleck – it's all the same thing. Go while the sun is high.

GRETEL: Yes, and hurry back. We'll race on the canal tonight if the mother lets us.

HANS: Your spinning wheel wants a new treadle, Mother.

DAME BRINKER: You can make it, Hans.

HANS: So I can. That will take no money. But you need feathers and wool and meal and...

DAME BRINKER: There, there! That will do. Your silver cannot buy everything. Ah, Hans, if our stolen money would but come back on this bright Saint Nicholas Eve, how glad we

would be! Only last night I prayed that the good saint might never give the thieves a wink of sleep till they brought it back! That, or else brighten our wits that we might find it ourselves. Not a sight have I had of it since the day before the dear father was hurt.

HANS: *(Sadly)* **I know, Mother, though you have almost pulled down the cottage in searching.**

DAME BRINKER: But it was of no use. Hiders make best finders.

HANS: Do you think the father could tell us where it is?

DAME BRINKER: I do, and then I don't. I never hold the same belief in the matter two days. Mayhap the father paid it off for the great silver watch we have been guarding since that day. But, no, I'll never believe it.

HANS: The watch was not worth a quarter of the money, Mother.

DAME BRINKER: No, indeed! And your father was a shrewd man up to the last moment. He was too steady and thrifty for silly doings.

HANS: Where did the watch come from, I wonder?

DAME BRINKER: That we shall never know, Hans. I have shown it to the father many a time, but he does not know it from a potato. When he came in that dreadful night to supper, he handed the watch to me and told me to take good care of it until he asked for it again. Just as he opened his lips to say more, Broom Klatterboost came flying in with word that the dike was in danger. Ah, the waters were terrible that week! My man, alack, caught up his tools and ran out. That was the last I ever saw of him in his right mind. He was brought in again by midnight, nearly dead, with his poor head all bruised and cut. The fever passed off in time, but never the dullness; that grew worse every day. We shall never know.

HANS: Aye, Mother, you have done bravely to keep the watch. Many a one would have tossed it off for gold long ago.

DAME BRINKER: And more shame for them! I would not do it.

Besides, the gentry are so hard on us poor folks that if they saw such a thing in our hands, even if we told all, they might suspect the father of...

HANS: *(Angrily)* **They would not dare to say such a thing, Mother! If they did, I'd...**

DAME BRINKER: Hans, you are a true, brave lad. We will never part company with the watch. In his dying hour the dear father might wake and ask for it.

GRETEL: Might wake, mother? Wake and know us?

DAME BRINKER: Aye, child. Such things have been.

HANS: But you are right, Mother, we must never give up the watch. For the father's sake, we will guard it always. The money, though, may come to light when we least expect it.

DAME BRINKER: Never! There is no chance. One thousand guilders! and all gone in a day! One thousand guilders! Oh, whatever did become of them? If they went in an evil way, the thief would have confessed by this on his dying bed; he would not dare to die with such guilt on his soul!

HANS: He may not be dead yet. Any day we may hear of him.

DAME BRINKER: Ah, child, what thief would ever come here? It was always neat and clean, thank God! but not fine; for the father and I saved and saved that we might have something laid by. Little and often soon fills the pouch. We found it so, in truth; besides, the father had a goodly sum already, for service done at the time of the great inundation. Every week we had a guilder left over, sometimes more, for the father worked extra hours and could get high pay for his labor. Every Saturday night we put something by, except the time when you had the fever, Hans, and when Gretel came. At last the pouch grew so full that I mended an old stocking and commenced again. Now that I look back, it seems that the money was up to the heel in a few sunny weeks. There was great pay in those days if a man was quick at engineer work. The stocking went on

filling with copper and silver, and gold. You may well open your eyes, Gretel. I used to laugh and tell the father it was not for poverty I wore my old gown. And the stocking went on filling, so full that sometimes when I woke at night, I'd get up, soft and quiet, and go feel it in the moonlight. Then, on my knees, I would thank our Lord that my little ones could in time get good learning, and that the father might rest from labor in his old age. Sometimes, at supper, the father and I would talk about a new chimney and a good winter-room for the cow. Every week the father would take out the stocking and drop in the money and laugh and kiss me as we tied it up together. But now, up with you Hans! There you sit gaping and the day a-wasting. It's high time you were on your way.

HANS: *(Almost in a whisper)* **Have you ever tried, Mother, to ask the father where the money is? Surely he knows!**

DAME BRINKER: Yes, child, often. But the father only laughs, or he stares at me so strange I am glad to ask no more. When you and Gretel had the fever last winter, and our bread was nearly gone and I could earn nothing, for fear you would die while my face was turned, oh, I tried then! I smoothed his hair and whispered to him soft as a kitten, about the money, where it was, who had it? Alack! He would pick at my sleeve and whisper gibberish till my blood ran cold. At last, while Gretel lay whiter than snow and you were raving on the bed, I screamed to him, it seemed as if he must hear me: "Raff, where is our money? Do you know where it is? The money in the pouch and the stocking in the big chest?" But I might as well have talked to a stone.

HANS: Mother, let us try to forget this money. I am big and strong. Gretel, too, is very quick and willing. Soon all will be prosperous with us again. Why, we would rather see you bright and happy than have all the silver in the world.

Wouldn't we, Gretel?

GRETEL: *(Sobbing)* **The mother knows it.**

DAME BRINKER: Oh, I am blessed to have such children as you! How can I ever be poor when I have such riches!

From

THE TRIMMED LAMP

By O. Henry

O. Henry's stories are filled with remarkably true-to-life characters, colorful language, and wonderful surprise endings. He was especially adept at creating strong young women who knew their own minds. In *The Trimmed Lamp*, he presents three young women of New York City who were known in the late nineteenth century as "shop girls," who worked in stores or factories, earned a modest living, and dreamed of the future.

CHARACTERS: NANCY, LOU, CARRIE.

SCENE: A park bench somewere in the city, where NANCY, LOU, and CARRIE are catching a moment of relaxation after their day's work.

(LOU is dressed in a gaudy, tightfitting outfit with a plumed hat and an ermine scarf and gloves. NANCY and CARRIE are more modestly and neatly dressed, a bit shoddy, but definitely in fashion.

LOU: **Ain't you cold, Nance, in that thin outfit? What a chump you are for working in that old store for eight dollars a week! I made eighteen fifty last week at the laundry. Of course, ironing ain't as swell work as selling lace behind a counter, but it pays. None of us ironers make less than ten dollars a week, and I don't know that it's any less respectful work.**

NANCY: *(Holding her head high)* **You can have it, Lou. I'll take my eight dollars a week and hall bedroom. I like to be among nice things and swell people. And look what a chance I've got! Why, one of our glove girls married a Pittsburgh steel-maker, or blacksmith, or something, the other day, worth a million dollars. I'll catch a swell myself someday. What show would a girl have in a laundry?**

LOU: **Why, that's where I met Dan. He came in for his Sunday shirt and collars and saw me at the first board, ironing. He said he noticed my arms first, how round and white they was.** *(She preens, stretching out her arms.)*

NANCY: *(Sweetly scornful)* **Really, Lou, how come you wear such clothes as you do? It shows fierce taste.**

LOU: **I paid sixteen dollars for this outfit! It's worth twenty-five! A woman left it to be laundered and never called for it. The boss sold it to me. Better talk about that ugly, plain thing you've got on!**

NANCY: This "ugly plain thing" was copied from one that Mrs. Van Alstyne Fisher was wearing. The girls say her bill in the store last year was twelve thousand dollars. I made this myself. It cost me a dollar and a half. Ten feet away you couldn't tell it from hers.

LOU: Oh, well, if you want to starve and put on airs, go ahead! But I'll take my job and good wages, and after hours, give me something as fancy and attractive to wear as I am able to buy!

CARRIE: Well, I'm sure Nancy will stay in the store, as I will. It's something to be surrounded by beautiful things that simply breathe of taste and refinement. If you're in an atmosphere of luxury every day, it's yours, whether your money pays for it, or another's.

NANCY: I learn so much from the women who come in to the store. *(She demonstrates as she talks.)* **I copy and practice a gesture from one, the lifting of an eyebrow from another, a manner of walking, of carrying a purse, of smiling, or greeting a friend, or addressing "inferiors" in station.**

CARRIE: And Mrs. Van Alstyne Fisher is Nancy's best beloved model. Her voice is as clear as silver, as perfect in articulation as a thrush.

NANCY: I shall practice until I can speak exactly the way Mrs. Van Alstyne Fisher does. And from my counter I can hear the finest music from the music room. You can't imagine how many works of the great composers I now recognize.

LOU: But what's the point? What's all this for?

CARRIE: Why, to catch a man, of course! And not just *any* man. Nancy's so particular. She's waiting for a millionaire!

LOU: A millionaire! *(Laughs.)*

NANCY: They come into the store all the time. I've learned to discriminate.

CARRIE: Which means she stands by the window and watches the automobiles in the street. One day a gentleman bought

four dozen handkerchiefs and wooed her over the counter until it was just shameless! After he left, I said to Nancy, "What's wrong? You didn't warm up to that fellow at all. He looks the swell article to me."

NANCY: *(Coolly)* **And I said, "Him? Not for me. I saw him drive up outside. A twelve horsepower machine and an Irish chauffeur! And you saw the kind of handkerchiefs he bought - silk! Give me the real thing or nothing, if you please."**

LOU: So you go after your unknown "catch," eat dry bread, and tighten your belt on your eight dollars a week! Well, not me! I'll stick to my eighteen fifty in the laundry and I'll stick to my Dan. Of course, Dan is always wanting me to marry him right away, but why should I? I'm independent. I can do as I please with the money I earn, and he would never agree for me to keep on working afterwards. Oh, Nance, what do you want to stick to that old store for, and half starve and half dress yourself? I could get you a place in the laundry right now if you'd come. It seems to me you could afford to be a little less stuck-up if you could make a good deal more money.

NANCY: I don't think I'm stuck-up, Lou. I'd rather live on half-rations and stay where I am. But I don't expect to be always behind a counter. I'm learning something new every day. I'm right up against refined and rich people all the time, even if I do only wait on them.

LOU: And you really think you'll be right up against a millionaire some day?

NANCY: I haven't selected one yet. I've been looking them all over.

CARRIE: Goodness! The idea of picking over 'em! *(Laughs.)* **You can bet Nancy won't let one get by her, even if he's a few dollars shy.** *(Sighs.)* **But then, what's the use? Millionaires don't think about working girls like us.**

NANCY: It might be better for them if they did. Some of us could teach them how to take care of their money.

LOU: If one was to speak to me, I know I'd have a duck-fit!

NANCY: That's because you don't know any. I speak to them all the time. The only difference between swells and other people is you have to watch 'em closer. And I may settle for less if he has good taste and a good name. *(Glancing at LOU)* **Don't you think that red silk lining is just a little too bright for that coat, Lou?**

LOU: *(Looking closely at NANCY's jacket)* **Well, no, I don't. But it may seem so beside that faded-looking thing you've got on.**

NANCY: *(Calmly)* **This jacket has exactly the cut and fit of one that Mrs. Van Alstyne Fisher was wearing the other day. This material cost me three ninety-eight. I suppose hers cost a hundred more.**

LOU: Oh, well, it don't strike me as millionaire bait. I shouldn't wonder if I catch one before you do. *(Laughs.)*

CARRIE: I don't know, Lou. Nancy is just keeping her lamp trimmed, so to speak.

LOU: A trimmed lamp? She looks pretty dim if you ask me. *(Laughs gaily.)* **There's Dan.** *(Waves.)* **We're off to the vaudeville show. Dan's got the tickets. We're going to look at the stage diamonds, since we can't shake hands with the real sparklers!** *(Still laughing, she waves at the girls and runs out.)* **Dan! Dan! Here I am!**

CARRIE: *(With a sigh)* **Her Dan is certainly constant and faithful enough.**

NANCY: *(Looking off in the direction of Dan)* **He's nice. He saves his money and dresses modestly. He's the kind of man you tend to forget when he's around, but you remember him well enough when he's not.**

CARRIE: Why, Nance! I didn't know you cared for him at all. He's not a millionaire!

NANCY: No, but he has good sense. He'll make some lucky girl a good catch someday.

CARRIE: Why, hasn't Lou already caught him?

NANCY: *(Still looking off, she links arms with CARRIE.)* **I think I have the price of a vaudeville ticket, Carrie. And I'll stand treat for you. Let's go!** *(She leads a rather surprised CARRIE off after LOU and DAN.)*

From

MOBY DICK

By Herman Melville

Herman Melville's classic story of the great white whale, *Moby Dick,* published in 1851, became his most famous book, resulting from his own rich experience on the seas. The variety of memorable characters in the novel offers a feast for the reader, including Captain Ahab of the whaleboat *Pequod*, with his ivory peg leg and cruelly scarred face, and his crew of ship's mates, harpooneers, and whaling seamen.

CHARACTERS: CAPTAIN AHAB, of the *Pequod;* STARBUCK, Chief Mate; TASHTEGO, Harpooneer.

SCENE: Captain Ahab sights the great white whale that haunts him, and incites his crew to share his fanatic excitement.

AHAB: *(Livid with excitement)* **What do ye do when ye see a whale, men?**

MEN: Sing out for him!

AHAB: Good! And what do ye next, men?

MEN: Lower away, and after him!

AHAB: It's a white whale, I say, a white whale! Skin your eyes for him, men; look sharp for white water; if ye see but a bubble, sing out!

TASHTEGO: Captain Ahab, that white whale must be the same that some call Moby Dick.

AHAB: Moby Dick? Do ye know the white whale then, Tash?

TASHTEGO: Does he fan-tail a little curious, sir, before he goes down? And has he a curious spout, too, very bushy, and a good many iron in his hide?

AHAB: Corkscrew! Aye, the harpoons lie all twisted and wrenched in him. Aye, his spout is a big one, like a whole shock of wheat, and white as a pile of our Nantucket wool after the great annual sheep-shearing. Aye, Tashtego, and he fan-tails like a split jib in a squall. Death and devils, men, it is Moby Dick ye have seen. Moby Dick!

STARBUCK: Captain Ahab, I have heard of Moby Dick – but was it not Moby Dick that took off thy leg?

AHAB: Who told thee that? Aye, Starbuck, aye, my hearties all round, it was Moby Dick that dismasted me; Moby Dick that brought me to this dead stump I stand on now. Aye, aye, it was that accursed white whale that made a poor pegging lubber of me for ever and a day. Aye, and I'll chase him round Good Hope and round the Horn and round the

Norway Maelstrom and round perdition's flames before I give him up. And this is what ye have shipped for, men, to chase that white whale on both sides of land, and over all sides of earth, till he spouts black blood and rolls fin out. What say ye, men, will ye splice hands on it, now? I think ye do look brave.

TASHTEGO: Aye, aye! A sharp eye for the white whale; a sharp lance for Moby Dick!

AHAB: God bless ye! But what's this long face about, Mr. Starbuck? Wilt thou not chase the white whale? Art not game for Moby Dick?

STARBUCK: I am game for his crooked jaw, and for the jaws of death, too, Captain Ahab, if it fairly comes in the way of the business we follow; but I came here to hunt whales, not my commander's vengeance. How many barrels will thy vengeance yield thee even if thou gettest it, Captain Ahab? It will not fetch thee much in our Nantucket market.

AHAB: Nantucket market! Hoot! If money's to be the measurer, man, and the accountants have computed their great countinghouse the globe, by girdling it with guineas, one to every three parts of an inch, then, let me tell thee, that my vengeance will fetch a great premium here!

STARBUCK: Vengeance on a dumb brute, that simply smote thee from blindest instinct! Madness! To be enraged with a dumb thing, Captain Ahab, seems blasphemous.

AHAB: All visible objects, man, are but as pasteboard masks. But in each event, in the living act, the undoubted deed, there, some unknown but still reasoning thing puts forth the mouldings of its features from behind the unreasoning mask. If man will strike, strike through the mask! How can the prisoner reach outside except by thrusting through the wall? To me, the white whale is that wall, shoved near to me. Sometimes I think there's naught beyond. He tasks me; he heaps me; I see in him outrageous

strength, with an inscrutable malice sinewing it. That inscrutable thing is chiefly what I hate, and be the white whale agent, or be the white whale principal, I will wreak that hate upon him. Talk not to me of blasphemy, man; I'd strike the sun if it insulted me. For could the sun do that, then could I do the other; since there is ever a sort of fair play herein, jealousy presiding over all creations.

Attend now, my braves. Drink, ye harpooneers!! Drink and swear, ye men that man the deathful whaleboats bow! Death to Moby Dick! God hunt us all, if we do not hunt Moby Dick to his death!

TASHTEGO: Death to Moby Dick! *(He exits.)*

STARBUCK: *(Under his breath)* **God keep me – keep us all!**

AHAB: *(Sitting down, looking out over the sea)* **Oh, time was, when as the sunrise nobly spurred me, so the sunset soothed. No more. This lovely light, it lights not me. All loveliness is anguish to me, since I can ne'er enjoy. Gifted with the high perception, I lack the low, enjoying power; damned, most subtly and most malignantly! Damned in the midst of Paradise! But what I've dared, I've willed; and what I've willed, I'll do!**

They think me mad – Starbuck does; but I'm demoniac! I am madness maddened! That wild madness that's only calm to comprehend itself! The prophecy was that I should be dismembered, and aye! I lost this leg. I now prophesy that I will dismember my dismemberer. Now, then, be the prophet and the fulfiller one. The path to my fixed purpose is laid with iron rails, whereon my soul is grooved to run. Over unsounded gorges, through the rifled hearts of mountains, under torrents' beds, unerringly I rush! Naught's an obstacle, naught's an angle to the iron way!

STARBUCK: *(Watching him, quietly)* **My soul is more than matched; she's overmanned, and by a madman! Insufferable sting, that sanity should ground arms on such**

a field! But he drilled deep down, and blasted all my reason out of me! I think I see his impious end, but feel that I must help him to it. Will I, nill I, the ineffable thing has tied me to him; tows me with a cable I have no knife to cut. Horrible old man! Who's over him, he cries; aye, he would be a democrat to all above; look, how he lords it over all below! Oh, I plainly see my miserable office, to obey, rebelling; and worse yet, to hate with touch of pity! For in his eyes I read some lurid woe would shrivel me up, had I it. Yet is there hope. Time and tide flow wide. The hated whale has the round watery world to swim in, as the small goldfish has its glassy globe. His heaven-insulting purpose, God may wedge aside. I would up heart, were it not like lead. But my whole clock's run down; my heart the all-controlling weight, I have no key to lift again.

A Dramatic Reading of

OUR HIRED GIRL

By James Whitcomb Riley

The down-home poetry of the Hoosier Poet, James Whitcomb Riley, tells of everyday delights of another time, when something as simple as a custard pie could make a day worth-while. The dialect is pure Hoosier (from the state of Indiana) and fits the poem perfectly. The characters may mime the actions of smelling the pies, running away, eating the scraps of dough, mowing the lawn with a scythe, etc.

CHARACTERS: NARRATOR, a young girl or boy; LIZABUTH ANN, the hired girl; THE RAGGEDY MAN, a hired man.

NARRATOR: Our hired girl, she's 'Lizabuth Ann;
An' she can cook best things to eat!
She ist puts dough in our pie-pan,
An' pours in sompin' at's good an' sweet;
An' nen she salts it all on top
With cinnamon; an' nen she'll stop
An' stoop an' slide it, ist as slow,
In the' old cook-stove, so's 'twon't slop
An' git all spilled; nen bakes it, so
It's custard-pie, first thing you know!
An' nen she'll say,
LIZABUTH ANN: Clear out o' my way!
They's time fer work, an' time fer play!
Take yer dough, an' run, child, run!
Er I can't git no cookin' done!
NARRATOR: When our hired girl 'tends like she's mad,
An' says folks got to walk the chalk
When she's around, er wisht they had!
I play out on our porch and talk
To Th' Raggedy Man 'at mows our lawn;
An' he says,
RAGGEDY MAN: Whew!
NARRATOR: An' nen leans on
His old crook-scythe, and blinks his eyes,
An' sniffs all 'round an' says,
RAGGEDY MAN: I swawn!
Ef my old nose don't tell me lies,
It 'pears like I smell custard-pies!
NARRATOR: An' nen *he'll* say,
RAGGEDY MAN: Clear out o' my way!
They's time fer work, and time fer play!

Take yer dough, an' run, child, run!
Er she cain't git no cookin' done!
NARRATOR: Wunst our hired girl, when she
Got the supper, an' we all et,
An' it wuz night, and Ma an' me
An' Pa went where the "Social" met –
An' nen when we come home, an' see
A light in the kitchen door, an' we
Heerd a maccodeun*, Pa says,
"Lan' – O' Gracious, who can her beau be?"
An' I marched in, an' Lizabuth Ann
Wuz parchin' corn for The Raggedy Man!
Better say,
LIZABUTH ANN: Clear out' o the way!
They's time fer work, and time fer play!
RAGGEDY MAN: Take the hint, an' run, child, run!
Er we cain't git no *courtin'* done!

**This is probably the child's conception of an accordion.*

From

CYRANO de BERGERAC

By Edmond Rostand

One of the most popular characters in modern French literature, Cyrano de Bergerac is a skilled, poetic swordsman possessed of a hot temper, a passionate soul, and an extremely large nose, all of which combine to make him and Edmond Rostand's seventeenth-century tragi-comedy theatrical favorites. The play begins at the Hotel de Bourgogne in Paris where Cyrano has driven the lamentable actor Montfleury from the stage. Cyrano hates this man because he "mouths his verse and moans his tragedy and heaves up like a hod-carrier lines that ought to soar on their own wings." But once the actor is gone, several of the play's patrons protest the action and come to regret the subsequent performance of the great-nosed Cyrano.

CHARACTERS: CYRANO de BERGERAC, THE MEDDLER, VALVERT.

MEDDLER: The great Montfleury! Did you know the Duc de Candale was his patron? Who is yours?

CYRANO: No one.

MEDDLER: No one? No patron?

CYRANO: I said no.

MEDDLER: And when do you leave Paris?

CYRANO: That's as may be.

MEDDLER: The Duc de Candale has a long arm.

CYRANO: Mine is longer... *(Drawing his sword)* **...by three feet of steel.**

MEDDLER: *(Backing away)* **Yes, yes, but do you dream of daring ...**

CYRANO: I do dream of daring. *(Returns his sword to his belt.)* **Tell me, why are you staring at my nose?**

MEDDLER: Oh, I wasn't staring!

CYRANO: *(Moving closer to him)* **Does it astonish you?**

MEDDLER: *(In confusion)* **Your grace misunderstands me.**

CYRANO: Is it long and soft and dangling, like a trunk? Or crooked, like an owl's beak?

MEDDLER: I never said a word about it.

CYRANO: Perhaps a pimple ornaments the end of it? Or a fly parading up and down? What is this portent? This phenomenon?

MEDDLER: But I have been careful not to look at...your nose.

CYRANO: And why not, if you please? Does it disgust you? Does its color appear to you unwholesome?

MEDDLER: Oh, by no means!

CYRANO: Or its form obscene?

MEDDLER: Not in the least!

CYRANO: Then why assume this deprecating manner? Possibly you find it just a trifle large?

MEDDLER: Oh, no! Small, very small, infinitesimal!

CYRANO: *(Roaring)* **What? How? You accuse me of absurdity?**

Small – *my* nose? It is magnificent! You pug! You knob! You button-head! Know that I glory in this nose of mine, for a great nose indicates a great man, genial, courteous, intellectual, virile, courageous, as I am, and such as you, poor wretch, will never dare to be even in imagination. For that face of yours – that blank, inglorious concavity which my right hand finds... *(He strikes the MEDDLER)* **...on top of you, is as devoid of pride, of poetry, of soul, of picturesqueness, of contour, of character, of *nose* in short, as that...** *(Takes him by the shoulders and turns him around)* **...which at the end of that limp spine of yours my left foot discovers...** *(Kicks him.)*

MEDDLER: *(Fleeing)* **Help! Help! Call the guard!**

CYRANO: *(Turning to others in the room)* **Take notice, all who find this feature of my countenance a theme for comedy! When the humorist is noble, then my custom is to show appreciation proper to his rank – more heartfelt – and more pointed.** *(Hand on sword)*

VALVERT: Observe, my friends, I will put this fellow in his place. *(Walks up to CYRANO with an affected air.)* **Ah, your nose...hem! Your nose is...rather large!**

CYRANO: *(Gravely)* **Rather, Valvert. Rather.**

VALVERT: *(Simpering)* **Oh, well...**

CYRANO: Is that all?

VALVERT: *(Turns away with a shrug.)* **Well, of course...**

CYRANO: *(Stopping him)* **Ah, no, young sir! You are too simple. Why, you might have said, oh, a great many things! Mon dieu, why waste your opportunity? For example, thus: Aggressive: "I, sir, if that nose were mine, I'd have it amputated – on the spot!" Or friendly: "How do you drink with such a nose? You ought to have a cup made specially." Or descriptive: "Tis a rock – a crag – a cape – a cape? say rather, a peninsula!" Or inquisitive: What is that receptacle – a razor-case or a portfolio?" Or kindly: "Ah, do you love the little birds so much that when they come and sing**

to you, you give them this to perch on?" Or cautious: "Take care, a weight like that might make you top-heavy." Or eloquent: "When it blows, the typhoon howls and the clouds darken." Or dramatic: "When it bleeds – the Red Sea!" Or parodying Faustus in the play – "Was this the nose that launched a thousand ships and burned the topless towers of Illium?"

These, my dear sir, are things you might have said had you some tinge of letters, or of wit to color your discourse. But wit – you never had an atom; and of letters, you need but three to write you down – an ass! Moreover, if you had the invention, here before these folks to make a jest of me – be sure you would not then articulate the twentieth part of half a syllable of the beginning! For I say these things lightly enough myself, but I allow none else to utter them.

VALVERT: *(Choking)* **Oh, these arrogant grand airs from a clown! Look at him! Not even gloves! No ribbons – no lace – no buckles on his shoes!**

CYRANO: I carry my adornments on my soul. I do not dress up like a popinjay; but inwardly, I keep my daintiness. I do not bear with me, by any chance, an insult not yet washed away – a conscience yellow with unpurged bile – an honor frayed to rags, a set of scruples badly worn. I go caparisoned in gems unseen, trailing white plumes of freedom, garlanded with my good name – no figure of a man, but a soul clothed in shining armor, hung with deeds for decorations, twirling – thus – a bristling wit, and swinging at my side courage, and on the stones of this old town making the sharp truth ring, like golden spurs!

VALVERT: But you –

CYRANO: But I have no gloves! A pity too! I had one – the last one of an old pair – and lost that. Very careless of me. Some gentleman offered me an impertinence. I left it – in his face.

VALVERT: Dolt! Bumpkin! Fool! Insolent puppy! Jobbernowl!

CYRANO: *(Removes his hat and bows.)* **Ah, yes? And I, Cyrano-Savinien-Hercule De Bergerac...** *(He draws his sword and pinions his adversary against the wall)* **...shall see that you die exquisitely!**

From

ROB ROY

By Sir Walter Scott

Sir Walter Scott's romantic Waverly novel, *Rob Roy*, was published in 1817, and became popular as both an adventure story of the heroic Scottish outlaw, and as a historical novel. An early eighteenth-century "Robin Hood" type of hero, Rob Roy fights for justice for his Highlander people against oppression by the English on the border of Scotland and England. While the novel centers around the character of a young English gentleman, Frank Osbaldistone, it is Rob Roy, who figures prominently in Frank's fortunes, who captures the attention and imagination of the reader. When Rob Roy is lured into an ambush, captured, and made a prisoner by his enemy, the Duke of Montrose, young Osbaldistone is sent by Rob Roy's wife to deliver a message from the Highlanders. Upon being admitted to the Duke's camp in the wild highlands, he begins his perilous mission.

CHARACTERS: ROB ROY, a Scottish outlaw; THE DUKE OF MONTROSE, his enemy; FRANK OSBALDISTONE, a young English gentleman.

SCENE: DUKE is seated on a large rock. ROB ROY, bound securely around his arms, reclines on the ground to one side. FRANK approaches.

FRANK: *(With a deep, respectful bow to the DUKE)* **My lord duke, my name is Francis Osbaldistone, of London. I have been an involuntary witness to the defeat the king's soldiers suffered today at the pass of Loch Ard. The Highland victors threaten every species of extremity to the English prisoners they have taken and to the Low Country in general, unless their chief, Rob Roy MacGregor, who this morning you have made prisoner, is returned to them promptly and uninjured.**

DUKE: *(Composedly)* **I should be extremely sorry to expose the unfortunate gentlemen who have been made prisoners to the cruelty of these barbarians, but it is folly to suppose that I will deliver up the author of these disorders and offenses. You may return to those who sent you and inform them that I shall certainly cause Rob Roy MacGregor to be executed, by break of day, as an outlaw taken in arms and deserving death by a thousand acts of violence. I should be most justly held unworthy of my situation and commission did I act otherwise. I well know how to protect the country against this outlaw and his band; and if they injure a hair of the head of any of the unfortunate gentlemen whom an unlucky accident has thrown into their power, I will take such ample vengeance that the very stones of their glens shall sing woe for it this hundred years to come!**

FRANK: My lord, there is obvious danger in such a course of action. I entreat you to make me the bearer of such terms

that might be the means of saving lives. Allow me to convey to you the message of Helen MacGregor, the wife of Rob Roy, who bade me tell you, thus: "That if you injure a hair of her husband's head and do not set him at liberty within the space of twelve hours, there is not a farmer but shall find his barnyard burnt, and not a laird or heritor who shall not lay his head on the pillow at night with the assurance of being a live man in the morning. And if the twelve hours expire without the safe return of Rob Roy, then she will send you her prisoners, each bundled in a plaid and chopped into as many pieces as there are checks in the tartan."

DUKE: *(Rises and paces a short way, appearing to be troubled.)* **It is a hard case. I do feel it as such. But I have a paramount duty to perform to the country.** *(After a pause)* **Rob Roy must die!**

FRANK: Consider, my lord, that perhaps it would be more advisable to detain him at Stirling Castle, as a pledge for the submission and dispersion of his band. It would be a great pity to expose the country to plunder, especially now when the long nights approach and it will be difficult to guard every point. I assure you, my lord, the unfortunate prisoners face certain doom. Also, I have just recently learned that the Highlandmen you thought to buy off to your side have deserted you and made a separate peace with your enemies.

DUKE: *(Angrily)* **Yes, it is so! It is the fate of all alliances.** *(Pacing again)* **I suppose we cannot attempt to penetrate farther into the country, unsupported by friendly Highlanders.**

FRANK: It would be perfect madness, sir.

DUKE: *(Staring at ROB ROY)* **Do you see him, Mr. Osbaldistone? Do you see him there? Let me make you sensible, by your own eyes and ears, of the extreme unfitness of leaving him space for further outrage. MacGregor! Come here!**

ROB ROY: *(Gets to his feet and approaches the DUKE with a bold, dignified bow.)* **My lord duke.**

DUKE: It is long since we have met, MacGregor.

ROB ROY: It is so, my lord. *(Twisting in his bonds)* **I could have wished it had been when I could have better paid the compliments I owe to your grace – but there's a good time coming.**

DUKE: No time like the present, for the hours are fast flying that must settle your last account with all mortal affairs. I do not say this to insult your distress, but you must be aware yourself that you draw near the end of your career. I do not deny that you may sometimes have done less harm than others of your unhappy trade, and that you may occasionally have exhibited marks of talent and even of a disposition which promised better things. But you are aware how long you have been the terror and the oppressor of a peaceful neighborhood, and by what acts of violence you have maintained and extended your usurped authority. You know, in short, that you have deserved death and that you must prepare for it.

ROB ROY: My lord, although I may well lay my misfortunes at your grace's door, yet I will never say that you yourself have been the willful and witting author of them. For if I had thought so, your grace would not this day be sitting in judgment on me, for you have been three times within good rifle distance of me when you were thinking only of the red deer, and few people have known me miss my aim. But as for them that have abused your grace's ear and set you up against me, a man that was once as peaceful a man as any in the land, and made your name the warrant for driving me to utter extremity, I have some amends of them, and for all that your grace now says, I expect to live to have more.

DUKE: *(His anger rising)* **I know that you are a determined and**

impudent villain who will keep his oath if he swears to mischief, but it shall be my care to prevent you. You have no enemies but your own wicked actions. And you will do well, sir, to warn your wife and family and followers to beware how they use the gentlemen they hold hostage, as I will requite tenfold on them and their kin and allies, the slightest injury done to any of his majesty's liege subjects.

ROB ROY: My lord, none of my enemies will allege that I have been a bloodthirsty man, and were I now with my folk, I could rule four or five hundred wild Highlanders as easy as your grace the eight or ten lackeys and footboys of yours. But if your grace means to take the head away from a house, you may lay your account there will be misrule among the members.

DUKE: It is your very sense and cunning that have so long maintained your reign. A mere Highland robber would have been put down in as many weeks as he had flourished years. But your gang, without you, shall no more be dreaded as a permanent annoyance. It will no longer exist than a wasp without its head, which may sting once, perhaps, but be instantly crushed into annihilation.

ROB ROY: You speak like a boy, my lord, who thinks the old gnarled oak can be twisted as easily as the young sapling. Can I forget that I have been branded an outlaw, stigmatized as a traitor with a price set on my head as if I had been a wolf; my family treated as the dam and cubs of the hill-fox whom all may torment, vilify, degrade, and insult the very name which came to me from a long and noble line of mortal ancestors, and denounce, as if it were a spell to conjure up the devil with? *(Furious)* **You shall find, my lord, that my name *is* indeed a spell to raise the devil! You shall hear of my vengeance! I, the miserable Highland drover, bankrupt, stripped of all, dishonored and hunted down because the avarice of others grasped at more than I**

could pay – I shall burst on my enemies in an awful change! Oh, it more than frets my patience, my lord, to be hunted like an otter or a salmon upon the shallows, and to have as many sword-cuts made and pistols flashed at me that would try a saint's temper, much more a Highlander who is not famous for the gift of patience!

DUKE: Say what you must, but I inform you herewith that I shall certainly cause you to be executed, by break of day!

ROB ROY: And I say, my lord, that my peril may be less than you think. Of those men you have summoned to take me and keep me, there may be some that have no will that I shall be either taken or kept, and some who may be afraid to act against me, and so I bid your grace be wary. And remember, at least, that I and my people have not been unprovoked. We are a rude and ignorant people, violent and passionate, but we are not a cruel people. The land might be at peace and in law for us, did they allow us to enjoy the blessings of peaceful law. But we have been a persecuted generation!

DUKE: And next you will tell me that persecution makes wise men mad?

ROB ROY: What must it do then to men like me, living as our fathers did a thousand years since and possessing scarce more than they did? Can we view the bloody edicts against us, hanging, hounding, and hunting down an ancient and honorable name, as deserving better treatment than that which enemies give to enemies? Here I stand, who have been in twenty frays and never hurt any man but when I was in hot blood, and yet there are those who would betray me and hang me like a masterless dog at the gate of any great man that has an ill-will against me!

DUKE: Enough! I shall myself see you escorted to Duchray tonight and order your execution in the morning. Hold yourself ready! *(He exits.)*

ROB ROY: *(Turns to FRANK.)* **I know not what to make of you, Mr. Osbaldistone. You appear where least expected and always unlikely to be in my company, considering what I have been, what I have been forced to become and, above all, what I am.**

FRANK: Sir, I should be most happy to learn that there is some honorable chance of your escape.

ROB ROY: I thank ye. You are a kindhearted and honorable man, and I assure you, sir, my lord Duke of Montrose has not seen the last of Rob Roy MacGregor!

From

DR. JEKYLL AND MR. HYDE

By Robert Louis Stevenson

In Robert Louis Stevenson's tale of psychological terror and suspense, a respected London scientiest, Dr. Henry Jekyll, and a grotesque man-monster, Edward Hyde, represent a mysterious conflict between good and evil that results in a hideous murder. Hyde is a prime suspect in the crime, and Jekyll's lawyer friend, Utterson, is concerned that Jekyll's strange protégé, Hyde, has dangerously influenced and overwhelmed the doctor.

CHARACTERS: MR. UTTERSON, a lawyer and Jekyll's friend; POOLE, Jekyll's butler; DR. JEKYLL'S VOICE.

SCENE: DR. JEKYLL's butler, POOLE, has urgently summoned UTTERSON to the house. They stand outside the door of DR. JEKYLL's laboratory where he has locked himself in, refusing to see anyone.

POOLE: Mr. Utterson, there is something very wrong. You know the doctor's ways – how he shuts himself up to work. But I'm afraid tonight. I've been afraid for a week, and I can bear it no more. I think there's been foul play.

UTTERSON: Foul play?! What you mean, Poole?

POOLE: I don't know, sir. But come, as gently as you can, to the door. I want you to hear, but not be heard. *(They move quietly to the door; POOLE taps on it.)* **Mr. Utterson, sir, asking to see you.**

JEKYLL'S VOICE: *(From the other side of the door)* **Tell him I cannot see anyone.**

POOLE: Thank you, sir. *(Draws UTTERSON away from the door.)* **You heard?**

UTTERSON: *(Puzzled)* **Yes.**

POOLE: Was that my master's voice?

UTTERSON: It... it seems much changed.

POOLE: Changed! Have I been twenty years in this man's house, to be deceived about his voice? No, sir! My master's been made away with eight days ago, when we heard him cry out upon the name of God. And who's in there instead of him, and why it stays there, is a thing I cannot begin to understand!

UTTERSON: This is a very wild tale, Poole. Come, sit down. *(They sit on a bench.)* **Now suppose it were as you imagine – that Dr. Jekyll has been...murdered. What could induce the murderer to stay?**

POOLE: I don't know, sir, but all this last week, whatever it is that lives beyond that door has been crying night and day for some sort of medicine. And I have been ordered by notes passed under the door to go flying to all the whole-sale chemists in town. And every time I have brought the stuff back, there is another note telling me to return it because it was not pure. This drug is wanted bitter bad, sir, whatever for. And the worst of it, sir, is that I've seen him!

UTTERSON: Seen him? Well, of course, you've seen him.

POOLE: Not my master, sir. *Him*!

UTTERSON: What do you mean?

POOLE: It was this way, sir. I came in suddenly from the garden and it seems he had slipped out of the laboratory to look for this drug. He was digging away in the crates at the end of the passage. He looked up when I came in, gave a kind of cry, and whipped back into the laboratory and slammed and locked the door. It was only for a moment that I saw him, but the hair stood upon my head like quills! Oh, sir, if that was my master, why had he a mask upon his face? If that was my master, why did he cry out like a rat and run from me?

UTTERSON: This is very strange, Poole, but I think I begin to see daylight. Your master is plainly seized with one of those maladies that both torture and deform the sufferer. This must be causing the alteration in his voice. Hence the mask and the avoidance of his friends, and his eagerness to find the drug that may cure him.

POOLE: Sir, that *thing* I saw was not my master! *(Looking around, fearfully)* **My master is a tall, fine man, and this...was like a dwarf! No, sir, that thing in the mask was never Dr. Jekyll! God knows what it was, but never my master! It is the belief of my heart that murder has been done!**

UTTERSON: Then it is my duty to make certain. Much as I desire to spare your master's feelings, I consider it my duty

to have that door broken down.

POOLE: Ah! Now, that's talking, sir!

UTTERSON: But...who is going to do it?

POOLE: Why, you and me, sir! There's an axe in the passage and a poker in the kitchen.

UTTERSON: That's very well said, Poole, and whatever comes of it, I shall make it my business to see you are no loser. But, do you realize that we are about to place ourselves in a position of some peril?

POOLE: You may say that, sir, indeed!

UTTERSON: Then answer me this. The masked figure that you saw – did you recognize it?

POOLE: Well, sir, it went so quickly and was so doubled up, that I could hardly swear to that. But if you mean was it Mr. Hyde? Why, yes, I think it was! It had the same bigness and had the same quick, light way with it. And then, who else could have got in by the outside door with a key! But that's not all. Did you ever meet Mr. Hyde, sir?

UTTERSON: Yes. I spoke with him one evening in a dark street. He gave me an impression of deformity without any nameable malformation. He had a displeasing smile and bore himself with a sort of murderous mixture of timidity and boldness that seemed to force a feeling of loathing, disgust – fear. He seemed hardly human! And I thought at the time that if ever I read Satan's signature upon a face, it was on his!

POOLE: Then you know as well as the rest of us, the servants, sir, that there was something queer about him, something that gave a man a turn. I don't know rightly how to say it, sir, beyond this – that you felt in your marrow kind of cold and thin.

UTTERSON: Yes, I know I felt something of what you describe.

POOLE: Well, when that masked thing like a monkey jumped from among the chemicals and whipped into the labora-

tory, something went down my spine like ice! Oh, I know it's not evidence, Mr. Utterson. I'm book-learned enough to know that. But a man has his feelings, and I give you my Bible word, it was Mr. Hyde!

UTTERSON: Yes, my fears incline to the same point. Evil was sure to come of that connection. Truly, I believe you, Poole. Poor Jekyll is killed and his murderer, for what purpose God alone can tell, is still lurking in his victim's room!

POOLE: *(Creeps to the door and listens.)* **Listen, sir! Footsteps.** *(UTTERSON listens at the door.)* **So it will walk all day, sir, and the better part of the night. Only when a new sample comes from the chemist is there a bit of a break. Ah, it's an ill conscience that's such an enemy to rest! There's blood foully shed in every step of it! Oh, sir, put your heart in your ears and tell me, is that the doctor's foot?**

UTTERSON: *(Listens, then sighs.)* **That is not Jekyll's heavy tread. Is there never anything else?**

POOLE: Once I heard it weeping.

UTTERSON: Weeping!

POOLE: Yes, sir, like a woman, or a lost soul!

UTTERSON: Our name must be vengeance. Bring the tools. We can delay no longer. *(POOLE exits. UTTERSON moves to the door and shouts.)* **Jekyll! Can you hear me? I demand to see you!** *(There is no reply.)* **I give you fair warning. My suspicions are aroused and I must and shall see you! If not by fair means, then by foul; if not by your consent, then by brute force!**

JEKYLL'S VOICE: *(In agony)* **Utterson, for God's sake, have mercy! Go away!**

POOLE: *(Returns with axe and poker.)* **That voice, sir!**

UTTERSON: Not Jekyll's. It's Hyde's! Down with the door, Poole! Now! *(POOLE and UTTERSON raise their tools as the lights black out.)*

A Dramatic Reading of

MORTE D'ARTHUR

From Idylls of the King

By Alfred Lord Tennyson

Alfred Lord Tennyson based his literary epic, *Idylls of the King*, on the romantic legends of King Arthur told by Sir Thomas Malory in the fifteenth century. Camelot, The Round Table, the sword Excalibur, The Holy Grail, and other familiar images of the Arthurian time were vividly and beautifully recreated by Tennyson. The epic of Arthur ends with his death after his final battle against the evil forces led by Mordred.

CHARACTERS: NARRATOR, KING ARTHUR, SIR BEDIVERE.

NARRATOR: So all day long the noise of battle roll'd
Among the mountains by the winter sea,
Until King Arthur's table, man by man,
Had fallen in Lyonnesse about their lord,
King Arthur; then, because his wound was deep,
The bold Sir Bedivere uplifted him,
Sir Bedivere, the last of all his knights,
And bore him to a chapel nigh the field,
A broken chancel with a broken cross,
That stood on a dark strait of barren land.
On one side lay the ocean, and on one
Lay a great water, and the moon was full.
Then spake King Arthur to Sir Bedivere:
KING ARTHUR: The sequel of today unsolders all
The goodliest fellowship of famous knights
Whereof this world holds record. Such a sleep
They sleep – the men I loved. I think that we
Shall never more, at any future time,
Delight our souls with talk of knightly deeds,
Walking about the gardens and the halls
Of Camelot, as in the days that were.
I perish by this people which I made –
Tho' Merlin sware that I should come again
To rule once more – but let what will be, be,
I am so deeply smitten thro' the helm
That without help I cannot last till morn.
Thou therefore take my brand Excalibur,
Which was my pride; for thou rememberest how
In those old days, one summer noon, an arm
Rose up from out the bosom of the lake,
Clothed in white samite, mystic, wonderful,
Holding the sword – and how I row'd across

**And took it, and have worn it, like a king;
And, wheresoever I am sung or told
In aftertime, this also shall be known.
But now delay not; take Excalibur,
And fling him far into the middle mere;
Watch what thou seest, and lightly bring me word.
SIR BEDIVERE: It is not meet, Sir King, to leave thee thus,
Aidless, alone, and smitten thro' the helm.
A little thing may harm a wounded man.
Yet I thy hest will all perform at full,
Watch what I see, and lightly bring thee word.
NARRATOR: So saying, from the ruin'd shrine he stept
And in the moon athwart the place of tombs,
Where lay the mighty bones of ancient men,
Old knights, and over them the sea-wind sang
Shrill, chill, with flakes of foam. He, stepping down
Came on the shining levels of the lake.
By zigzag paths and juts of pointed rock,
There drew he forth the brand Excalibur,
And o'er him, drawing it, the winter moon,
Brightening the skirts of a long cloud, ran forth
And sparkled keen with frost against the hilt;
For all the haft twinkled with diamond sparks,
Myriads of topaz-lights, and jacinth-work
Of subtlest jewelry. He gazed so long
That both his eyes were dazzled, as he stood,
This way and that dividing the swift mind,
In act to throw; but at the last it seem'd
Better to leave Excalibur conceal'd
There in the many-knotted water-flags,
That whistled stiff and dry about the marge.
So strode he back slow to the wounded king.
Then spake King Arthur to Sir Bedivere:
KING ARTHUR: Hast thou perform'd my mission which I gave?**

What is it thou hast seen, or what hast heard?
SIR BEDIVERE: I heard the ripple washing in the reeds,
And the wild water lapping on the crag.
KING ARTHUR: Thou hast betray'd thy nature and thy name,
Not rendering true answer, as beseem'd
Thy fealty, nor like a noble knight;
For surer sign had follow'd, either hand,
Or voice, or else a motion of the mere.
This is a shameful thing for men to lie.
Yet now, I charge thee, quickly go again
As thou art lief and dear, and do the thing
I bade thee, watch, and lightly bring me word.
NARRATOR: Then went Sir Bedivere a second time
Across the ridge, and paced beside the mere,
Counting the dewy pebbles, fix'd in thought;
But when he saw the wonder of the hilt,
How curiously and strangely chased, he smote
His palms together, and he cried aloud:
SIR BEDIVERE: And if indeed I cast the brand away,
Surely a precious thing, one worthy note,
Should thus be lost forever from the earth,
Which might have pleased the eyes of many men.
What good should follow this, if this were done?
What harm, undone? Deep harm to disobey,
Seeing obedience is the bond of rule.
Were it well to obey then, if a king demand
An act unprofitable, against himself?
The King is sick, and knows not what he does.
What record, or what relic of my lord
Should be to aftertime, but empty breath
And rumours of a doubt? But were this kept,
Stored in some treasure-house of mighty kings,
Some one might show it at a joust of arms,
Saying, "King Arthur's sword, Excalibur,

Wrought by the lonely maiden of the lake;
Nine years she wrought it, sitting in the deeps
Upon the hidden bases of the hills."
So might some old man speak in the aftertime
To all the people, winning reverence;
But now much honour and much fame were lost.
NARRATOR: So spake he, clouded with his own conceit,
And hid Excalibur the second time,
And so strode back slow to the wounded king.
Then spoke King Arthur, breathing heavily:
KING ARTHUR: What is it thou hast seen, or what hast heard?
SIR BEDIVERE: I heard the water lapping on the crag,
And the long ripple washing in the reeds.
NARRATOR: To whom replied King Arthur, much in wrath:
KING ARTHUR: Ah, miserable and unkind, untrue,
Unknightly, traitor-hearted! Woe is me!
Authority forgets a dying king,
Laid widow'd of the power in his eye
That bow'd the will. I see thee what thou art,
For thou, the latest-left of all my knights,
In whom should meet the offices of all,
Thou wouldst betray me for the precious hilt;
Either from lust of gold, or like a girl
Valuing the giddy pleasure of the eyes.
Yet, for a man may fail in duty twice,
And the third time may prosper, get thee hence;
But if thou spare to fling Excalibur,
I will arise and slay thee with my hands.
NARRATOR: Then quickly rose Sir Bedivere, and ran,
And, leaping down the ridges lightly, plunged
Among the bulrush-beds, and clutch'd the sword,
And strongly wheel'd and threw it. The great brand
Made lightnings in the splendor of the moon,
And flashing round and round, and whirl'd in an arch

Shot like a streamer of the northern morn,
Seen where the moving isles of winter shock
By night, with noises of the Northern sea.
So flash'd and fell the brand Excalibur;
But ere he dipt the surface, rose an arm
Cloth'd in white samite, mystic, wonderful,
And caught him by the hilt, and brandish'd him
Three times, and drew him under in the mere.
And lightly went the other to the King.
Then spoke King Arthur, drawing thicker breath:

KING ARTHUR: Now see I by thine eyes that this is done.
Speak out; what is it thou hast heard, or seen?

SIR BEDIVERE: Sir King, I closed mine eyelids, lest the gems
Should blind my purpose, for I never saw,
Nor shall see, here or elsewhere, till I die,
Not tho' I live three lives of mortal men,
So great a miracle as yonder hilt.
Then with both hands I flung him, wheeling him;
But when I look'd again, behold an arm,
Clothed in white samite, mystic, wonderful,
That caught him by the hilt, and brandish'd him
Three times, and drew him under in the mere.

KING ARTHUR: My end draws nigh; 'tis time that I were gone.
Make broad thy shoulders to receive my weight,
And bear me to the margin; yet I fear
My wound hath taken cold, and I shall die.

NARRATOR: So saying, from the pavement he half rose,
Slowly, with pain, reclining on his arm,
And looking wistfully with wide blue eyes
As in a picture. Him Sir Bedivere
Remorsefully regarded thro' his tears,
And would have spoken, but he found not words;
Then took with care, and kneeling on one knee,
O'er both his shoulders drew the languid hands,

And rising bore him thro' the place of tombs.
Then saw they how there hove a dusky barge,
Dark as a funeral scarf from stem to stern,
Beneath them; and descending they were ware
That all the decks were dense with stately forms,
Black-stoled, black-hooded, like a dream – by these
Three queens with crowns of gold – and from them rose
A cry that shiver'd to the tingling stars,
And as it were one voice, an agony
Of lamentation, like a wind that shrills
All night in a waste land, where no one comes,
Or hath come, since the making of the world.
Then murmur'd Arthur:
KING ARTHUR: Place me in the barge.
NARRATOR: So to the barge they came. There those three queens
Put forth their hands, and took the king, and wept.
But she that rose the tallest of them all
And fairest laid his head upon her lap
And loosed the shatter'd casque, and chafed his hands,
And call'd him by his name, complaining loud,
And dropping bitter tears against his brow
Striped with dark blood; for all his face was white
And colourless, and like the wither'd moon
Smote by the fresh beam of the springing east;
So like a shatter'd column lay the king;
Not like that Arthur who, with lance in rest,
From spur to plume a star of tournament,
Shot thro' the lists of Camelot, and charged
Before the eyes of ladies and of kings.
SIR BEDIVERE: Ah! my lord Arthur, whither shall I go?
Where shall I hide my forehead and my eyes?
For now I see the true old times are dead,
When every morning brought a noble chance,
And every chance brought out a noble knight.

Such times have been not since the light that led
Thy holy Elders with the gift of myrrh.
But now the whole Round Table is dissolved
Which was an image of the mighty world;
And I, the last, go forth companionless,
And the days darken round me, and the years,
Among new men, strange faces, other minds.

KING ARTHUR: The old order changeth, yielding place to new,
And God fulfills himself in many ways,
Lest one good custom should corrupt the world.
Comfort thyself; what comfort is in me?
I have lived my life, and that which I have done
May He within himself make pure! but thou,
If thou shouldst never see my face again,
Pray for my soul. More things are wrought by prayer
Than this world dreams of. Wherefore, let thy voice
Rise like a fountain for me night and day.
For what are men better than sheep or goats
That nourish a blind life within the brain,
If, knowing God, they lift not hands of prayer
Both for themselves and those who call them friend?
For so the whole round earth is every way
Bound by gold chains about the feet of God.

NARRATOR: So said he, and the barge with oar and sail
Moved from the brink, like some full-breasted swan
That, fluting a wild carol ere her death,
Ruffles her pure cold plume, and takes the flood
With swarthy webs. Long stood Sir Bedivere
Revolving many memories, till the hull
Look'd one black dot against the verge of dawn,
And on the mere the wailing died away.

A Dramatic Reading From

MAUD MULLER

By John Greenleaf Whittier

New England poet, John Greenleaf Whittier, conceived the idea for his ballad of *Maud Muller*, when he took a trip to Maine and stopped to rest his horse under an apple tree. In a field nearby was a beautiful young girl working in the hay, who talked with him but seemed ashamed of her bare feet and suntanned skin. Whittier used this simple, everyday incident as the basis for his tale of "what might have been."

This story-poem may be acted out by Maud and The Judge, with the Narrator to one side. Simple props, such as a rake, a tin cup, and a wine glass, may also be used.

CHARACTERS: NARRATOR, MAUD MULLER, THE JUDGE.

NARRATOR: Maud Muller on a summer's day
Raked the meadow sweet with hay.
Beneath her torn hat glowed the wealth
Of simple beauty and rustic health.
Singing, she wrought, and her merry glee
The mock-bird echoed from his tree.
But when she glanced to the far-off town,
White from its hill-slope looking down,
The sweet song died, and a vague unrest
And a nameless longing filled her breast;
A wish that she hardly dared to own,
For something better than she had known.
The Judge rode slowly down the lane,
Smoothing his horse's chestnut mane.
THE JUDGE: I drew my bridle in the shade
Of the apple-trees, to greet the maid,
And ask a draft from the spring that flowed
Through the meadow across the road.
She stooped where the cool spring bubbled up,
And filled for me her small tin cup,
And blushed as she gave it, looking down
On her feet so bare, and her tattered gown.
"Thanks!" said I then; "A sweeter draft
From a fairer hand was never quaffed."
I spoke of the grass and flowers and trees,
Of the singing birds and the humming bees;
Then talked of the haying, and wondered whether
The cloud in the west would bring foul weather.
NARRATOR: And Maud forgot her brier-torn gown
And her graceful ankles bare and brown;
And listened while a pleased surprise
Looked from her long-lashed hazel eyes.

At last, like one who for delay
Seeks a vain excuse, he rode away.
Maud Muller looked and sighed:
MAUD MULLER: Ah me! That I the Judge's bride might be!
He would dress me up in silks so fine,
And praise and toast me at his wine.
My father should wear a broadcloth coat;
My brother should sail a painted boat.
I'd dress my mother so grand and gay,
And the baby should have a new toy each day.
And I'd feed the hungry and clothe the poor,
And all should bless me who left our door.
NARRATOR: The Judge looked back as he climbed the hill,
And saw Maud Muller standing still.
THE JUDGE: A form more fair, a face more sweet,
Ne'er hath it been my lot to meet.
And her modest answer and graceful air
Show her wise and good as she is fair.
Would she were mine, and I today
Like her, a harvester of hay;
No doubtful balance of rights and wrongs,
Nor weary lawyers with endless tongues,
But low of cattle and song of birds,
And health and quiet and loving words.
Then I thought of my sisters, proud and cold,
And my mother, vain of her rank and gold.
So, closing my heart, I then rode on.
MAUD MULLER: And I was left in the field alone.
NARRATOR: But the lawyers smiled that afternoon,
When he hummed in court an old love-tune;
And the young girl mused beside the well
Till the rain on the unraked clover fell.
THE JUDGE: I wedded a wife of richest dower,
Who lived for fashion, as I for power.

Yet oft in my marble hearth's bright glow,
I watched a picture come and go;
And sweet Maud Muller's hazel eyes
Looked out in their innocent surprise.
Oft, when the wine in my glass was red,
I longed for the wayside well instead;
And closed my eyes on my garnished rooms
To dream of meadows and clover-blooms.
I, a proud man, sighed, with a secret pain.
"Ah, that I were free again!
Free as when I rode that day,
Where the barefoot maiden raked her hay!"

MAUD MULLER: I wedded a man unlearned and poor,
And many children played round my door.
But care and sorrow, and childbirth pain,
Left their traces on heart and brain.
And oft, when the summer sun shone hot
On the new-mown hay in the meadow lot,
And I heard the little spring brook fall
Over the roadside, through the wall,
In the shade of the apple-tree again
I saw a rider draw his rein.
And gazing down with timid grace,
I felt his pleased eyes read my face.
Sometimes my narrow kitchen walls
Stretched away into stately halls;
The weary wheel to a spinet turned,
The tallow candle an astral burned,
And for him who sat by the chimney lug,
Dozing and grumbling o'er pipe and mug,
A manly form at my side I saw,
And joy was duty and love was law.
Then I took up my burden of life again,
Saying only, "It might have been."

NARRATOR: Alas for maiden, alas for Judge,
For rich repiner and household drudge!
God pity them both! And pity us all,
Who vainly the dreams of youth recall.
For of all sad words of tongue or pen,
The saddest are these:
THE JUDGE & MAUD MULLER: It might have been!

Scenes for Four or More Performers

From

MARJORIE DAW

By Thomas Bailey Aldrich

Thomas Bailey Aldrich was a poet, novelist, magazine writer, an editor of *The Atlantic Monthly*, and a writer of popular short stories. In *Marjorie Daw*, written in 1873, his cleanly drawn characters, clever dialogue through a series of letters, and unexpected ending offer a very pleasant reading experience. Dr. Dillon, a New York physician, writes to Mr. Edward Delaney at The Pines, near Rye, New York, about a young patient of his, John Flemming, and begins a chain of events intended to cheer up an invalid, but which have unexpected results.

CHARACTERS: DR. DILLON; EDWARD DELANEY, a young lawyer; JOHN FLEMMING, an invalid; WATKINS, a serving-man.

SCENE: DILLON sits at one side at his desk. JOHN FLEMMING lies on a sofa at center, with a lap desk on his left knee, and his right leg in a cast. On the opposite side is EDWARD DELANEY, seated at a small table. The action moves smoothly from one actor to the next.

DILLON: *(Writes a moment, then puts down his pen and picks up his letter to read aloud.)* **To Edward Delaney, Esquire, August 8th: My dear sir, I am happy to assure you that your anxiety is without reason. Flemming will be confined to the sofa for three or four weeks and will have to be careful at first how he uses his leg. A fracture of this kind is always a tedious affair. Flemming is doing perfectly well physically, but I must confess that his irritable state of mind causes me a great deal of uneasiness. He is the last man in the world who ought to break his leg. You know how impetuous he is ordinarily, what a soul of restlessness and energy, never content unless he is rushing at some object like a sportive bull at a red shawl, but amiable withal. He is no longer amiable. He has a complete set of Balzac's works, twenty-seven volumes piled up near his sofa, to throw at Watkins whenever that exemplary serving-man appears with his meals. At times he sits with bowed head, regarding his splintered limb, silent, sullen, despairing. He refuses to eat, does not even read the newspapers. Books, except as projectiles for Watkins, have no charms for him. His state is truly pitiable. In a young fellow of twenty-four, with plenty of money and seemingly not a care in the world, the thing is monstrous! I am at my wit's end to know what to prescribe for him. You are Flemming's intimate friend. Write to him, distract his**

mind, cheer him up! I am, my dear sir, with great respect, etc, etc. *(He rises, folding the letter.)* **I do hope this will be of some help to poor Flemming.** *(He exits.)*

DELANEY: *(In the act of writing a letter)* **August ninth. My dear Jack, I had a line from Dillon this morning and was rejoiced to learn that your hurt is not so bad as reported. I can imagine how tranquil and saintly you are with your leg in a trough! It is awkward, to be sure, just as we had promised ourselves a glorious month at the seaside, but we must make the best of it. It is unfortunate, too, that my father's health renders it impossible for me to leave him. I cannot come to you, dear Jack, but I have hours of unemployed time on hand, and I will write you a whole post office full of letters if that will divert you. I wish I were a novelist. It is so pleasant here. Picture to yourself a large white house just across the road from me, a self-possessed, high-bred piece of architecture with its nose in the air. Sometimes a young woman appears on the piazza. There is a hammock there which is very becoming when one is eighteen and has golden hair, and dark eyes, and an emerald-colored illusion dress looped up after the fashion of a Dresden china shepherdess. All this splendor goes into that hammock and sways there like a pond lily in the golden afternoon. The window of my room looks down on that piazza, and so do I. Drop me a line, Jack. State your case.** *(He folds the letter and exits.)*

JOHN FLEMMING: *(Writing on the lap desk)* **August 11th. Your letter, dear Ned, was a godsend. Fancy what a fix I am in! I, who never had a day's sickness since I was born! My left leg weighs three tons! It is embalmed in spices and smothered in layers of fine linen, like a mummy. I can't move! I lie from morning till night on a lounge, staring into the hot street. Old Dillon fancies that I have something on my mind. Nonsense! I am only restless as the devil under this**

confinement. Take a man who has never had so much as a headache or a toothache in his life, strap one of his legs in a section of water-spout, keep him in a room in the city for weeks, with the hot weather turned on, and then expect him to smile and purr and be happy! It is preposterous! The only exercise I take is heaving Balzac at Watkins. Your letter is the first consoling thing I have had since my disaster ten days ago. It really cheered me up for half an hour. Write me more about that little girl in the hammock. Dark eyes and golden hair! I shall be a bear until I hear from you again. What is her name? Who is she? Who's her father? Where's her mother? Who's her lover? You cannot imagine how this will occupy me. *(He folds letter.)* **Watkins!** *(WATKINS, an old serving man of great patience and forbearance, enters.)* **Post this letter at once!**

WATKINS: Yes, sir. *(He takes the letter and starts out. FLEMMING leans over the edge of the sofa, picks up a large book. WATKINS glances over his shoulder, then neatly side-steps as DELANEY heaves the book after him, missing him.)*

DELANEY: *(Enters and sits at his writing table.)* **August twelfth. Dear Jack, very well, the sick pasha shall be amused. The little girl is swinging in the hammock at this moment. Her name is Daw, only daughter of Mr. Richard Daw, ex-colonel and banker. Mother dead. Old, rich family. This is where father and daughter pass eight months of the twelve, the rest of the year in Baltimore and Washington. She is called Marjorie – Marjorie Daw. Sounds odd at first, doesn't it? But after you say it over to yourself half a dozen times, you like it. There's a pleasing quaintness to it, something prim and violet-like. I saw the little beauty face to face at a party on the lawn. We talked about the weather – and *you*. The weather has been disagreeable for several days, and so have you. I told her of your accident and how it had frustrated all our summer plans. Miss Marjorie asked all**

manner of leading questions concerning you. Positively, I think I made her like you. And she is a girl whom you would like immensely. By the way, how is your leg? *(He folds letter, and exits.)*

FLEMMING: *(Writing)* **August seventeenth. Dear Ned, they are curing me. I haven't hurled anything at Watkins since last Sunday. That Miss Daw must be a charming person. I like her already. Asked a lot of questions about me, did she? I wonder you don't fall in love with her. I am ripe to do it myself. About my leg – it's better.** *(He folds the letter.)* **Watkins!** *(WATKINS enters, takes the letter, turns to leave, pauses, looks back. FLEMMING has closed his eyes for a nap. WATKINS sighs with relief and exits with the letter.)*

DELANEY: *(Enters and sits down to write.)* **August twentieth. Dear Jack, you ask me why I do not fall in love with Marjorie Daw. It would be impossible for me to fall in love with a woman who seems to be interested only in someone else. You! She has all but confessed to me her interest in you. And with what modesty and dignity! She has tacitly acknowledged to me – a third party – the love she feels for a man she has never seen. And the effect which you tell me was produced on you by my casual mention of an unknown girl swinging in a hammock is certainly as strange. Is it possible that two people who have never met, and who are hundreds of miles apart, can exert a magnetic influence on each other? I understand neither you nor her.** *(Folds letter and exits.)*

FLEMMING: *(Writing)* **August twenty-seventh. Dear Ned, I am now able to walk with the aid of a cane. I feel that as my leg grows stronger, my head becomes weaker. I must see Miss Daw! I will come there the instant Dillon thinks I am strong enough to stand the journey.** *(Folds letter.)* **Watkins!** *(WATKINS enters, takes letter, and exits.)*

DELANEY: *(Hurries in and writes.)* **August 28th. Dear Jack, I**

advise you not to come. Wait until you are fully recovered. Marjorie knows you only through me. You are to her an abstraction, a figure in a dream, from which the faintest shock would awaken her. Do you not see that every hour you remain away, Marjorie's glamour deepens and your influence over her increases? But you must bear in mind that the chances are ten to five that if you do come to know her, she will fall far short of your ideal, and you will not care for her in the least. You must not dream of coming here. Besides, her father would not tolerate it for a moment. I fear the effect of your abrupt appearance. It simply must not happen. *(Folds letter and hurries out.)*

FLEMMING: *(Writing)* **August thirty-first. Dear Ned, I am determined to come. I must see this precious girl! Dillon says I am in no condition to take so long a journey, that the air of the coast would be the worse thing possible for me, but I will not be advised by either Dillon or you!** *(Folds letter.)* **Watkins!** *(WATKINS enters, takes letter, exits.)*

DELANEY: *(Dashes in, sits at table, and writes hurriedly.)* **September first. Dear Jack, I write in great haste. I am in the utmost perplexity. Marjorie has told her father everything! If you come, it would be fatal to your interests and hers. Though he loves Marjorie tenderly, he is capable of going to any lengths if opposed. He has already locked her in her room. Stay where you are!** *(Folds letter, dashes out.)*

FLEMMING: *(Writing furiously)* **September second. Locked in her room! That settles it! I must come! I shall leave by the 12:15 express.** *(Using a cane, he struggles up and hobbles off, waving the letter.)* **Watkins! Post this letter and pack my bags!** *(DELANEY rushes in, reads a letter in dismay, then scoops up all the letters from his table, and dashes out.)* **There's no time to lose!** *(There is a pause. The sofa and two tables are taken off. A bench is brought in. FLEMMING enters, using cane, leaning on WATKINS, who carries his bags.)*

FLEMMING: Are you sure he wasn't in?

WATKINS: Quite sure, sir. Mr. Delaney has gone to Boston. He left yesterday and his servant did not know when he was expected to return.

FLEMMING: Did he leave any message for me?

WATKINS: Yes, sir. A letter. *(He pulls the letter from his pocket.)*

FLEMMING: *(Snatching letter)* **This is all very strange, Watkins. This is The Pines?**

WATKINS: Yes, sir.

FLEMMING: And that is where Delaney lives, over there?

WATKINS: Yes, sir.

FLEMMING: But there isn't any... *(He looks around, puzzled.)* **Wait for me back at the station.**

WATKINS: Yes, sir. *(He exits with bags.)*

FLEMMING: *(Sits on bench and tears open letter. He reads aloud.)* **"My dear Jack, I am horror stricken at what I have done! When I began this correspondence, I had no other purpose than to relieve the tedium of your sick chamber. Dillon told me to cheer up you. I tried to. I tried to make a little romance to interest you, something soothing and idyllic, and by Jove, I did it only too well! I am in sackcloth and ashes! I am a dog of an outcast! I fly from the wrath to come when you arrive at The Pines. Dear Jack, there isn't any great white house across the road. There isn't any piazza. There isn't any hammock. Jack – there isn't any Marjorie Daw!"** *(He looks up in astonishment. The letter drops from his hand.)*

From

THE WIZARD OF OZ

By L. Frank Baum

L. Frank Baum's popular story, *The Wizard of Oz*, has entertained readers since it was first published in 1900. Dorothy's adventures in the Land of Oz begin after she and her little dog Toto are blown there by a Kansas cyclone, and all the memorable characters she meets there have become favorites with children and adults alike.

CHARACTERS: DOROTHY, WITCH OF THE NORTH, THE SCARECROW, THE TIN WOODMAN, THE COWARDLY LION.

SCENE: DOROTHY has just landed in Oz, stepping out of the windblown farmhouse that carried her there, and is looking about her.

DOROTHY: *(To her little dog who sits in her basket)* **My goodness, Toto, where are we? This certainly doesn't look like Kansas!**

WITCH OF THE NORTH: *(Enters; a beautiful lady, carrying a wand, and smiling graciously)* **You are welcome, most noble Sorceress, to the land of the Munchkins. We are very grateful to you for killing the Wicked Witch of the East, and for setting our people free from bondage.**

DOROTHY: *(With a curtsy)* **You are very kind, but there must be some mistake. I am not a sorceress, and I haven't killed anyone.**

WITCH OF THE NORTH: Your house did, then, for it fell on her.

DOROTHY: *(Looking at the protruding legs of the dead witch)* **Oh, dear! Whatever shall we do?**

WITCH OF THE NORTH: There is nothing to be done now, my dear. The Wicked Witch of the East has held all the Munchkins in bondage for many years, making them slave for her day and night. Now they are all set free, thanks to you.

DOROTHY But who are the Munchkins? *(Looking around)* **I don't see anyone.**

WITCH: They are very shy.

DOROTHY: Are you a Munchkin?

WITCH: No, but I am their friend. I am the Witch of the North.

DOROTHY: *(Steps back in fright.)* **Oh, my! Are you a real witch?**

WITCH: Yes, indeed, but I am a good witch.

DOROTHY: I thought all witches were wicked.

WITCH: Oh, no, that is a great mistake. There were four witches in Oz, and the ones who live in the North and South are

good witches. I know this is true for I am one of them myself, and cannot be mistaken. But now that you have killed the Witch of the East, the Witch of the West is the only wicked witch left in Oz.

DOROTHY: But Aunt Em told me that the witches were all dead many years ago.

WITCH: Who is Aunt Em?

DOROTHY: She is my aunt who lives in Kansas where I come from.

WITCH: Kansas? I do not know where that is. Is it a civilized country?

DOROTHY: Oh, yes.

WITCH: Then that accounts for it. I believe there are no witches left in the civilized countries. But you see, the Land of Oz has never been civilized, for we are cut off from the rest of the world. We still have witches and wizards among us.

DOROTHY: Wizards? Who are they?

WITCH: Oz himself is the Great Wizard. *(In a whisper)* **He is more powerful than all the witches together and lives in the City of Emeralds.**

DOROTHY: I'm sure it would be a lovely place to visit, but I am anxious to get back to my Aunt and Uncle. Can you help me find my way?

WITCH: *(Thinking)* **All the Land of Oz is surrounded by a great desert and none could live who tried to cross it. I'm afraid, my dear, you will have to stay here.**

DOROTHY: *(Starting to cry)* **Oh, but I can't! I must get back to Kansas!**

WITCH: Don't cry. Let me consult my magic a moment. *(She waves her wand in the air, looking up.)* **My magic says, "Let Dorothy go to the City of Emeralds." Is your name Dorothy?**

DOROTHY: Yes.

WITCH: Then you must go to the City of Emeralds. Perhaps the great Oz will help you.

DOROTHY: How do I get there?

WITCH: You must walk. It is a long journey through a country that is sometimes pleasant and sometimes dark and terrible. However, I will use all the magic arts I know of to keep you from harm.

DOROTHY: Won't you go with me?

WITCH: No, I cannot, but I will give you my kiss. No one will dare hurt a person who has been kissed by the Witch of the North. *(Kisses DOROTHY on her forehead.)* **And take the shoes from the Wicked Witch of the East. She was proud of them, and there is a secret charm connected with them, but what it is I never knew.**

DOROTHY: *(Puts on the shoes.)* **They fit me perfectly.**

WITCH: *(Pointing off)* **The road to the City of Emeralds is paved with yellow brick, so you cannot miss it. When you get to Oz, do not be afraid of him. Just tell him your story and ask him to help you. Goodbye, my dear.**

DOROTHY: Goodbye. And thank you! *(As the WITCH exits, DOROTHY looks around.)* **A road paved with yellow brick. Oh, there it is!** *(She moves to one side, not noticing the SCARECROW propped on his pole. As she passes him, he winks at her. She stops and looks up in surprise.)*

SCARECROW: Good day.

DOROTHY: Gracious! Did you speak?

SCARECROW: Certainly! How do you do?

DOROTHY: I'm pretty well, thank you. How do you do?

SCARECROW: I'm afraid I'm not feeling well at all, for it is very tiresome being perched up here night and day to scare away crows.

DOROTHY: Can't you get down?

SCARECROW: No, for there is a pole stuck up my back. If you will please take it away, I shall be greatly obliged to you. *(DOROTHY takes out the pole; the SCARECROW wobbles, totters, then slides to the ground in a heap.)*

DOROTHY: Oh, dear! Let me help you. *(Helps him up.)* **Are you hurt?**

SCARECROW: Not a bit. Thank you very much. I feel like a new man. Now, tell me, who are you and where are you going?

DOROTHY: My name is Dorothy and I'm going to the City of Emeralds to ask the Great Oz to send me back to Kansas.

SCARECROW: Where is the City of Emeralds and who is the Great Oz?

DOROTHY: Why, don't you know?

SCARECROW: No, indeed. I don't know anything. You see, I am stuffed with straw, so I have no brains.

DOROTHY: Oh, I'm awfully sorry. Oz is a Great Wizard.

SCARECROW: Do you think if I go to the City of Emeralds with you, that the Great Oz would give me some brains?

DOROTHY: I cannot tell, but you may come with me if you like.

SCARECROW: Thank you. You see, I don't mind my legs and arms and body being stuffed, because I cannot get hurt. If anyone treads on my toes or sticks a pin into me, it doesn't matter, for I can't feel it. But if my head stays stuffed with straw instead of brains, how am I ever to know anything?

DOROTHY: I understand. I'll ask Oz to do all he can for you.

SCARECROW: That's very kind of you. Shall we be on our way?

DOROTHY: Yes. We just have to follow this yellow brick road. Be careful. There seems to be a great many holes in it.

SCARECROW: *(Takes a couple of steps, stumbles and falls.)* **Oh, my! How clumsy I am!**

DOROTHY: *(Helping him up)* **Are you hurt?**

SCARECROW: Not in the least. And I'm not afraid of falling again. Actually, there is only one thing in the world I am afraid of. A lighted match! *(As they link arms and start to walk off, they hear a groaning sound.)*

DOROTHY: Oh, my! What was that?

SCARECROW: I can't imagine. It came from over there. *(Points to one side where the TINMAN stands stiffly.)*

DOROTHY: What a strange looking man? *(Approaches him.)* **Excuse me, but did you groan?**

TINMAN: Yes, I did. I've been groaning for more than a year, and no one has heard me until now.

DOROTHY: Oh, dear! You poor man! What can I do to help you?

TINMAN: Get my oilcan and oil my joints. They are rusted so badly that I can't move them at all.

DOROTHY: *(Picks up oilcan from the ground.)* **Where should I oil you first?**

TINMAN: Oil my neck first, then my arms. *(He twists his head and moves his arms stiffly at first, then freely, as Dorothy oils him.)* **Oh, this is a great comfort. I have been holding that axe in the air ever since I rusted. Now if you will kindly oil the joints of my legs?**

DOROTHY: There! Are you all right now?

TINMAN: *(Lifts his legs one at a time.)* **Oh, yes, thank you! I might have stood there forever if you hadn't come along. You have certainly saved my life.** *(Walks stiffly about.)* **How did you happen to be here?**

DOROTHY: We are on our way to see the Great Oz.

TINMAN: Why do you want to see the Great Oz?

DOROTHY: I want him to send me back to my home in Kansas.

SCARECROW: And I want him to put a few brains in my head.

TINMAN: Do you suppose he would give me a heart?

DOROTHY: I guess so. It would be as easy as giving the Scarecrow some brains, I should think.

TINMAN: Then if you'll allow me to join you, I will go to the Great Oz and ask him to help me.

DOROTHY: Of course!

TINMAN: You had better put my oilcan in your basket, for if I should get caught in the rain and rust again, I'll need it badly. *(DOROTHY puts the oilcan in her basket, and linking arms with the SCARECROW and the TINMAN, is about to start off when the COWARDLY LION suddenly bounds in and roars* *loudly at them. DOROTHY screams as the LION knocks down the SCARECROW and tries to bite the TINMAN.)*

DOROTHY: Oh! Stop that! *(She smacks the LION sharply on his nose.)* **Don't you dare bite my friend! You ought to be ashamed of yourself! A big beast like you trying to bite us!** *(She helps the SCARECROW up.)*

COWARDLY LION: Ouch! *(Rubbing his nose)* **Ow! Ow! I didn't bite anybody!**

DOROTHY: Well, you tried to. You are nothing but a big coward!

LION: *(Sighs, hangs his head.)* **I know it. But I can't help it.**

DOROTHY: What makes you a coward?

LION: I don't know. *(Sadly)* **I suppose I was born that way. All the other animals in the forest expect me to be brave, for the Lion is always thought to be the King of Beasts. I learned that if I roared very loudly,** *(Roars)* **everything was frightened and got out of my way. But if an elephant or a tiger tried to fight me, I would run away, for I'm such a coward.**

SCARECROW: But the king of beasts shouldn't be a coward.

LION: *(Wiping a tear away with his tail)* **I know it. It is my great sorrow, and it makes my life very unhappy. But whenever there is danger, my heart begins to beat fast.**

TINMAN: Well, that proves you have a heart, at least. I don't have one.

LION: Perhaps if I had no heart, I should not be a coward.

SCARECROW: Do you have any brains?

LION: I suppose so. I never looked to see.

SCARECROW: I'm going to the Great Oz to ask him to give me some.

TINMAN: And I'm going to ask him to give me a heart.

DOROTHY: And I'm going to ask him to send me back to Kansas.

LION: Oh? Do you think this Great Oz could give me some courage?

DOROTHY: Why don't you come with us and ask him?

LION: If you don't mind, I will, for you can help scare away any

other wild beasts we may meet along the way.

DOROTHY: Then let's be off. This way! The yellow brick road will lead us to the City of Emerald – and the Great Oz. *(The four link arms and march off.)*

From

THE DECAMERON

By Giovanni Boccaccio

The Decameron is a fourteenth century masterpiece created by Italy's master storyteller and recognized "man of letters," Giovanni Boccaccio. Using the Great Plague of 1348 as a background, Boccaccio made his central characters three charming and well-bred young men and seven beautiful and well-educated young women who leave the city of Florence to go to a villa in the country where they hope to escape the terrible ravages of the plague. There, over a period of ten days, the ten young people entertain each other by telling stories. The third story on the first day is told by the young lady, Filomena.

CHARACTERS: FILOMENA, a young woman; SALADIN, sultan of Egypt; MELCHIZEDEK, a Jewish moneylender; the RICH MAN.

SCENE: FILOMENA sits at one side, as the storyteller, speaking to the audience as her companions.

FILOMENA: I am reminded of the story of a moneylender who once found himself in a perilous situation. Have we not all heard fine things concerning God and the truth of our religion, and wondered about them? After hearing my story, you may all wish to be more cautious in answering questions addressed to you. It is a fact, my sweet companions, that just as folly often destroys men's happiness and casts them into misery and despair, so prudence may rescue the wise from dreadful perils and guide them firmly to safety and reward. In my little tale, Saladin, whose great worth had raised him from humble beginnings to the sultanate of Egypt and brought him many victories over Saracen and Christian kings, had spent all of his great treasure on the wars and in acts of generosity. He suddenly found himself in need of a great sum of money and called to his presence the Jewish moneylender, Melchizedek, who carried out his business in Alexandria. He knew that Melchizedek would have enough money to lend on short notice, if only he could be persuaded to part with it. He also knew that Melchizedek was a miserly man who would not loan his money freely of his own will. Saladin did not wish to take the money by force, so he picked his brains to find a way to compel Melchizedek to assist him, and finally resolved to use force in the guise of reason. When Melchizedek appeared before him, he gave him a cordial reception and invited him to sit down beside him. *(SALADIN and MELCHIZEDEK enter together and sit on a bench, one beside the other.)*

SALADIN: O man of excellent worth, I have heard of your great wisdom and knowledge of the ways of God. Will you tell me which of the three laws, Jewish, Saracen, or Christian, you deem to be the one true Law?

FILOMENA: Melchizedek, who was a very wise man, realized that Saladin was trying to pick a quarrel with him, and that if he praised one of the three laws over the other two, the Sultan would succeed in his aim. Therefore, to avoid falling into Saladin's trap, he sharpened his wits very quickly and readily gave answer.

MELCHIZEDEK: My lord, your question is a good one, and my answer will be found in a story.

SALADIN: Ah! I am fond of stories. Begin!

MELCHIZEDEK: There was once a great and wealthy man who possessed in his immense treasury of jewels a precious and beautiful ring. *(The RICH MAN enters, admiring a large and beautiful ring on his finger.)* **It was such a valuable ring that he wished to leave it to the son who would be his heir.**

RICH MAN: I will bequeath this ring to one of my sons, but which one? Ah! The one who finds it among his possessions, or the one to whom I shall give it personally, shall be my heir and the other two will honor and respect him as the head of the family.

MELCHIZEDEK: The man's three sons were all virtuous and obedient, and he loved each of them equally. Each son hoped to receive the ring and take precedence over his brothers, and each did all that he could to persuade his father to leave him the ring when he died. But the man could not decide which son would inherit the ring. He loved each one and wished to please them all.

RICH MAN: There is only one thing I can do. Secretly, I will have two more rings made exactly like this one, and my sons will not be able to tell which is the original. Each will know

that I love and honor him. *(He leaves, obviously pleased with his decision.)*

MELCHIZEDEK: So the man secretly commissioned a master craftsman to make two more rings, and when he was dying, he called each of his sons to him in turn and gave one ring to each. After his death, his sons were eager to succeed to his title and estate and each son produced his ring to prove his right as heir. But when they saw that all three rings were exactly alike, they could not determine which was the original, and the question of who was the rightful heir remained in abeyance – with no one holding the title. To this day it has never been settled. And I say to you, my lord, that the same applies to the three laws which God the Father granted his three peoples. Each considers itself the legitimate heir to God's estate, each believes it possesses the one true Law, and each observes God's commandments as they know them. But, as with the rings, the question as to which of them is right, or the one true Law, remains in abeyance.

FILOMENA: When Saladin saw that Melchizedek had ingeniously sidestepped the trap he had set for him, he admired his cleverness and wisdom, and decided to make his great need known to him and ask him outright for his assistance.

MELCHIZEDEK: My lord, I will gladly provide you with everything you require.

FILOMENA: Saladin later repaid him in full and gave him many magnificent gifts besides. He became his lifelong friend and always kept him at his court in a state of importance and honor. *(SALADIN and MELCHIZEDEK exit. FILOMENA watches them go.)*

A Dramatic Reading From

THE PIED PIPER OF HAMELIN

By Robert Browning

Robert Browning, well known as a major English poet, also wrote plays in verse. Some of his shorter poems often lent themselves to dramatization, such as *The Pied Piper of Hamelin,* which tells a story in verse with vivid characterization and delightful use of language.

CHARACTERS: NARRATOR, the MAYOR, TOWN WOMAN, TOWN MAN, the PIED PIPER.

NARRATOR: Hamelin town's in Brunswick,
By famous Hanover City.
The River Weser, deep and wide,
Washes its wall on the southern side;
A pleasanter spot you never spied.
But when begins my ditty,
Almost five hundred years ago,
To see the townsfolk suffer so
From vermin was a pity.
TOWN MAN: Rats! They fought the dogs and killed the cats!
TOWN WOMAN: And bit the babies in the cradles!
And ate the cheeses out of the vats
And licked the soup from the cook's own ladles!
TOWN MAN: Split open the kegs of salted sprats!
Made nests inside men's Sunday hats!
TOWN WOMAN: And even spoiled the women's chats
By drowning their speaking
With shrieking and squeaking
In fifty different sharps and flats!
NARRATOR: At last the people in a body
To the Town Hall came flocking.
TOWN MAN: 'Tis clear, say we, our Mayor's a noddy!
TOWN WOMAN: And as for our Corporation – shocking!
To think we buy gowns lined with ermine,
TOWN MAN: For dolts that can't or won't determine
What's best to rid us of our vermin!
Rouse up, sirs! Give your brains a racking
To find the remedy we're lacking.
TOWN WOMAN: Or, sure as fate, we'll send you packing!
NARRATOR: At this the Mayor and Corporation
Quaked with a mighty consternation.

An hour they sat in council.
At length the Mayor broke silence:
MAYOR: For a guilder I'd my ermine gown sell.
I wish I were a mile hence!
It's easy to bid one rack one's brains.
I'm sure my poor head aches again,
I've scratched it so, and all in vain.
Oh, for a trap, a trap, a trap!
NARRATOR: Just as he said this, what should hap
At the chamber door but a gentle tap!
MAYOR: Bless us!
NARRATOR: Cried the Mayor!
MAYOR: What's that? Only a scraping of shoes on the mat?
Anything like the sound of a rat
Makes my heart go pit-a-pat!
Come in!
NARRATOR: The Mayor cried, looking bigger.
And in did come the strangest figure!
His queer long coat from heel to head
Was half of yellow and half of red.
And he himself was tall and thin
With sharp blue eyes, each like a pin.
He advanced to the council table, and...
PIED PIPER: Please, your honors...
NARRATOR: Said he.
PIED PIPER: I'm able, By means of a secret charm, to draw
All creatures living beneath the sun
That creep or swim or fly or run
After me so as you never saw!
And I chiefly use my charm
On creatures that do people harm,
The mole and toad and newt and viper,
And people call me the Pied Piper.
NARRATOR: And here they noticed round his neck

A scarf of red and yellow stripe,
To match with his coat of the self-same check.
And at the scarf's end hung a pipe.
And his fingers, they noticed, were ever straying
As if impatient to be playing.

PIED PIPER: Yet...

NARRATOR: Said he...

PIED PIPER: Poor piper as I am, In Tartary I freed the Cham,
Last June, from his huge swarms of gnats.
I eased in Asia the Nizam
Of a monstrous brood of vampire bats.
And as for what your brain bewilders,
If I can rid your town of rats,
Will you give me a thousand guilders?

MAYOR: One? Fifty thousand!

NARRATOR: Was the exclamation of the astonished Mayor and Corporation.
Into the street the piper stepped,
Smiling first a little smile,
As if he knew what magic slept
In his quiet pipe the while.
Then, like a musical adept,
To blow the pipe his lips he wrinkled,
And green and blue his sharp eyes twinkled
Like a candle-flame where salt is sprinkled.
And ere three shrill notes the pipe uttered,
You heard as if an army muttered,
And the muttering grew to a grumbling.

TOWN MAN: And the grumbling grew to a mighty rumbling.

TOWN WOMAN: And out of the houses the rats came tumbling!
Great rats, small rats, lean rats, brawny rats!

TOWN MAN: Brown rats, black rats, grey rats, tawny rats!
Grave old plodders, gay young friskers!

TOWN WOMAN: Fathers, mothers, uncles, cousins!

Cocking tails and pricking whiskers!
Families by tens and dozens...
TOWN MAN: Brothers, sisters, husbands, wives,
Followed the Piper for their lives.
TOWN WOMAN: From street to street he piped, advancing;
And step for step they followed dancing,
Until they came to the River Weser
Wherein all plunged and perished!
NARRATOR: You should have heard the Hamelin people
Ringing the bells till they rocked the steeple!
MAYOR: Go!
NARRATOR: Cried the Mayor.
MAYOR: And get long poles.
Poke out the nests and block up the holes!
Consult with carpenters and builders,
And leave in our town not even a trace of the rats!
NARRATOR: When suddenly, up the face of the Piper perked in the Marketplace.
With a...
PIED PIPER: First, if you please, my thousand guilders!
MAYOR: A thousand guilders!
NARRATOR: The mayor looked blue. So did the Corporation, too.
MAYOR: To pay this sum to a wandering fellow
With a gipsy coat of red and yellow! Beside...
NARRATOR: Quoth the Mayor with a knowing wink...
MAYOR: Our business was done at the river's brink.
We saw with our eyes the vermin sink,
And what's dead can't come to life, I think.
So, friend, we're not the folks to shrink
From the duty of giving you something for drink,
And a matter of money to put in your poke;
But as for the guilders, what we spoke
Of them, as you very well know, was in joke.
Besides, our losses have made us thrifty.

A thousand guilders? Come, take fifty.
NARRATOR: The Piper's face fell, and he cried:
PIED PIPER: No trifling! I can't wait!
Beside, I've promised to visit by dinner time,
Baghdad, and accept the prime
Of the Head-Cook's pottage, all he's rich in,
For having left, in the Caliph's kitchen
Of a nest of scorpions no survivor.
With him I proved no bargain-driver.
With you, don't think I'll bate a stiver!
And folks who put me in a passion
May find me pipe after another fashion!
MAYOR: How?
NARRATOR: Cried the Mayor...
MAYOR: D'ye think I brook
Being worse treated than a cook?
Insulted by a lazy ribald
With idle pipe and vesture piebald?
You threaten us, fellow?
Do your worst! Blow your pipe there till you burst!
NARRATOR: Once more he stepped into the street
And to his lips again
Laid his long pipe of smooth straight cane,
And ere he blew three notes (such sweet
Soft notes as yet musicians cunning
Never gave the enraptured air)...
TOWN MAN: There was a rustling that seemed like a bustling
Of merry crowds justling at pitching and hustling!
TOWN WOMAN: Small feet were pattering, wooden shoes clattering;
Little hands clapping and little tongues chattering!
TOWN MAN: And, like fowls in a farmyard when barley is scattering,
Out came the children running!

TOWN WOMAN: All the little boys and girls
With rosy cheeks and flaxen curls,
And sparkling eyes and teeth like pearls;
TOWN MAN: Tripping and skipping, ran merrily after
The wonderful music with shouting and laughter.
MAYOR: The Mayor was dumb, and the Council stood
As if they were changed into blocks of wood,
Unable to move a step, or cry
To the children merrily skipping by;
Could only follow with the eye
That joyous crowd at the Piper's back.
But how the Mayor was on the rack!
And the wretched Council's bosoms beat
As the Piper turned from the High Street
To where the Weser rolled its waters
Right in the way of their sons and daughters!
TOWN MAN: However, he turned from south to west
And to Koppelberg Hill his steps addressed.
TOWN WOMAN: And after him the children pressed.
Great was the joy in every breast.
MAYOR: He never can cross that mighty top!
He's forced to let the piping drop,
And we shall see our children stop!
NARRATOR: When lo, as they reached the mountainside,
A wondrous portal opened wide,
As if a cavern was suddenly hollowed;
And the Piper advanced and the children followed.
And when all were in to the very last,
The door in the mountainside shut fast!
TOWN WOMAN: Alas! Alas for Hamelin!
TOWN MAN: The Mayor sent east, west, north, and south,
To offer the Piper, by word of mouth,
Wherever it was men's lot to find him,
Silver and gold to his heart's content...

TOWN WOMAN: If he'd only return the way he went
And bring the children behind him!
NARRATOR: But when they saw t'was a lost endeavor,
And Piper and dancers were gone forever,
They made a decree that lawyers never
Should think their records dated duly
If, after the day of the month and year,
These words did not as well appear:
MAYOR: And so long after what happened here
On the twenty-second of July,
Thirteen hundred and seventy-six...
NARRATOR: And the better in memory to fix
The place of the children's last retreat,
They called it the Pied Piper's Street.
And opposite the place of the cavern,
They wrote the story on a column,
How their children were stolen away.
And there it stands to this very day.

A Dramatic Reading From

THE DIVERTING HISTORY OF JOHN GILPIN

(Showing How He Went Farther Than He Intended and Came Home Safe Again)

By William Cowper

William Cowper (pronounced Cooper), a widely read English poet, known mainly for his hymns, and verses about nature and the ordinary things in life, displayed his humorous side in the ballad of John Gilpin.

CHARACTERS: NARRATOR; JOHN GILPIN; MRS. GILPIN, his wife; the CALENDAR (A dervish).

NARRATOR: John Gilpin was a citizen of credit and renown;
A trainband captain eke was he of famous London town.
John Gilpin's spouse said to her dear:
MRS. GILPIN: Though wedded we have been
These twice ten tedious years, yet we
No holiday have seen.
Tomorrow is our wedding day,
And we will then repair
Unto the Bell at Edmonton
All in a chaise and pair.
My sister and my sister's child,
Myself, and children three,
Will fill the chaise, so you must ride
On horseback after we.
NARRATOR: He soon replied:
JOHN GILPIN: I do admire
Of womankind but one,
And you are she, my dearest dear;
Therefore it shall be done.
I am a linendraper bold,
As all the world doth know,
And my good friend the calendar
Will lend his horse to go.
NARRATOR: Quoth Mrs. Gilpin:
MRS. GILPIN: That's well said,
And for that wine is dear,
We will be furnished with our own
Which is both bright and clear.
NARRATOR: John Gilpin kissed his loving wife;
O'erjoyed was he to find,
JOHN GILPIN: That though on pleasure she is bent,

She has a frugal mind.
NARRATOR: The morning came, the chaise was brought,
But yet was not allowed
To drive up to the door lest all
Should say that she was proud.
So three doors off the chaise was stayed,
Where they did all get in
Six precious souls, and all agog
To dash through thick and thin.
Smack went the whip,
Round went the wheels,
Were never folks so glad:
The stones did rattle underneath,
As if Cheapside were mad.
John Gilpin at his horse's side
Seized fast the flowing mane;
And up he got, in haste to ride,
JOHN GILPIN: But soon came down again.
For saddle tree scarce reached had I
My journey to begin,
When turning round my head, I saw
Three customers come in.
So down I came, for loss of time,
Although it grieved me sore,
Yet loss of pence, full well I knew
Would trouble me much more.
T'was long before the customers
Were suited to their mind,
When Betty screaming came downstairs,
"The wine is left behind!"
Good lack! Quoth I, yet bring it me,
My leathern belt likewise,
In which I bear my trusty sword
When I do exercise.

NARRATOR: Now Mistress Gilpin (careful soul)
Had two stone bottles found,
To hold the liquor that she loved,
And keep it safe and sound.
Each bottle had a curling ear,
Through which the belt he drew;
And hung a bottle on each side,
To make his balance true.
Now see him mounted once again
Upon his nimble steed,
Full slowly pacing o'er the stones,
With caution and good heed.
But finding soon a smoother road
Beneath his well-shod feet,
The snorting beast began to trot,
JOHN GILPIN: Which galled me in my seat!
"So, fair and softly!"
NARRATOR: John, he cried,
But John, he cried in vain;
That trot became a gallop soon,
In spite of curb and rein.
JOHN GILPIN: So stooping down, as needs I must
Who could not sit upright,
I grasped the mane with both my hands,
And eke with all my might.
NARRATOR: Away went Gilpin, neck or nought;
Away went hat and wig!
JOHN GILPIN: I little dreamt, when I set out,
Of running such a rig!
The wind did blow, my cloak did fly,
Like streamer long and gay,
Till, loop and button failing both,
At last it flew away!
NARRATOR: Then might all people well discern

The bottles he had slung;
A bottle swinging at each side,
As hath been said or sung.
JOHN GILPIN: The dogs did bark, the children screamed,
Up flew the windows all!
And every soul cried out, "Well done!"
As loud as he could bawl!
NARRATOR: Away went Gilpin! Who but he?
His fame soon spread around;
He carries weight! He rides a race!
'Tis for a thousand pound!
And still as fast as he drew near,
'Twas wonderful to view
How in a trice the turnpike men
Their gates wide open threw.
JOHN GILPIN: And now, as I went bowing down,
My reeking head full low,
The bottles twain behind my back
Were shattered at a blow!
Down ran the wine into the road,
Most piteous to be seen,
Which made my horse's flanks to smoke
As they had basted been.
NARRATOR: Thus all through merry Islington
These gambols he did play,
Until he came into the
Wash Of Edmonton so gay.
At Edmonton his loving wife
From the balcony spied
Her tender husband, wondering much
To see how he did ride.
MRS. GILPIN: Stop, stop, John Gilpin! Here's the house!
NARRATOR: They all at once did cry.
MRS. GILPIN: The dinner waits, and we are tired.

NARRATOR: Said Gilpin:
JOHN GILPIN: So am I!
NARRATOR: But yet his horse was not a whit
Inclined to tarry there;
For why? His owner had a house
Full ten miles off, at Ware.
Away went Gilpin out of breath,
JOHN GILPIN: And sore against my will,
Till at my friend the calendar's
My horse at last stood still.
NARRATOR: The calendar, amazed to see
His neighbor in such trim,
Laid down his pipe, flew to the gate,
And thus accosted him:
THE CALENDAR: What news? What news? Your tidings tell.
Tell me you must, and shall!
Say why bareheaded you are come,
Or why you come at all?
NARRATOR: Now Gilpin had a pleasant wit,
And loved a timely joke;
JOHN GILPIN: And thus unto the calendar
In merry guise I spoke.
I came because your horse would come,
And if I well forebode.
My wig and hat will soon be here –
They are upon the road.
NARRATOR: The calendar, right glad to find
His friend in merry pin,
Returned him not a single word,
But to the house went in.
Whence straight he came with hat and wig,
A wig that flowed behind,
A hat not much the worse for wear,
Each comely in its kind.

THE CALENDAR: I held them up, and in my turn
Thus showed my ready wit;
My head is twice as big as yours,
They therefore needs must fit.
But let me scrape the dirt away
That hangs upon your face;
And stop and eat, for well you may
Be in a hungry case.

JOHN GILPIN: Said I, It is my wedding day,
And all the world would stare,
If wife should dine at Edmonton,
And I should dine at Ware.
So turning to my horse, I said,
I am in haste to dine;
T'was for your pleasure you came here,
You shall go back for mine.

NARRATOR: Ah, luckless speech, and bootless boast!
For which he paid full dear;
For while he spake, a braying ass
Did sing most loud and clear;

JOHN GILPIN: Whereat my horse did snort, as he
Had heard a lion roar,
And galloped off with all his might
As he had done before.

NARRATOR: Away went Gilpin, and away
Went Gilpin's hat and wig;
He lost them sooner than at first,
For why? They were too big.
Now Mistress Gilpin, when she saw
Her husband posting down
Into the country far away,
She pulled out half a crown;

NARRATOR: And thus unto a youth she said:
Who drove them to the Bell;

MRS. GILPIN: This shall be yours, when you bring back
My husband safe and well.
NARRATOR: The youth did ride, and soon did meet
John coming back amain;
Whom in a trice he tried to stop,
By catching at his rein.
JOHN GILPIN: But not performing what he meant,
And gladly would have done,
The frighted steed he frighted more,
And made him faster run!
NARRATOR: Away went Gilpin, and away
Went postboy at his heels,
The postboy's horse right glad to miss
The lumbering of the wheels.
Six gentlemen upon the road,
Thus seeing Gilpin fly,
With postboy scampering in the rear,
They raised the hue and cry:
"Stop thief! Stop thief! A highway man!"
JOHN GILPIN: Not one of them was mute;
And all and each that passed that way
Did join in the pursuit.
And now the turnpike gates again
Flew open in short space,
The tollmen thinking as before,
That Gilpin rode a race.
And so I did, and won it, too,
For I got first to town,
Nor stopped till where I had got up
I did again get down.
NARRATOR: Now let us sing, "Long live the king,
And Gilpin, long live he!"
And when he next doth ride abroad,
May I be there to see!

From

THE COUNT OF MONTE CRISTO

By Alexandre Dumas

Alexandre Dumas' exciting novel, *The Count of Monte Cristo*, traces the life of one of literature's best-known characters, Edmond Dantes, the young sailor who is the victim of a devilish scheme by his enemies. He is arrested on his wedding day, wrongly accused of a political crime, and imprisoned for fourteen years. After making a daring escape, he secures the fabulous treasure of his prisoner friend, the Abbe Faria, who died in prison and willed all his possessions to him. Rich beyond belief, Dantes then assumes the identity of the mysterious Count of Monte Cristo, and vows to find his enemies and avenge his wrongs. Written in 1845, and set in the post-Napoleonic era in France, the story of suspense, love, intrigue, and adventure has remained a favorite with readers, actors, and filmmakers. Edmond Dantes' troubles begin on the day his ship, the *Pharaon*, docks at Marseilles on the 24th of February, 1815.

CHARACTERS: EDMOND DANTES, a sailor; MERCEDES, a beautiful Catalan girl; FERNAND, a Catalan fisherman; CADEROUSSE, a drunken tailor; DANGLARS, a supercargo (ship's clerk).

SCENE: The Cafe La Reserve in Marseilles, where MERCEDES and FERNAND sit at a table to one side, and DANGLARS and CADEROUSSE sit, drinking, at a table on the other side.

FERNAND: *(In love with MERCEDES and determined to have her)* **Mercedes, Easter is nearly here. It is the right time for a wedding. You know I love you!** *(Grasping her hand)* **Give me an answer.**

MERCEDES: I have answered you a hundred times, Fernand. *(Gently withdrawing her hand)* **I have never encouraged you. I have always been fond of you as a brother, but my heart belongs to another.**

FERNAND: Yes, you have always been cruelly frank with me. But I have dreamed for ten years of being your husband. I will not lose hope!

MERCEDES: We have been brought up together. You know me. When I say that you must be satisfied with my friendship, then believe me, for that is all I can give you.

FERNAND: Is this your final answer?

MERCEDES: *(Firmly)* **I love Edmond Dantes, and no other man will ever be my husband!**

FERNAND: *(His voice trembling)* **You will always love him?**

MERCEDES: As long as I live. *(He pounds the table in frustration.)* **Oh, I understand you, Fernand. You would be revenged on him because I do not love you. But think of this. You would lose my friendship if he were conquered, and see that friendship change to hate if you were the conqueror. You must not give way to evil thoughts. I cannot be your wife, but I will always be your friend and sister.**

FERNAND: *(Bowing his head in deep disappointment a moment, then, looking up at her and speaking between his teeth)* **And if Edmond Dantes should die?**

MERCEDES: Then I too shall die!

FERNAND: What if he forgets you? His ship has been gone four long months.

EDMOND: *(Rushes into the cafe, eagerly looking around; he joyously discovers MERCEDES.)* **Mercedes!**

MERCEDES: He is here! He has not forgotten me! *(Running to him)* **Edmond!** *(Their embrace of love and joy is like a knife thrust to FERNAND who watches them with a look of menace.)*

EDMOND: *(Seeing FERNAND)* **Mercedes, who is this gentleman?** *(His hand goes to the knife in his belt.)*

MERCEDES: He will be your best friend, Edmond, for he is my cousin, Fernand, the man whom, after you, I love best in the world. Don't you recognize him?

EDMOND: Yes, so it is. *(Extending his hand)* **Fernand.** *(FERNAND only stares at MERCEDES.)* **Mercedes, I did not rush home to you to find an enemy here.**

MERCEDES: *(Angrily, to FERNAND)* **An enemy! Fernand is not your enemy. He will grasp your hand in friendship.** *(FERNAND slowly rises, barely touches EDMOND's hand, then rushes to the door, unable to control his rage.)* **Fernand!**

EDMOND: Let him go. Come, sit with me. *(He draws her to a seat at the table.)* **I am too happy to be near you again to allow anything or anyone to distract me. I have come home to make you my wife. And I have great hopes that my master, Monsieur Morrel, will soon make me captain of the *Pharaon*.**

MERCEDES: Then I can know no greater happiness! *(EDMOND and MERCEDES sit together, talking softly, unaware of anything around them, especially the two men at the opposite table.)*

CADEROUSSE: *(Waving a wine bottle)* **Fernand! Come, join us. Come! Can you not spend a little time with your friends?**

(FERNAND looks at EDMOND and MERCEDES, then throws himself into a chair next to CADEROUSSE and thrusts his head into his hands.) **Shall I tell you what you look like, Fernand?** *(With a coarse laugh)* **A rejected lover!**

DANGLARS: What are you saying, Caderousse? A man of Fernand's good looks is never unlucky in love.

CADEROUSSE: Ah, let me tell you how the land lies, Danglars. Fernand, whom you see here, is one of the bravest and best of the Catalans, to say nothing of being one of the best fishermen in Marseilles. He is in love with the beautiful Mercedes. Unfortunately, she appears to be in love with Edmond Dantes, the mate of the good ship *Pharaon*.

FERNAND: *(Furiously)* **Mercedes is tied to no man and is free to love anyone she chooses, isn't she?**

CADEROUSSE: But, I thought you were a Catalan, and I have always been told that a Catalan is not a man to be supplanted by a rival.

DANGLARS: *(Feigning pity)* **Poor fellow! He did not expect Dantes to return so suddenly. Perhaps he thought Dantes was dead.** *(Aside)* **If only he were!**

CADEROUSSE: When is the wedding to take place, Fernand?

FERNAND: *(Between his teeth)* **A date has not been fixed.**

CADEROUSSE: But surely a date will be set soon, as surely as Dantes will soon be made captain of the *Pharaon*, eh Danglars? *(Nudges him and laughs.)*

DANGLARS: *(With a sneer)* **Yes. Let us drink to "Captain" Edmond Dantes and the beautiful Catalan!**

FERNAND: Never! *(He dashes his cup to the floor.)*

CADEROUSSE: *(The wine is making him mellow and reckless.)* **To Edmond Dantes! Hello! Edmond! Are you too proud to speak to your friends?**

EDMOND: No, I am not proud, Monsieur Caderousse, but I am in love, and love is more apt to make a man blind than pride.

CADEROUSSE: Bravo! A good excuse! Good day to you, too, Madame Dantes!

MERCEDES: That is not yet my name, monsieur, and in my country it is bad luck to call a girl by her sweetheart's name before she marries him. Call me Mercedes, if you please.

DANGLARS: *(With a bow, scarcely hiding his scorn)* **Will you have your wedding soon, Monsieur Dantes?**

EDMOND: As soon as possible, Monsieur Danglars. We will have the betrothal feast here at Le Reserve, to which you are invited. And you, Monsieur Caderousse! And you, too, of course, Fernand. *(FERNAND turns away, unable to answer.)*

DANGLARS: You seem to be in a great hurry to be married, "Captain."

EDMOND: *(Smiling)* **Do not give me the title that does not yet belong to me. As Mercedes said, it might bring bad luck.**

DANGLARS: You have plenty of time. The *Pharaon* will not put out to sea again for at least three months.

EDMOND: One is always in a hurry to be happy, Monsieur, for when one has been at sea for many months, longing to hold the one he loves in his arms, it is difficult to believe in one's good fortune. However, I must go to Paris before I am married.

DANGLARS: *(Carefully)* **You have business in Paris?**

EDMOND: None of my own. I have a last commission of Captain LeClerc's to carry out. You remember I spoke of it on the ship.

DANGLARS: I remember. *(To himself)* **Dantes' star is on the ascendant. He will marry the splendid girl. He will become captain and laugh at us all unless...unless I take a hand in the affair.** *(Pauses.)* **He goes to Paris, no doubt, to deliver the letter Captain LeClerc gave him on his deathbed. This letter gives me an excellent idea.** *(He takes a drink of wine.)* **Dantes is not yet made captain of the *Pharaon*!** *(EDMOND and MERCEDES continue a soft conversation at their table.)*

FERNAND: *(Watches them, then suddenly buries his face in his arms.)* **They will drive me to despair!**

DANGLARS: *(Feigning sympathy)* **Then you *do* love this Mercedes?**

FERNAND: I adore her! And I would kill Edmond Dantes, but she has sworn she will die with him.

DANGLARS: Consider, would it not be sufficient if Dantes simply did not marry her? The marriage could easily be thwarted. *(As FERNAND looks up at him)* **Absence severs as well as death. If the walls of a prison were between Dantes and Mercedes, they would be as effectively separated as if they lay under a tombstone, would they not?**

CADEROUSSE: *(Very drunk)* **Yes, but a man can get *out* of prison, and if his name is Edmond Dantes, he will seek revenge!**

FERNAND: I am not afraid of Edmond Dantes!

CADEROUSSE: But why, I should like to know, would anyone put Dantes in prison? He is not a thief, or a murderer. I like Dantes! *(Downing a drink)* **Dantes! Your health!**

DANGLARS: Hold your tongue! You are drunk! *(To FERNAND)* **You see, there is no need to kill him.**

FERNAND: But how would he be arrested? Do you have the means?

DANGLARS: The means can be found. *(Leaning back, with a shrug)* **But then, why should I meddle in your affairs?**

FERNAND: *(Seizing his arm)* **Because you have some motive of personal hatred against Dantes. I can see it! And if you hate him as much as I, and you can find the means for his arrest, I will execute it!**

DANGLARS: *(Thinking a moment)* **I could write a letter...in a disguised hand...a denunciation revealing that during the voyage Dantes and I have just made, he touched at the Isle of Elba. I saw him land there. And, if someone were to denounce him to the king's procurer as a Bonapartist agent...**

FERNAND: I will denounce him!

DANGLARS: There is a safer and surer way. I could write that

Dantes has been entrusted with a letter for the usurper, for I know he has such a letter, and that he is to deliver it to the Bonapartist committee in Paris. Proof of this crime will be found upon arresting him, on his person, or in his cabin on board the *Pharaon*.

FERNAND: And if he is arrested and put in prison?

DANGLARS: You may yet win the hand of your Mercedes, and *I* will be made captain of the *Pharaon.*

DANTES: My dearest Mercedes, this joy that I feel affects me strangely. At this moment I am the happiest man alive, and that alarms me.

MERCEDES: How can this be? I have never been so happy, and I am not at all alarmed about anything.

DANTES: Happiness is like the enchanted palaces we read of in our childhood, where fiery dragons defend the gates and monsters must be overcome in order to gain admittance. I am lost in wonder to find myself about to become your husband, when I feel myself so unworthy. I wonder what monsters I must face before you are truly my own.

MERCEDES: Edmond, you are the worthiest man I know, and I love you!

DANGLARS: *(With a deadly stare across the room)* **You do well to have your doubts, Dantes! For you are about to meet a "monster" against which you will have no defense!**

From

THE THREE MUSKETEERS

By Alexandre Dumas

Alexandre Dumas' swashbuckling adventure of *The Three Musketeers* appeared in 1844 and remains to this day a favorite story of intrigue and daring in the time of Louis XIV in France. On his very first day in Paris, where the hot-blooded young Gascon, D'Artagnan, has come to seek his fortune in life, he loses an important letter, and while furiously pursuing the gentleman he believes has stolen it, encounters the three musketeers who will influence and change his life.

CHARACTERS: D'ARTAGNAN, a young Gascon; ATHOS, a Musketeer; PORTHOS, a Musketeer; ARAMIS, a Musketeer; a FRIEND OF ARAMIS.

D'ARTAGNAN: *(Dashes in.)* **Thief! Traitor! Stop!** *(As he runs across the street, he rams headfirst into ATHOS, who has been recently wounded in the shoulder, and who cries out in pain.)* **Excuse me, sir. Excuse me, but I am in a hurry!** *(He attempts to run off.)*

ATHOS: *(Seizing him firmly by his belt)* **You are in a hurry? Under that pretense, you run against me! You cause me great pain from a wound in my shoulder which you have probably opened afresh when I have just had it dressed! You say "excuse me" and you believe that that is sufficient? Not at all, my young man, not for Monsieur Athos!**

D'ARTAGNAN: *(Impatiently)* **Sir, I did not do it intentionally and, not doing it intentionally, I said "excuse me." It appears to me that that is quite enough. I am in great haste. Leave your hold, I beg of you, and let me go about my business.**

ATHOS: *(Releasing him)* **Monsieur, you are not polite. It is easy to perceive that you come from a distance.**

D'ARTAGNAN: *(Has started to leave, then turns back.)* **Monsieur, however far I may come, it is not you who can give me a lesson in good manners. I warn you. And if I were not in such haste, and if I were not running after someone, I should –**

ATHOS: Mister gentleman-in-a-hurry, you can find *me* without running after me. Do you understand me?

D'ARTAGNAN: I do. And where, Monsieur?

ATHOS: Near the Carmes Deschaux.

D'ARTAGNAN: At what hour?

ATHOS: About noon.

D'ARTAGNAN: About noon. That will do. I will be there.

ATHOS: Endeavor not to make me wait, for at a quarter past twelve I will cut off your ears as you run!

D'ARTAGNAN: Good! I will be there ten minutes before twelve! *(ATHOS bows and leaves, nursing his wounded shoulder. D'ARTAGNAN, pausing only a moment to look after him, suddenly turns to continue his pursuit, but before he takes a half-dozen steps, he runs into PORTHOS, who is wearing a very full cape. D'ARTAGNAN is caught in the folds of the cape, and PORTHOS, believing he is losing the garment, pulls it tighter around him, rolling D'ARTAGNAN inside of it. For a moment there is a struggle with the astounded PORTHOS and the furiously struggling D'ARTAGNAN.)*

PORTHOS: *(Making every effort to dislodge D'ARTAGNAN from inside the cape)* **Vertubleu! This fellow must be mad to run against people in this manner!**

D'ARTAGNAN: *(Reappearing from under the folds of the cape)* **Excuse me, but I am in such haste! I was running after someone and —**

PORTHOS: And do you always forget your eyes when you happen to be in a hurry? Monsieur, you stand a chance of getting chastised if you run against musketeers in this fashion.

D'ARTAGNAN: Chastised, Monsieur? The expression is strong.

PORTHOS: It is one that becomes Monsieur Porthos, a man accustomed to looking his enemies in the face!

D'ARTAGNAN: I always look my enemies in the face, Monsieur Porthos!

PORTHOS: Very well then. At one o'clock, behind the Luxembourg.

D'ARTAGNAN: At one o'clock! *(PORTHOS pulls his cloak about him firmly and leaves. D'ARTAGNAN turns to resume his chase, looking all around him, exasparated.)* **The man I was pursuing is nowhere in sight! And what a harebrained, stupid fellow I am! Are musketeers to be run against without warning? No! Ah, cursed Gascon that I am, I get from one hobble into another. Friend D'Artagnan, if you**

escape these two musketeers, of which there is not much chance, I would advise you to practice perfect politeness for the future. You must henceforth be admired and quoted as a model of it. To be obliging and polite does not necessarily make a man a coward. Look there, another musketeer and his friend. *(ARAMIS and his FRIEND appear in animated conversation. D'ARTAGNAN sees that ARAMIS lets a handkerchief fall from his pocket. D'ARTAGNAN rushes to them and attempts to retrieve the handkerchief, but ARAMIS firmly places his foot on it. However, D'ARTAGNAN, with great skill, removes the handkerchief and stands up with it. Very politely)* **I believe, Monsieur, that this is a handkerchief you would be sorry to lose? Such fine cambric! Such elegant embroidery on the initials!** *(ARAMIS snatches the handkerchief from D'ARTAGNAN. His FRIEND laughs.)*

FRIEND: *(Noticing the initials)* **Ah! will you persist in saying, most discreet Aramis, that you are not on good terms with Madame de Bois-Tracy, when that gracious lady has the kindness to lend you her handkerchief?**

ARAMIS: *(With a furious scowl at D'ARTAGNAN, but a mild expression to his friend)* **You are deceived, my friend. This handkerchief is not mine, and I cannot fancy why Monsieur has taken it into his head to offer it to me rather than to you. As a proof of what I say, here is mine in my pocket.** *(He draws forth his own handkerchief.)*

D'ARTAGNAN: *(Timidly, realizing that he has made a mistake)* **The fact is, I did not see the handkerchief fall from the pocket of Monsieur Aramis. He had his foot upon it, that is all, and I thought from his having his foot upon it, the handkerchief was his.**

ARAMIS: *(Coldly)* **You were deceived, my dear sir.** *(To his FRIEND)* **This handkerchief is as likely to have fallen from your pocket as mine, my friend.**

FRIEND: No, no, upon my honor! It is yours! *(Laughing)* **Keep it,**

my dear Aramis. It is not worth a quarrel. *(He bows and leaves, still laughing, much to ARAMIS' discomfort.)*

D'ARTAGNAN: Monsieur, you will excuse me, I hope.

ARAMIS: Permit me to observe to you, that you have not acted in this affair as a man of good breeding ought to have done.

D'ARTAGNAN: *(His temper rising again)* **What?**

ARAMIS: I suppose, Monsieur, that you are not a fool, and that you know very well that people do not tread upon pocket handkerchiefs without a reason. What the devil! Paris is not paved with cambric!

D'ARTAGNAN: Monsieur, you act wrongly in endeavoring to mortify me.

ARAMIS: Being a musketeer but for a time, I only fight when I am forced to do so, and always with great repugnance, but this time the affair is serious. Here is a lady compromised by you.

D'ARTAGNAN: By *us*, you mean.

ARAMIS: Oh, you take it up in that way do you? Well, I will teach you how to behave yourself. But not here. We are opposite the Hotel d'Arguilon, which is full of the cardinal's guards. How do I know that it is not his eminence who has honored you with the commission to bring him my head? Now I entertain a ridiculous partiality for my head. It seems to suit my shoulders so admirably. I have no objection to killing you, depend upon that, but quietly, in a snug remote place, where you will not be able to boast of your death to anybody.

D'ARTAGNAN: I agree, Monsieur, but do not be too confident.

ARAMIS: At two o'clock I shall have the honor of expecting you at the hotel of M. de Treville. *(He bows and exits.)*

D'ARTAGNAN: *(Bows.)* **And now it comes on noon and I must meet Monsieur Athos. Decidedly, I can't draw back, but at least if I am killed, I shall be killed by a musketeer – and on my very first day in Paris!** *(He paces.)* **Ah, musketeers!**

Perhaps I may yet make a friend of Athos, whose noble air and austere courage please me very much. And the same with Porthos, for did I not see the very plain backing of his baldrick when I was caught in his cape – and he seems so very vain about the gold facing of it! I may offer to relate this information to whoever might wish to hear it, and thereby escape being killed upon the spot. As for Aramis, I do not entertain much dread of him, for I perceive that he does not really wish to fight.

ATHOS: *(Enters, and greets D'ARTAGNAN with a low bow.)* **Monsieur, we may settle our business here, if you please. I have engaged two of my friends as seconds, but they are not yet come, at which I am astonished, as it is not at all their custom to be late.**

D'ARTAGNAN: I have no seconds, Monsieur, for having only arrived today in Paris, I as yet know no one.

ATHOS: *(After a moment)* **You know no one? But then, if I kill you, I shall have the air of a boy-slayer.**

D'ARTAGNAN: Not too much so, since you do me the honor to draw a sword with me while suffering from a wound which is very painful.

ATHOS: Very painful, upon my word, and you hurt me devilishly! But I will take the left hand. I use both hands equally.

D'ARTAGNAN: *(With a bow)* **If you would permit me, monsieur, I have a miraculous balsam for wounds given to me by my mother. I am sure that in less than three days this balsam would cure you, and at the end of three days, when you would be cured, it would still do me a great honor to cross swords with you.**

ATHOS: Pardieu, Monsieur! That's a proposition that pleases me; not that I accept it, but it savors of the gentleman a league off. I now foresee plainly that, if we don't kill each other, I shall hereafter have much pleasure in your conver-

sation. Ah, here comes Porthos at last.

D'ARTAGNAN: *(As PORTHOS enters)* **What! Monsieur Porthos is your second?**

ATHOS: He is, and here comes the other. *(ARAMIS enters.)*

D'ARTAGNAN: Your second witness is Monsieur Aramis?

ATHOS: He is. Are you not aware that we are never seen one without the others, and that we are called in the musketeers and the guards, at court and in the city, Athos, Porthos, and Aramis, or the three inseparables?

D'ARTAGNAN: *(Impressed)* **You are well named, gentlemen.**

PORTHOS: *(At sight of D'ARTAGNAN, stops abruptly.)* **Ah! What does this mean?**

ATHOS: This is the young gentleman I am going to fight with.

PORTHOS: Why, it is with him I am also going to fight!

D'ARTAGNAN: But not before one o'clock.

ARAMIS: I am also going to fight with this gentleman.

D'ARTAGNAN: *(Calmly)* **But not till two o'clock. And now that you are all assembled, gentlemen, permit me to say this. In case I should not be able to discharge my debt to all three, I pray you will excuse me. Monsieur Athos has the right to kill me first, which must abate by your valor in your own estimation, Monsieur Porthos, and render yours almost null, Monsieur Aramis. And now, gentlemen, guard!** *(He draws his sword.)*

ATHOS: *(Drawing his sword)* **It is very hot, and yet I cannot take off my doublet for I just now felt my wound begin to bleed again, and I should not like to annoy Monsieur with the sight of blood which he has not drawn from me himself.**

D'ARTAGNAN: Whether drawn by myself or another, I assure you I shall always view with regret the blood of so brave a gentleman. I will therefore fight in my doublet, as you do.

PORTHOS: Come, come! Enough of compliments. Please to remember we are waiting for our turns.

ARAMIS: Speak for yourself, when you are inclined to utter such

incongruities. For my part, I think what they say is very well said and quite worthy of two gentlemen.

ATHOS: When you please, Monsieur.

D'ARTAGNAN: I await your orders, Monsieur.

ARAMIS: *(Suddenly)* **Stop! The Cardinal's guards!**

PORTHOS: The guards! Sheathe your swords, gentlemen! Sheathe your swords!

ATHOS: It is too late. They have seen us. If we do not allow them to arrest us, they will charge upon us.

PORTHOS: There are five of them, and we are but three.

ATHOS: Then we shall be beaten and must die on the spot, for, on my part, I declare I will never appear before the captain of the guard as a conquered man.

D'ARTAGNAN: Gentlemen, allow me to correct your words, if you please. You said you were but three, but it appears to me we are four.

PORTHOS: But you are not one of us.

D'ARTAGNAN: That's true. I do not wear the uniform, but I am one of you in spirit. My heart is that of a musketeer. I feel it, Monsieur, and that impels me on. Try me, gentlemen, and I swear to you by my honor that I will not go hence if we are conquered.

ATHOS: What is your name, my brave fellow?

D'ARTAGNAN: D'Artagnan, Monsieur.

ATHOS: Well, then! Athos, Porthos, Aramis, – and D'Artagnan – forward! *(With drawn swords, all four move forward together, ready for the fight.)*

From

THE LUCK OF ROARING CAMP

By Bret Harte

The American West in the days of the California gold rush came vividly to life in Bret Harte's colorful short stories. His entertaining cast of miners, gamblers, thieves, fugitives, and camp women were drawn from life, and his situations were common to the people who lived in the Sierra foothills in the mid-nineteenth century. In *The Luck of Roaring Camp*, the birth of a baby is an unusual event that brings all activity to a standstill in the otherwise bustling mining camp. Outside a rude cabin on the bank of a river, some of the camp residents await the arrival of Cherokee Sal's child.

CHARACTERS: SANDY TIPTON, a miner; KENTUCK, a miner; STUMPY, a miner; JOHN OAKHURST, a gambler.

SCENE: A rough cabin with a small table, and a closed door, outside of which are assembled KENTUCK and SANDY in rough miner's dress, and JOHN OAKHURST, more meticulously dressed as a successful gambler.

SANDY: I reckon this is mighty rough on Sal. I ain't got no use for such as her, but still, I reckon it's rough.

OAKHURST: At a time when she is most in need of a woman's care, there is not another woman to be found in forty miles. It's strange to think of how often men die and go out of this camp, and tonight, a new life is about to come in.

SANDY: Seems to me they go out a lot quicker'n they come in.

KENTUCK: Stumpy has gone in to see what he can do for Sal. He's had experience in them things, havin' been a father himself at one time or another, and knowin' somethin' of doctorin'.

SANDY: I lay you three to five that Sal will get through it. She's stubborn enough.

KENTUCK: I lay you the same odds that the child will survive!

SANDY: And be a boy!

KENTUCK: And look like Sal, Lord help him!

OAKHURST: Listen! *(They all freeze, listening with rapt attention.)* **Do you hear that?**

SANDY: It ain't the pines a-moanin'.

KENTUCK: It ain't the river over the rocks, neither.

SANDY: It shore ain't the fire a-cracklin'.

KENTUCK: I never heard nuthin' like it before.

OAKHURST: Gentlemen, that is the first querulous cry of a newborn baby.

SANDY: *(Throwing his hat in the air)* **Yahoo! Sal done it! Let's explode a barrel of gunpowder!**

KENTUCK: Let's fire off every gun in camp!

OAKHURST: Gentlemen, out of consideration for the mother...

SANDY: Nobody around here ever had consideration for Sal before.

KENTUCK: We have to celebrate! Ain't nothin' like this ever happened before in Roaring Camp! Nor any other camp around these parts, neither!

OAKHURST: Here is Stumpy, ready to report.

STUMPY: *(Opens the cabin door and steps outside, rolling down his shirt-sleeves. He speaks calmly.)* **Gentlemen, I regret to say that Cherokee Sal has passed out of Roaring Camp forever. May her sinful soul find peace at last. But the child lives. Gentlemen, it is a boy.**

SANDY: A boy! Didn't I say so?

KENTUCK: A boy! Of course, it is! *(Suddenly)* **But Stumpy, can he live now? If his maw's passed on, how will he...**

SANDY: Milk! He'll need milk.

KENTUCK: Milk? Where we goin' to get milk in Roaring Camp?

STUMPY: *(Quietly)* **I believe Jinny can be of use.**

SANDY: Jinny? *(With a loud laugh)* **Jinny!**

KENTUCK: *(Laughing)* **Jinny's an ass!**

OAKHURST: A female ass, with a nursing colt. *(The laughter stops. SANDY and KENTUCK look thoughtful.)*

STUMPY: Jinny will do. Now, gentlemen, if you would like to see the newcomer, he is comfortably abed, wrapped in red flannel and stowed snug and tight in a candlebox on the table. Them as wishes to contribute anything toward the orphan will find a hat handy. *(He steps back inside and stands beside the table with an authoritative air. OAKHURST enters, removes his hat, and approaches the table reverently. SANDY and KENTUCK follow his example. All stand around the table, looking down at the infant in the candlebox.)*

SANDY: *(In awe)* **Is that him? Mighty small specimen.**

KENTUCK: Ain't bigger nor a derringer. *(He extends a forefinger* *curiously into the box.)* **Ain't got much color, neither. Oh! Lookee there! Will you look!**

SANDY: If he ain't took hold on your finger! Will you look at that!

KENTUCK: *(Embarrassed, but pleased, he laughs.)* **The dern little cuss! Let go, you!** *(He gently draws his finger away, looking at it, amazed.)* **He rastled with my finger! And he ain't even an hour old! The dern little cuss!**

OAKHURST: Stumpy, have you thought of sending the child over to Red Dog where female attention may be procured?

STUMPY: No, I ain't.

SANDY: And he won't! *We'll* adopt this here baby!

KENTUCK: He'll stay right here in Roaring Camp!

SANDY: If them fellows at Red Dog got hold of him, they'd most likely swap him for somethin' and he'd be gone for good! What do *they* know about babies!

KENTUCK: *(Holding his finger apart from the others)* **The dern little cuss! Rastled with my finger!**

OAKHURST: Perhaps a female nurse could be brought in to care for the child.

SANDY: *(With a snort)* **What *decent* woman could be prevailed upon to come to Roaring Camp? Nary a one as I know of. And we shore don't want no more of Sal's kind.**

OAKHURST: What do you say, Stumpy?

STUMPY: *(After a moment)* **Gentlemen, me and Jinny will be father and mother to this here baby. He will survive in Roaring Camp.**

OAKHURST: An original plan. Almost heroic. I like it. We'll send to Sacramento for certain articles...

SANDY: Toys! All babies has got to have toys! And clothes! The best that can be got!

KENTUCK: Lace! And frills! Damn the cost!

OAKHURST: Can you picture a rosewood cradle being packed by mule for eighty miles? It will be the talk of every camp

along the way. A rosewood cradle for...for...what are we going to call him, Stumpy?

STUMPY: Well, I hadn't thought. But, of course, he must have a name.

SANDY: A name! But...what name?

KENTUCK: One that means somethin' special – to be his own, you know?

OAKHURST: Gentlemen, I have a gambler's intuition that this baby will bring us luck.

SANDY: The luck! That's it!

STUMPY: Perhaps Tommy could be added, for convenience?

KENTUCK: Tommy Luck. It will fit him just fine.

OAKHURST: The mother is best not to have a part in it, and the father is unknown. It's better to take a fresh deal all round. Call him Luck and start him fresh.

SANDY: Who's to stand godfather?

STUMPY: Why, if there's goin' to be a godfather, I'd like to see who's got any better rights than me! Didn't I help Sal bring him to light?

KENTUCK: You did. Stumpy will stand godfather!

STUMPY: I will. And according to the laws of the State of California, I proclaim this child, Thomas Luck!

OAKHURST: We all stand witness. Thomas Luck!

SANDY: The Luck of Roaring Camp!

KENTUCK: *(Holding up his treasured finger)* Rastled with my finger, the dern little cuss!

From

RIP VAN WINKLE

By Washington Irving

In 1820, American author Washington Irving published *The Sketch Book*, a collection of nostalgic stories, including *Rip Van Winkle*. Dealing with Dutch folklore in the state of New York, particularly in the Catskill Mountains, *Rip Van Winkle* is the magical tale of a simple, good-natured man who is lured deep into the mountains by the spirits of Henry Hudson and the early Dutch settlers of the area. After drinking profusely from a flagon until his senses are overpowered and he falls asleep, he awakens twenty years later. As Rip wanders back to his home village, he is completely astonished and totally unable to understand what has happened.

CHARACTERS: RIP VAN WINKLE, a YOUNG MAN, an OLD MAN, an OLD WOMAN.

RIP: *(Enters, his clothes in tatters, his beard almost a foot long, carrying a rusty gun of the period. He looks around him, bewildered.)* **Surely, I did not sleep up there on the mountain all night! That flagon! Oh, that wicked flagon! What excuse shall I make to Dame Van Winkle? And my gun! I've lost it. There is nothing here but a rusty, worm-eaten old firelock. And my dog. Wolf! Where is he? Gone!** *(He takes a few steps and groans.)* **Ah, these mountain beds do not agree with me. If this frolic should lay me up with a fit of the rheumatism, I shall have a blessed time with Dame Van Winkle! There is no terror like that woman's tongue! It's like a sharp-edged tool – it only grows keener with constant use.** *(He winces, then looks around again.)* **There are people passing by – but I don't know them. And they don't seem to know me, from the surly way they are looking at me. I thought I knew everyone in the Catskill country. And it *is* the Catskill country. I know these mountains – these hills – this village. But these people – their clothes are not like mine.** *(As he looks down at his own clothes, he gasps.)* **What's this? Rags! And my beard? This is mine? A foot long! And gray! How can this be? I swear I was a young man when I fled the clamor of Dame Van Winkle's temper and climbed the mountain last night! Oh-h-h! That flagon! It has addled my poor head sadly.**

What's this? My own house? Gone to decay! The roof fallen in – the windows shattered – the doors off the hinges! And it is so quiet. No shrill voice ringing through the hall – no tumbling and shouting of the children. *(He turns, looking around in utter amazement.)* **The inn! The village inn where hung the sign painted with a jolly portrait of His Majesty King George the Third – it's gone!**

What is this rickety building in its place? And what's this? A new sign? The head of King George wearing a cocked hat? And a blue coat instead of a red? Holding a sword instead of a sceptre? And named – George Washington! *(He backs away, looking around in dismay.)* **Did I not spend many an evening here, smoking my pipe under this sign, with my good friends? But these people, I do not know them!** *(The YOUNG MAN, OLD MAN, and OLD WOMAN gather around him, looking at him curiously.)*

YOUNG MAN: Sir, you cut a quaint figure here. On which side did you vote?

RIP: *(Staring stupidly)* **Vote?**

YOUNG MAN: Are you a Federal or a Democrat?

RIP: A what?

YOUNG MAN: Why do you come to the election with a gun on your shoulder? Do you mean to breed a riot in the village?

RIP: Alas, neighbors, I am a poor, quiet man, a native of this place, and a loyal subject of the King, God bless him!

YOUNG MAN: A Tory! A spy! Away with him! *(He grabs RIP's arm.)*

OLD MAN: Hold! He looks harmless enough. Let him go. Now, answer, sir. What are you doing here? What are you looking for?

RIP: I mean no harm. I am merely searching for my neighbors whom I used to meet at this tavern.

OLD WOMAN: Who are these neighbors? Name them.

RIP: I don't see Nicholas Vedder here.

OLD WOMAN: Nicholas Vedder! Why, he is dead and gone these eighteen years!

RIP: Where is Brom Dutcher?

OLD MAN: He went off to the army in the beginning of the war. Some say he was killed at the storming of Stony Point. Others say he was drowned in a squall at the foot of Antony's Nose. I don't know. He never came back again.

RIP: And the schoolmaster, Van Bummel?

YOUNG MAN: He went off to the wars, too, and was a great militia general. He's now in Congress.

RIP: Wars? Congress? I don't understand. All these sad changes in my home, with my friends. *(Looking anxiously around)* **Does nobody here know Rip Van Winkle?**

OLD MAN: Rip Van Winkle? Why, it's twenty years since he went away from home with his gun and never has been heard of since.

RIP: Twenty years!

OLD WOMAN: His dog, the one he called Wolf, came home without him. But whether he shot himself or was carried away by the Indians, nobody can tell.

RIP: *(In a faltering voice)* **And his wife? Dame Van Winkle?**

OLD WOMAN: She died. Broke a bloodvessel in a fit of passion at a New England peddler. Terrible tempered woman! Who could blame Rip for running off?

RIP: *(With a sigh of relief)* **Well, there is a drop of comfort in knowing that! But see here, all of you, you must believe me. I am Rip Van Winkle! Once young, now old – I don't know how! Does nobody here recognize me?**

OLD MAN: *(Stares at him, closely, then exchanges a look with the OLD WOMAN.)* **Why, I believe it is! Sure enough! It is Rip Van Winkle!**

OLD WOMAN: Where have you been these twenty years?

RIP: I hardly know how to answer. I only know that everything is changed – and I'm changed. I went up to the mountain – I thought it was just last night – and I heard someone calling me. A voice I'd never heard before. And a strange man, a short, square-built old fellow, with thick bushy hair and a grizzled beard, and his dress of the old Dutch fashion, beckoned to me. He bore a stout keg on his shoulders and led me up the dry bed of a mountain stream. And as we climbed I heard long, rolling peals, like distant thunder, and we came to a high, wild place where there

was a company of odd-looking men playing at ninepins and all dressed in the quaint, outlandish fashion. Why, they reminded me of the figures in the old Flemish painting that hangs in the parlor of Dominie Van Shaik, the parson. You know, the one he brought over from Holland at the time of the settlement here. And the odd thing was, they maintained the gravest of faces, and the most mysterious silence, and whenever they rolled their balls, they echoed along the mountains like rumbling peals of thunder. Then they emptied the contents of the keg into long flagons, and I tasted it, too, and it had the flavor of excellent Hollands. Being a thirsty soul, I tasted, and tasted again, and again, until my eyes swam in my head and I felt myself dropping off to sleep. When I woke up, I was lying on the same green hill where I had first seen the old man with the keg on his shoulder. It was a bright, sunny morning – *this* very morning, and there was no sign of the strange old men with the keg, or the men playing at ninepins, or the flagon. And when I tried to find the dry stream bed, it wasn't dry at all, but full of fresh, rushing water! I swear to you, that is all I remember.

YOUNG MAN: *(Skeptical)* **I think we should take the old man's gun and put it away for safekeeping, and lock him up where he'll do no mischief.** *(Taps his head knowingly.)*

OLD MAN: No, no. There is something in what he says. We have all heard that the Catskill mountains are haunted by strange beings. Haven't we all heard, many a time, that the great Hendrick Hudson, the first discoverer of this river and country, kept a kind of vigil on the mountains every twenty years, with his crew from the *Half-Moon*.

OLD WOMAN: Yes! They come back to keep a guardian eye upon the river. Didn't my own father see them once in their old Dutch clothes, playing at ninepins in a hollow of the mountain, and hear, just as you say, the sound of their balls like

distant peals of thunder on a summer afternoon!

YOUNG MAN: That's only a story! A fairy tale! And this old man simply had a nightmare!

RIP: A nightmare? No! It was too real. Look at me! How did I change so, if it didn't really happen? When I fell asleep, the village – the country all around here was still a province of Great Britain. But now – you speak of a war...?

OLD MAN: Yes, the Revolutionary War.

RIP: Revolution?

OLD WOMAN: The country has thrown off the yoke of old England. We are no longer subjects of his Majesty George the Third, but free citizens of the United States!

RIP: United States?

OLD MAN: Look up there, high on that pole! See it? Our flag! The stars and stripes! And ours is now a government of the people.

RIP: I am no politician. I care not what sort of government it is, so long as it is not a petticoat government! My neck is out of the yoke of matrimony! I am free of Dame Van Winkle's tyranny, and I am a happy man!

OLD MAN: Come, sit down. You must tell your story again, and again, to everyone who will listen.

RIP: Not everyone will be as ready to listen as you, my friends.

OLD WOMAN: Oh, there may be some who will doubt you, and say that you're out of your head. *(She nods toward the YOUNG MAN.)* **But you needn't mind them. They are free to disagree, or agree, as they choose.**

OLD MAN: See there? Thunder clouds over the mountain! Rain coming, I'd say. And perhaps, soon, on this very summer's afternoon, the doubters will listen to the thunder rumbling.

RIP: *(Nodding)* **And perhaps they'll doubt no more!**

From

DAISY MILLER

By Henry James

Daisy Miller, published in 1878, is a very short novel by Henry James, and one of his more popular pieces. He presents a delightful portrait of a young, unsophisticated American girl from Schenectady, New York, who is spending a summer in Vevey, Switzerland, with her mother and younger brother. There she meets Winterbourne, a young American gentleman who is attracted by her innocent and direct manner and her way of doing what she pleases and talking to whomever she likes, regardless of whether or not such behavior by a young woman is considered proper by either American or European observers.

CHARACTERS: DAISY MILLER, a young American girl; FREDERICK WINTERBOURNE, an American man; EUGENIO, a courier (guide); MRS. COSTELLO, Winterbourne's aunt.

SCENE: Set in the garden of the Hotel Trois Couronnes, DAISY both enchants and puzzles her new acquaintance, WINTERBOURNE. DAISY and WINTERBOURNE lean on a railing, overlooking a lake. She wears a white muslin dress with many ruffles and flounces, which she fusses over in a natural way as she speaks.

DAISY: We are going to Rome for the winter, my mother and I, and my little brother Randolph. Are you a real American?

WINTERBOURNE: *(With a laugh)* **I hope so!**

DAISY: I wouldn't have taken you for an American. You seem more like a German.

WINTERBOURNE: Well, I have met Germans who spoke like Americans, but never an American who speaks like a German. Would you be more comfortable sitting down, Miss...Miss...?

DAISY: Miller. I am called Daisy, though my real name is Annie. And I like standing up and walking about. I'm from New York State, if you know where that is. My father's back in Schenectady. He has to look after his business. He doesn't like Europe. An English lady in the train asked me if we didn't all live in hotels in America. I told her I have never been in so many hotels in my life as since I came to Europe. I have never seen so many. It's nothing but hotels. But they are very good when once you get used to their ways, and Europe is perfectly sweet. I am not one bit disappointed. I have ever so many intimate friends who have been here ever so many times. And I have ever so many dresses and things from Paris. Whenever I put on a Paris dress, I feel as if I am in Europe.

WINTERBOURNE: It is a kind of wishing-cap for you?

DAISY: **Yes. It always makes me wish I was here. I am sure they send all the pretty dresses to America. You see the most frightful things here. The only thing I don't like is the society. There isn't any society here, or, if there is, I don't know where it keeps itself. I'm very fond of society, and I have always had a great deal of it, not only in Schenectady, but in New York. Last winter I had seventeen dinners given me, and three of them were by gentlemen. I have always had a great deal of gentlemen's society.**

WINTERBOURNE: **Have you?** *(He looks away a moment; to himself)* **She has the most charming nose I've ever seen.**

DAISY: **Have you been to that old castle?** *(Points with her parasol.)*

WINTERBOURNE: **The Chateau de Chillon? Yes, more than once. I suppose you have seen it?**

DAISY: **No, but I want to go there dreadfully.**

WINTERBOURNE: **It's a very pretty excursion. You can drive or go by the little steamer.** *(After a moment)* **I would like very much to go there again – with you.**

DAISY: *(Placidly)* **With me?**

WINTERBOURNE: **And with your mother, of course.**

DAISY: **I guess my mother won't go. She doesn't like to ride round in the afternoon. She suffers dreadfully from dyspepsia. But did you really mean that you would like to go there with me?**

WINTERBOURNE: **Most earnestly.**

DAISY: **Then we may arrange it. If Mother will stay with my brother Randolph, then I guess Eugenio will stay, too.**

WINTERBOURNE: **Eugenio?**

DAISY: **Our courier. He doesn't like to stay with Randolph. He's the most fastidious man I ever saw, but he's a splendid courier. But I guess he'll stay at home with Randolph if mother does, and then we can go to the castle. Oh, here comes Eugenio now.** *(In a friendly tone)* **Eugenio!**

EUGENIO: *(Impeccably dressed, enters, looks closely at WINTER-*

BOURNE, then bows to Daisy.) **I have the honor to inform Mademoiselle that luncheon is upon the table.**

DAISY: See here, Eugenio, I am going to that old castle.

EUGENIO: To the Chateau de Chillon? *(Sternly)* **Mademoiselle has made arrangements?**

DAISY: *(Just a little taken aback by his tone, she turns to WINTERBOURNE.)* **You won't back out, will you?**

WINTERBOURNE: I shall not be happy till we go!

EUGENIO: *(Icily)* **I think you had better not go to the Chateau with this gentleman, Mademoiselle.**

DAISY: I suppose you don't think it's proper. *(To WINTERBOURNE)* **Eugenio doesn't think *anything* is proper. But you *are* staying in the hotel, aren't you? And you are really an American?**

WINTERBOURNE: I shall have the honor of presenting to you a person who will tell you all about me – my aunt, Mrs. Costello, of New York.

DAISY: Your aunt? Is she that lady with the white hair in puffs, who never takes her meals in the dining room and has a headache every two days?

WINTERBOURNE: *(With a laugh)* **I believe you have described her perfectly.**

DAISY: I learned all about her from the chambermaid. I want to know her ever so much! I know I should like her. She must be very exclusive. I'm dying to be exclusive myself. Well, we *are* exclusive, mother and I. We don't speak to anyone, or they don't speak to us. I suppose it's about the same thing. Anyway, I shall be ever so glad to know your aunt. And we *will* go to that old castle some day. *(She smiles, puts up her parasol, and goes off on EUGENIO's arm.)*

WINTERBOURNE: *(Looking after her)* **I swear she has the bearing of a princess. An American princess! If only she were not so familiar with the courier!**

MRS. COSTELLO: *(Enters and sits on a bench. She is elderly, but* *beautifully dressed.)* **Frederick! Come and sit with me.**

WINTERBOURNE: Aunt! *(Crosses to her and kisses her on the cheek.)* **I didn't know you were coming out today.** *(Sits beside her.)* **But I'm very glad you have come. I must ask you, Aunt, if you have observed in the hotel an American family, the Millers, mother, daughter, and a little boy?**

MRS. COSTELLO: Oh, yes. I have observed them, heard them, and kept out of their way.

WINTERBOURNE: I am afraid you don't approve of them?

MRS. COSTELLO: They are very common. They are the sort of Americans that one does one's duty by in not accepting them.

WINTERBOURNE: Then you don't accept them?

MRS. COSTELLO: I can't, my dear Frederick. I would if I could, but I can't.

WINTERBOURNE: *(After a moment)* **The young girl is very pretty.**

MRS. COSTELLO: Of course, she's pretty, but she is very common. She has that charming look that they all have. I can't think where they pick it up. And she dresses in perfection. I can't think where they get their taste.

WINTERBOURNE: *(With a laugh)* **My dear Aunt, she is not a Commanche savage!**

MRS. COSTELLO: She is a young lady who has an intimacy with her mama's courier. And the mother is just as bad! They treat the courier like a familiar friend, like a gentleman. I shouldn't wonder if he dines with them. Very likely they have never seen a man with such good manners, such fine clothes, so like a gentleman. He probably corresponds to the young lady's idea of a count.

WINTERBOURNE: Well, I am not a courier, and yet she was very charming to me. We simply met here in the garden and talked.

MRS. COSTELLO: *Simply* met? And talked? Pray, what did you say?

WINTERBOURNE: **I said that I would take the liberty of introducing her to my admirable aunt in order to guarantee my respectability.**

MRS. COSTELLO: **And who is to guarantee hers?**

WINTERBOURNE: **Aunt! You are cruel! She is completely uncultivated, but she is wonderfully pretty and, in short, she is very nice. To prove that I believe it, I am going to take her to the Chateau de Chillon.**

MRS. COSTELLO: **You two are going there together? I should say that will prove just the contrary. How long have you known her?**

WINTERBOURNE: **Half an hour.**

MRS. COSTELLO: **Half an hour! Dear me! What a dreadful girl!**

WINTERBOURNE: *(Rises, steps away a few paces; after a moment)* **Aunt, do you really think then, that she is the sort of young lady who expects a man, sooner or later, to carry her off?**

MRS. COSTELLO: **I haven't the least idea what such young ladies expect a man to do. But I really think you had better not meddle with little American girls that are uncultivated, as you call them. You will be sure to make some great mistake. You are too innocent.**

WINTERBOURNE: *(Smiling)* **My dear Aunt, I am not innocent.**

MRS. COSTELLO: **You are too guilty, then?**

WINTERBOURNE: **You won't let me introduce the poor girl to you?**

MRS. COSTELLO: **Is it true that she is going to the Chateau de Chillon with you?**

WINTERBOURNE: **I think she fully intends it.**

MRS. COSTELLO: **Then, my dear Frederick, I must decline the honor of her acquaintance. I am an old woman, but I am not too old, thank heaven, to be shocked!**

WINTERBOURNE: **But don't the young girls in America do these things?**

MRS. COSTELLO: **I should like to see my granddaughters do them!**

WINTERBOURNE: *(Turns away, thoughtfully)* **Regardless, I am impatient to see her again. I have never met anyone quite like her. And regardless of anything, I *will* take her to the Chateau de Chillon!**

A Dramatic Reading From

THE SONG OF HIAWATHA

By Henry Wadsworth Longfellow

Henry Wadsworth Longfellow has been called the most widely-read American poet. A distinguished professor of modern languages at Harvard, he taught for many years and then began to write the poetry that all the world has come to recognize. His narrative poem, *The Song of Hiawatha,* is a free rendering of American Indian lore. In this excerpt, Hiawatha seeks and wins a wife. The actions of the story may be played out by the readers.

CHARACTERS: HIAWATHA, an Indian brave; NOKOMIS, his grandmother; ARROW-MAKER, an old man; MINNEHAHA, his daughter; NARRATOR.

HIAWATHA: As unto the bow the cord is,
So unto the man is woman,
Though she bends him, she obeys him,
Though she draws him, yet she follows,
Useless each without the other!

NARRATOR: Thus the youthful Hiawatha said within himself and pondered;
Much perplexed by various feelings,
Listless, longing, hoping, fearing,
Dreaming still of Minnehaha,
Of the lovely Laughing Water
In the land of the Dacotahs.

NOKOMIS: Wed a maiden of your people!

NARRATOR: Warning, said the old Nokomis.

NOKOMIS: Go not eastward, go not westward
For a stranger, whom we know not!
Like a fire upon the hearthstone
Is a neighbor's homely daughter;
Like the starlight or the moonlight
Is the handsomest of strangers!

NARRATOR: Thus dissuading spake Nokomis,
And my Hiawatha answered, only thus:

HIAWATHA: Dear old Nokomis,
Very pleasant is the firelight,
But I like the starlight better;
Better do I like the moonlight!

NARRATOR: Gravely then said old Nokomis:

NOKOMIS: Bring not here an idle maiden,
Bring not here a useless woman,
Hands unskillful, feet unwilling;

Bring a wife with nimble fingers,
Heart and hand that move together,
Feet that run on willing errands!
NARRATOR: Smiling, answered Hiawatha:
HIAWATHA: In the land of the Dacotahs
Lives the Arrow-Maker's daughter,
Minnehaha, Laughing Water,
Handsomest of all the women.
I will bring her to your wigwam.
She shall run upon your errands,
Be your starlight, moonlight, firelight,
Be the sunlight of my people!
NARRATOR: Still dissuading, said Nokomis:
NOKOMIS: Bring not to my lodge a stranger
From the land of the Dacotahs!
Very fierce are the Dacotahs!
Often is there war between us,
There are feuds yet unforgotten,
Wounds that ache and still may open!
NARRATOR: Laughing, answered Hiawatha:
HIAWATHA: For that reason, if no other,
Would I wed the fair Dacotah,
That our tribes might be united,
That old feuds might be forgotten,
And old wounds be healed forever!
NARRATOR: Thus departed Hiawatha
To the land of the Dacotahs,
To the land of handsome women.

At the doorway of his wigwam
Sat the ancient Arrow-Maker
In the land of the Dacotahs,
Making arrow-heads of jasper.
At his side in all her beauty

Sat the lovely Minnehaha,
Sat his daughter, Laughing Water,
Plaiting mats of flags and rushes.
Of the past the old man's thoughts were,
And the maiden's of the future.
Through their thoughts they heard a footstep,
Heard a rustling in the branches,
And with glowing cheeks and forehead,
With a deer upon his shoulders,
Hiawatha stood before them.
Straight the ancient Arrow-Maker
Looked up gravely from his labor,
Laid aside the unfinished arrow,
Bade him enter at the doorway,
Saying, as he rose to meet him,

ARROW-MAKER: Hiawatha, you are welcome.

NARRATOR: At the feet of Laughing Water
Hiawatha laid his burden;
Threw the red deer from his shoulders.
And the maiden looked up at him,
Looked up from her mat of rushes,
Said, with gentle look and accent:

MINNEHAHA: You are welcome, Hiawatha.

HIAWATHA: *(To ARROW-MAKER)* **After many years of warfare,**
Many years of strife and bloodshed,
There is peace between the Ojibways
And the tribe of the Dacotahs.
That this peace may last forever,
And our hands be clasped more closely,
And our hearts be more united,
Give me as my wife this maiden,
Minnehaha, Laughing Water,
Loveliest of Dacotah women!

NARRATOR: And the ancient Arrow-Maker

Paused a moment ere he answered;
Smoked a little while in silence,
Looked at Hiawatha proudly,
Fondly looked at Laughing Water,
And made answer very gravely:
ARROW-MAKER: Yes, if Minnehaha wishes.
Let your heart speak, Minnehaha.
NARRATOR: And the lovely Laughing Water
Seemed more lovely as she stood there.
Neither willing nor reluctant,
As she went to Hiawatha,
Softly took the seat beside him,
While she said, and blushed to say it:
MINNEHAHA: I will follow you, my husband.
NARRATOR: This was Hiawatha's wooing!
Thus it was he won the daughter
Of the ancient Arrow-Maker,
In the land of the Dacotahs.
From the wigwam he departed,
Leading with him Laughing Water.
Hand in hand they went together
Through the woodland and the meadow,
Left the old man standing lonely
At the doorway of his wigwam.
And the ancient Arrow-Maker
Turned again unto his labor,
Sat down by his sunny doorway,
Murmuring to himself, and saying:
ARROW-MAKER: Thus it is our daughters leave us,
Those we love, and those who love us.
Just when they have learned to help us,
When we are old and lean upon them,
Comes a youth with flaunting feathers,
With his flute of reeds, a stranger

Wanders piping through the village,
Beckons to the fairest maiden,
And she follows where he leads her,
Leaving all things for the stranger!

NARRATOR: Thus it was that Hiawatha
To the lodge of old Nokomis
Brought the moonlight, starlight, firelight,
Brought the sunlight of his people,
Minnehaha, Laughing Water,
Handsomest of all the women
In the land of the Dacotahs.

A Fable From

THE PANCHATANTRA

Composed in the second century, *The Panchatantra's* fables of India are shrewd little stories about the art of living wisely. Here is one dealing with the conflict between education, or book-learning, and common sense.

CHARACTERS: NARRATOR, 1ST BRAHMAN YOUTH, 2ND BRAHMAN YOUTH, 3RD BRAHMAN YOUTH, GUMPTION.

NARRATOR: Men of learning and noble birth often lack common sense. The saying is true: "Book-learning people rightly cherish; but gumption's best of all to me. Bereft of gumption, you shall perish like to the Lion-maker's three."

I'll tell you of four brahman youths who were great friends. Three of them were men of science, but none had any common sense. The fourth had plenty of common sense, but no mind for science and learning. Once they took counsel with each other.

1ST YOUTH: What good is science to us, if we cannot take it to some foreign country and win the favor of great men and make our fortunes?

2ND YOUTH: Then we must go to the Eastern Country.

3RD YOUTH: We'll go today.

GUMPTION: Tomorrow would be better.

NARRATOR: And so it came to pass, and the four friends set off on their journey. After they had gone a little way, one of the youths said to the others:

1ST YOUTH: There is one among us, he who is called Gumption, who has no learning. He has only common sense, and a man can't win favor with a prince or a king without learning. Whatever I get, I'll not give him a share, so let him go home again and leave us to ourselves.

2ND YOUTH: Hey, you! Gumption! Go home. You have no learning and are therefore of no use to us.

3RD YOUTH: Wait. It is not right that we send him away. Remember, we have played together since we were boys. Let him come with us. He is a pleasant fellow and shall have a share in the riches we win.

NARRATOR: So they went on together, the four of them, until they came to a jungle. There they found the bones and leav-

ings of a dead lion.

1ST YOUTH: Ha! Now we can put our book-learning to the test. Here lies some sort of dead creature. With our great learning we will put it back together and bring it to life. I'll assemble the bones.

2ND YOUTH: I'll add flesh and blood and the hide.

3RD YOUTH: And when the two of you have done all that, I will breathe the breath of life into this creature.

GUMPTION: Wait! Can't you see that this is a lion? If you bring him back to life, he will kill us and eat us.

1ST YOUTH: Stupid! Is all our learning to go for nothing?

3RD YOUTH: What good is our education if we don't put it to use?

2ND YOUTH: You know nothing about it. Get out of our way.

GUMPTION: Very well, if you insist. But wait until I climb a tree before you make the lion alive again.

NARRATOR: And so Gumption quickly climbed a tree, and his three friends brought the lion to life. But the moment this happened, the lion sprang up and killed the three friends, just as Gumption had predicted. Afterwards, Gumption climbed safely down from the tree and went home. So, you see, the saying was perfectly true: "Book-learning people rightly cherish; but gumption's best of all to me. Bereft of gumption you shall perish like to the Lion-makers three."

From

HEIDI

By Johanna Spyri

Heidi is Swiss author Johanna Spyri's best-known work, written in 1881. Heidi is a little orphan who has lived with her grandfather high in the Swiss Alps since she was very young. She loves tending the goats and living in her beautiful mountain home where she leads a free and happy life. But when she is eight years old, she is taken by her Aunt Dete to Frankfurt, Germany, to be educated and to act as a companion to an invalid child, Clara Sesemann.

CHARACTERS: HEIDI, age 8; DETE, her aunt; MISS ROTTENMEIER, a housekeeper; CLARA SESEMANN, age 12, an invalid.

SCENE: The reluctant HEIDI and her determined aunt, who does not wish to be responsible for her, arrive at the Sesemann house where they are met by the haughty housekeeper, MISS ROTTENMEIER.

DETE: *(With a curtsy)* **Miss Rottenmeier, I have brought the child who has come to be a companion for Herr Sesemann's daughter.**

MISS ROTTENMEIER: *(Looking displeased)* **Indeed! What is your name, child?**

HEIDI: Heidi. *(She looks around the room, curiously.)*

MISS ROTTENMEIER: What? That's no Christian name for a child. You were not christened that. What name did they give you when you were baptized?

HEIDI: I do not remember.

MISS ROTTENMEIER: What a way to answer! Dete, is the child a simpleton or only saucy?

DETE: *(Giving HEIDI a poke)* **If the lady will allow me, I will speak for the child, for she is very unaccustomed to strangers. She is certainly not stupid nor saucy, for she does not know what it means. She speaks exactly as she thinks. Today is the first time she has been in a gentleman's house and she does not know good manners. But she is docile and very willing to learn if the lady will kindly have patience. She was christened Adelheid, after her mother, my sister, who has died.**

MISS ROTTENMEIER: Adelheid! Well, that's a name that one can pronounce. But I must tell you, Dete, that I am astonished to see so young a child. I told you that I wanted a companion of the same age as the young lady of the house, one who could share her lessons and all her other occupa-

tions. Fräulein Clara is now over twelve. What age is this child?

DETE: I have lost count of her exact age, but I believe she is ten, or thereabouts.

HEIDI: Grandfather told me I was eight. *(DETE pokes her again.)*

MISS ROTTENMEIER: What? Only eight? Four years too young! Of what use is such a child to me? And what have you learned, child? What books have you read?

HEIDI: None.

MISS ROTTENMEIER: What? How did you learn to read, then?

HEIDI: I have never learned to read, nor my friend, Peter, either.

MISS ROTTENMEIER: Mercy upon us! Is it possible you cannot read? What have you learned then?

HEIDI: Nothing.

MISS ROTTENMEIER: Dete! This is not at all the sort of companion you led me to expect. How could you think of bringing me a child like this?

DETE: *(Firmly, but respectfully)* **If the lady will allow me, the child is exactly what I thought you required, a child altogether different and not at all like other children. Now I must go, but I will come again soon to see how she is getting on.** *(Curtsies and hurries out.)*

MISS ROTTENMEIER: Wait! Wait! Are you really going to leave her here? Stop! *(She hurries out after her.)*

CLARA: *(Who has watched all this with amusement, now beckons to HEIDI)* **Come here to me.** *(HEIDI goes to her.)* **Would you like to be called Heidi or Adelheid?**

HEIDI: I am never called anything but Heidi.

CLARA: Then I shall always call you by that name. My name is Clara. Are you pleased to be here in Frankfurt?

HEIDI: No, but I shall go home again tomorrow and take grandfather some white rolls.

CLARA: Well, you are a funny child! You have come here expressly to stay with me and share my lessons. There will

be some fun times, too, since you cannot read, for lessons are often dreadfully dull. Now they will be much more amusing. But why do you not like Frankfurt?

HEIDI: There are only buildings and streets here. I cannot see the mountains. Tomorrow I will go back home again where it is so beautiful. The sky is wide and blue and the sun smiles brightly and the fir trees murmur softly where I live.

CLARA: I think you will learn to like it here, especially when you learn to read.

HEIDI: I don't think I can learn to read.

CLARA: Oh, yes, Heidi! You must learn. Every lady must, and the tutor is very good and never gets angry. He comes every morning at ten o'clock and we will have lessons until two.

HEIDI: I don't think I will like it. Already I miss the mountains and the beautiful valleys.

CLARA: You must tell me all about them, Heidi, for I have never seen mountains and valleys. I have always been ill and have not often been out of doors. I cannot walk, you see, and must sit in this chair, and be carried to my bed.

HEIDI: Then I will help you, and I'll tell you everything about my village and my grandfather, and my friend Peter, and all our goats. They all have names and...

MISS ROTTENMEIER: *(Returns, very upset.)* **Well, Adelheid, your aunt has gone and you are to stay here after all. There is no help for it. You are not at all what I wished for Clara, but you will have to do until I can write to her father. Come along to your room.** *(She exits.)*

CLARA: Don't be sad, Heidi. You and I will be happy together. Miss Rottenmeier is in charge of everything while my father is traveling at his business, but she does everything according to my wishes.

MISS ROTTENMEIER: *(Angrily, from Off-stage)* **Adelheid!**

CLARA: Run along, Heidi. I will see you again at dinner.

HEIDI: Will there be white rolls for dinner?

CLARA: Oh, yes, and many other good things.

HEIDI: Then I will be there. *(She goes out.)*

CLARA: Oh, she is going to brighten my days! This dreary old house will not be the same now that she is here! I can hardly wait until dinner to see her again!

From

OLDTOWN FOLKS

By Harriet Beecher Stowe

In her novel, *Oldtown Folks,* published in 1869, Harriet Beecher Stowe presents a realistic picture of New England life shortly after the Revolutionary War. The residents of the village of Oldtown, Massachusetts, were based on people Mrs. Stowe knew well, and she brings them vividly to life in a natural and familiar way through their everyday tasks, troubles, manners, and opinions. Mrs. Stowe was especially talented in establishing strong-willed women with unforgettable names. In this scene, Miss Mehitable Rossiter, a plain, fiftyish spinster living in genteel poverty, has decided to adopt an orphaned little girl who has run away from Miss Asphyxia Smith, a strict, no-nonsense woman who mistreated her. Miss Mehitable shares her concerns and feelings with her close friends and neighbors.

CHARACTERS: MISS MEHITABLE ROSSITER, MRS. BADGER, MISS LOIS BADGER, MISS ASPHYXIA SMITH.

SCENE: MISS MEHITABLE, MRS. BADGER, and MISS LOIS BADGER are seated around a comfortable table in MRS. BADGER's kitchen.

MISS MEHITABLE: Now I suppose I'm about as fit to undertake to bring up a child as the old Dragon of Wantley, but as you two seem to have a surplus of children on your hands, I'm willing to take the girl and do what I can for her.

MRS. BADGER: Dear Miss Mehitable, what a mercy it'll be to her!

MISS LOIS: *(Gently)* **If you feel that you can afford it, of course.**

MISS MEHITABLE: Well, the fowls of the air and the lilies of the field are taken care of somehow, as we are informed. My basket and store are not much to ask a blessing on, but I have a sort of impression that an orphan child will make it none the less likely to hold out.

MRS. BADGER: There'll always be a handful of meal in the barrel and a little oil in the cruse for you, I'm sure. The word of the Lord stands sure for that. Little Tina is a pretty child, and an engaging one.

MISS LOIS: It is more than kind of you to take her, Miss Mehitable.

MISS MEHITABLE: One never knows what may be found in the odd corners of an old maid's heart. There are often unused hoards of maternal affection enough to set up an orphan asylum; but it's like iron filings and a magnet – you must try them with a live child, and if there is anything in 'em, you find it out. That little girl made an instant commotion in the dust and rubbish of my forlorn old garret, and brought to light a deal that I thought had gone to the moles and the bats long ago. She will do me good, I can feel, with her little pertnesses and her airs and fancies. If you could

know how chilly and lonesome an old house gets sometimes, particularly in autumn when the equinoctial storm is brewing! A lively child is a godsend, even if she turns the whole house topsy-turvy!

MISS LOIS: Well, a child can't always be a plaything. It's a solemn and awful responsibility.

MISS MEHITABLE: And if I don't take it, who will? If a better one would, I wouldn't. I've no great confidence in myself. I profess no skill in human cobbling. I can only give house room and shelter and love, and let come what will come.

MRS. BADGER: The Lord will bless you for your goodness to the orphan.

MISS MEHITABLE: I don't know about it's being goodness. I take a fancy to her. I hunger for the child. There's no merit in wanting your bit of cake, and maybe taking it when it isn't good for you. But let's hope all's well that ends well. Since I have fairly claimed her for mine, I begin to feel a fierce right of property in her, and you'll see me fighting like an old hen with anybody that should try to get her away from me. You'll see me made an old fool of by her smart little ways and speeches, and I am already proud of her beauty. Did you ever see a brighter little minx? Depend upon it, she is of good blood. You'll never make me believe that she will not be found to belong in some way to some reputable stock.

MRS. BADGER: Well, we know nothing about her parents, except that the mother was a wandering woman, sick, and a stranger, who was taken down and died over in Needmore. Then Miss Asphyxia took the girl, although why I will never know! There was never a worse woman for trying to do for a child!

MISS MEHITABLE: One can tell by the child's manner of speaking that she has been brought up among educated people. She is no little rustic. Poor little thing! How she

must have suffered in the hands of Miss Asphyxia! But now she is my little one. *My* little one. *(She pauses a moment.)* **Forgive me, but only a few hours ago I was sitting in my old, windy, lonesome house, alone with the memories of dead friends and feeling that I was walking to the grave in a dismal solitude. Now it is as if I have awoke from a dark dream and found myself sole possessor of beauty, youth, and love in a glowing little form, all my own, with no mortal to dispute it! I have a mother's right in a child. I may have a daughter's love.**

MISS LOIS: You may, indeed, Miss Mehitable. But be wary of Miss Asphyxia. She may not take her loss quietly.

MRS. BADGER: I should like to talk to that woman! I wonder folks can be so mean as to strike a child the way she did! I wonder what such folks think of themselves and where they expect to go!

MISS LOIS: *(Looking out the window)* **Well, mother, as true as you live, here's Miss Asphyxia Smith hitching her horse at our picket fence.**

MRS. BADGER: Is she! Well, let her come right in. She's welcome, I'm sure! And I shall certainly speak my mind!

MISS MEHITABLE: *(Calmly)* **It is best, I suppose, to settle this now and be done with it.**

MISS ASPHYXIA: *(Enters, dressed in her Sunday best, looking grim and angry.)* **Good morning, Mrs. Badger. Miss Badger. Miss Rossiter.**

THE LADIES: Miss Smith.

MISS ASPHYXIA: *(After an uncomfortable pause)* **I come over, Mis' Badger, to see about a gal of mine that has run away.**

MRS. BADGER: *(Briskly)* **Run away, did she? And good reason she *should* run away! All I wonder at is that you have the face to come to a Christian family after her! Well, she is provided for, and you've no call to be inquiring anything about her. So I advise you to go home and attend to your**

own affairs, and leave children to folks that know how to manage them better than you do.

MISS ASPHYXIA: *(Wrathfully)* **I expected this, but I ain't a person that's a-goin' to take sass from no one! No deacon's wife is a-goin' to turn up her nose at me! Mis' Badger, I defy you to say that I hain't done well by that little gal! She had everything pervided for her that a child could want; a good clean bed and plenty o' bedclothes, and good whole clothes to wear, and her belly full o'good victuals every day, and me a-teachin' and a-trainin' on her enough to wear the very life out o' me – for I always hated younguns! Why, what did she think I was a-goin' to do for her? I didn't make a lady of her, to be sure! I was a-fetchin' her up to work for her livin' as I was fetched up. I hadn't nothin' more'n she, and just look at me now! There ain't many folks that can turn off as much work in a day as I can. And I've got as pretty a piece of property, and as well seen to, as most any around, and all I've got – house and lands – is my own earnin's, honest. So there! There's folks like you, I s'pose, that thinks they can afford to keep tavern for all sorts of stragglers and runaways. Well, I never was one o' them sort of fools! So come now, Mis' Badger, have it out! I ain't afraid of you. I'd just like to have you tell me what I coulda done more nor better for that child!**

MRS. BADGER: *(Bristling)* **Done! Why, you've done what you'd no business to! You'd no business to take a child in at all! You haven't got a grain of motherliness in you. Why, look at nature! That might teach you that more than meat and drink and clothes is wanted for a child. Hens brood their chickens and keep 'em warm under their wings. Cows lick their calves and cosset 'em! And there's our old cat will lie an hour on the kitchen floor and let her kittens lug and pull at her, atween sleeping and waking, just to keep 'em warm and comfortable. It's *broodin'* that young creatures**

want, and you haint' got a bit of broodin' in you! Your heart's as hard as a millstone! Sovereign Grace may soften it some day, but nothin' else can. You're a poor, old, hard, worldly woman, Miss Asphyxia Smith! That's what you are! If Divine Grace could have broken in upon you and given you a heart to love that child, you might have brought her up, 'cause you're a smart woman, and an honest one – that nobody denies! But as for broodin' a child...

MISS MEHITABLE: *(In a conciliatory, polite tone of voice)* **My good Miss Smith, by your own account, you must have had a great deal of trouble with Tina. Now I propose for the future to relieve you of it altogether.** *(With a slight smile)* **It strikes me that there are radical differences of nature which would prevent her growing up like yourself. I don't doubt you conscientiously intended to do your duty by her, but I beg you to believe that you need have no further trouble with her.**

MISS ASPHYXIA: Goodness gracious, the child ain't much to fight over! She was nothin' but a plague, and I'd rather have done all she did any day, than to a-had her under my feet. I hate younguns anyway!

MISS METHITABLE: Then why do you object to parting with her?

MISS ASPHYXIA: Who said I objected? I don't care nothin' about parting with her. All it is, when I begin a thing, I like to go through with it. But if folks think they're able to bring up a beggar child bettern' I can, it's their lookout and none of mine! I wasn't aware that Parson Rossiter left so much of an estate that you could afford to bring up other folks' children.

MISS MEHITABLE: *(Good-naturedly)* **Our estate isn't much, but we shall make the best of it.**

MISS ASPHYXIA: Well, you mark my words, Miss Rossiter, that child will never grow up a smart woman with *your* bringin' up. She'll just run right over you and you'll let her have her

way in everything.

MISS MEHITABLE: I dare say you are quite right, Miss Smith. I haven't the slightest opinion of my own powers in that line, but she may be happy with me, for all that.

MISS ASPHYXIA: Happy! Oh, well, if folks is a-goin' to talk about *that*, I hain't got time to waste. It don't seem to me that that's what this world's for.

MISS MEHITABLE: What *is* it for then?

MISS ASPHYXIA: Why, for hard work! That's all I ever found it for! And who's a-goin' to stop to quiddle with younguns, I should like to know? T'aint me, that's certain! You're welcome to the girl. I just wanted you to know that what I begun I'd a-gone through with if you hadn't stepped in, and I didn't want no reflections on my good name! Good mornin'! *(She exits brusquely.)*

MRS. BADGER: *(With finality)* **Good morning!**

MISS MEHITABLE: To think of a creature so dry and dreary, so devoid even of the conception of enjoyment in life! Hurrying through life without a moment's rest – and all for what?

MISS LOIS: For my part, Mother, I think you went down a bit too hard on her.

MRS. BADGER: *(Cheerily)* **Not a bit. Such folks ought to be talked to! It may set her to thinking and do her good!**

MISS MEHITABLE: *(Rising)* **Well, I have a very serious responsibility at my time of life to charge myself with the upbringing and education of a child. But I feel I am blessed by her, and if all goes well, so will she be with me. God willing!**

MRS. BADGER: Amen!

MISS LOIS: Amen!

A Dramatic Reading From

THE KING OF BRENTFORD'S TESTAMENT

By William Makepeace Thackeray

Best known as the author of the English social satire, *Vanity Fair,* and other novels, Thackeray also wrote excellent essays, sketches, and poetry. An example of his half-humorous, half-pathetic ballads is *The King of Brentford's Testament.* The readers of this poem are encouraged to act out the story as it is read, portraying the characters as they are described, and using appropriate actions to enhance the reading.

CHARACTERS: NARRATOR, THE KING OF BRENTFORD, HIS LAWYER, PRINCE THOMAS, PRINCE NED.

NARRATOR: The noble King of Brentford
Was old and very sick,
He summoned his physicians
To wait upon him quick.
They stepped into their coaches
And brought their best physic.
They crammed their gracious master
With potion and with pill;
They drenched him and they bled him;
They could not cure his ill.
THE KING: Go fetch
NARRATOR: Says he
THE KING: My lawyer ; I'd better make my will.
NARRATOR: The monarch's royal mandate
The lawyer did obey;
The thought of six-and-eightpence
Did make his heart full gay.
LAWYER: What is't
NARRATOR: Says he
LAWYER: Your Majesty
Would wish of me today?
THE KING: The doctors have belaboured me
With potion and with pill;
My hours of life are counted,
O man of tape and quill!
Sit down and mend a pen or two,
I want to make my will.
O'er all the land of Brentford
I'm lord, and eke of Kew;
I've three-per-cents and five-per-cents;
My debts are but a few;

And to inherit after me
I have but children two.
Prince Thomas is my eldest son;
A sober prince is he,
And from the day we breeched him
Till now – he's twenty-three –
He never caused disquiet
To his poor mamma or me.
At school they never flogged him;
At college, though not fast,
Yet his little-go and great-go
He creditably passed,
And made his year's allowance
For eighteen months to last.
He never owed a shilling,
Went never drunk to bed,
He has not two ideas
Within his honest head;
In all respects he differs
From my second son, Prince Ned.
When Tom has half his income
Laid by at the year's end,
Poor Ned has ne'er a stiver
That rightly he may spend,
But sponges on a tradesman,
Or borrows from a friend.
Ned drives about in buggies,
Tom sometimes takes a 'bus;
Ah, cruel fate, why made you
My children differ thus?
Why make of Tom a dullard,
And Ned a genius?

LAWYER: You'll cut him with a shilling!

NARRATOR: Exclaimed the man of wits.

THE KING: I'll leave my wealth
NARRATOR: Said Brentford,
THE KING: Sir Lawyer, as befits,
And portion both their fortunes unto their several wits.
LAWYER: Your grace knows best,
NARRATOR: The lawyer said,
LAWYER: On your commands I wait.
THE KING: Be silent, sir!
NARRATOR: Says Brentford,
THE KING: A plague upon your prate!
Come take your pen and paper,
And write as I dictate.
NARRATOR: The will as Brentford spoke it
Was writ and signed and closed;
He bade the lawyer leave him,
And turned him round and dozed;
And next week in the churchyard
The good old King reposed.
Tom, dressed in crepe and hatband,
Of mourners was the chief,
In bitter self-upbraidings
Poor Edward showed his grief.
Tom hid his fat white countenance
In his pocket handkerchief.
And when the bones of Brentford,
That gentle King and just,
With bell and book and candle
Were duly laid in dust,
THOMAS: Now gentleman,
NARRATOR: Says Thomas,
THOMAS: Let business be discussed.
When late our sire beloved
Was taken deadly ill,
Sir Lawyer, you attended him

(I mean to tax your bill);
And, as you signed and wrote it,
I prithee read the will.
NARRATOR: **The lawyer wiped his spectacles,**
And drew the parchment out;
And all the Brentford family
Sat eager round about.
Poor Ned was somewhat anxious,
But Tom had ne'er a doubt.
LAWYER: *(Reading from the parchment)* **My son, as I make ready**
To seek my last long home,
Some cares I had for Neddy,
But none for thee, my Tom;
Sobriety and order
You ne'er departed from.
Ned hath a brilliant genius
And thou a plodding brain;
On thee I think with pleasure,
On him with doubt and pain.
THOMAS: **You see, good Ned,**
NARRATOR: **Says Thomas,**
THOMAS: **What he thought about us twain.**
LAWYER: *(Reading)* **Though small was your allowance,**
You saved a little store;
And those who save a little
Shall get a plenty more.
NARRATOR: **As the lawyer read this compliment,**
Tom's eyes were running o'er.
LAWYER: *(Reading)* **And though my lands are wide,**
And plenty is my gold,
Still better gifts from Nature
My Thomas, do you hold;
A brain that's thick and heavy,
A heart that's dull and cold.

Too dull to feel depression,
Too hard to heed distress,
Too cold to yield to passion
Or silly tenderness.
March on – your road is open
To weath, Tom, and success.
Ned sinneth in extravagance,
And you in greedy lust.

NED: I 'faith,

NARRATOR: Says Ned,

NED: Our father
Is less polite than just.

LAWYER: *(Reading)* **In you, son Tom, I've confidence,**
But Ned I cannot trust.
Wherefore my lease and copyholds,
My lands and tenements,
My parks, my farms, and orchards,
My houses and my rents,
My Dutch stock and my Spanish stock,
My five and three-per-cents,
I leave to you, my Thomas -

NED: What, all?

NARRATOR: Poor Edward said.

NED: Well, well, I should have spent them,
And Tom's a prudent head.

LAWYER: *(Reading)* **I leave to you, my Thomas,**
To you IN TRUST for Ned.

NARRATOR: The wrath and consternation
What poet e'er could trace
That at this fatal passage
Came o'er Prince Tom his face;
The wonder of the company
And honest Ned's amaze?

NED: Tis surely some mistake,

NARRATOR: Good-naturedly cries Ned.
The lawyer answered gravely,
LAWYER: Tis even as I said.
'Twas thus his gracious Majesty
Ordained on his death-bed.
See, here the will is witnessed,
And here's his autograph.
NED: In truth, our father's writing,
NARRATOR: Says Edward with a laugh.
NED: But thou shalt not be a loser, Tom;
We'll share it half and half.
LAWYER: Alas, my kind young gentleman,
This sharing cannot be;
'Tis written in the testament
That Brentford spoke to me,
THE KING: *(As the voice of the testament)* **"I do forbid Prince Ned to give**
Prince Tom a halfpenny!
He hath a store of money,
But ne'er was known to lend it;
He never helped his brother,
The poor he ne'er befriended;
He hath no need of property
Who knows not how to spend it.
Poor Edward knows but how to spend
And thrifty Tom to hoard;
Let Thomas be the steward then,
And Edward be the lord.
And as the honest laborer
Is worthy his reward.
I pray Prince Ned, my second son,
And my successor dear,
To pay to his intendant
Five hundred pounds a year;

And to think of his old father
And live and make good cheer."
NARRATOR: Such was old Brentford's honest testament,
He did devise his moneys for the best,
And lies in Brentford church in peaceful rest.
Prince Edward lived, and money made and spent;
But his good sire was wrong, it is confessed;
To say his son, young Thomas, never lent.
He did. Young Thomas lent at interest,
And nobly took his twenty-five percent.

Long time the famous reign of Ned endured
O'er Chiswick, Fulham, Brentford, Putney, Kew;
But of extravagance he ne'er was cured.
And when both died, as mortal men will do,
Twas commonly reported that the steward
Was very much the richer of the two.

From

THE ADVENTURES OF TOM SAWYER

By Mark Twain

Mark Twain's wonderful story, *The Adventures of Tom Sawyer,* was published in 1876, and has delighted readers of all ages since. The book is worthy of a first reading and many, many re-readings, for its depiction of childhood in a quiet Mississippi River town where children made their own entertainment and dealt simply and practically with life's little everyday problems. In this reading, Tom Sawyer, himself, acts as a narrator and recalls a few of the favorite moments from the book.

CHARACTERS: TOM SAWYER, a boy; AUNT POLLY, his aunt; HUCKLEBERRY FINN, his friend; BECKY THATCHER, his girl; ALFRED TEMPLE, a spoiled boy.

TOM SAWYER: *(Enters, licking his jam-covered fingers and holding an overflowing jar.)* **Ummm-mm! Strawberry jam!** *(He nods to audience.)* **Ain't nothin' Tom Sawyer likes better! That's me, Tom Sawyer. Most likely you've heard of me. I've been around a long time in a story that was written by Mr. Mark Twain. He knew a lot about boys, having been one himself, of course, and a lot of things he remembered in himself as a boy he relived through me. I live with my Aunt Polly in the little town of St. Petersburg, Missouri, on the banks of the great Mississippi River.**

AUNT POLLY: *(Enters, looking around.)* **Tom! Tom Sawyer!**

TOM: Uh-oh! There's Aunt Polly lookin' for me. I'd better hide. *(He ducks down, as AUNT POLLY looks all around, raising and lowering her spectacles.)* **My aunt never looks through her spectacles. They are simply for show. She could see through a pair of stove lids just as well!**

AUNT POLLY: Tom? Now where is that boy, I wonder? *(TOM slips behind her and follows her about.)* **You, Tom! I never did see the beat of that boy! If I ever get hold of him, I'll –** *(She catches sight of him behind her and seizes him by the collar.)* **There you are! What have you been doing?**

TOM: *(Meekly, hiding jam behind his back)* **Nothin', Aunt.**

AUNT POLLY: Nothing! Look at your hand! And look at your mouth! What is that truck?

TOM: *(Innocently)* **Why, I don't know, Aunt.**

AUNT POLLY: Well, I know! It's jam, that's what it is! Forty times I've said I'd skin you if you didn't let that jam alone. Hand me that switch! *(She points off.)*

TOM: *(Giving her his most appealing look)* **Yes'm.** *(He slowly goes off, returns slowly with the switch, and hands it to her. She* *takes a firm grip on his collar, bends him over, and raises the switch. He cringes and sniffs. She hesitates. He is encouraged and sniffs louder. She hardens her look, raises the switch again and is about to lower it.)* **Oh, quick, Aunt! Look behind you! Quick!**

AUNT POLLY: *(Gasping)* **What? What's behind me?** *(She drops switch, grabs up her skirts, and looks behind her. TOM laughs and runs off.)* **Oh, hang that boy!** *(Laughs gently.)* **Can't I ever learn anything? Ain't he played me tricks enough like that for me to be looking out for him by this time? But, my goodness, he never plays the same trick twice in a row, and how am I to know what's comin'? Ah, well, he's my own dead sister's boy, poor thing, and I ain't got the heart to lash him somehow. Still, I've got to do my duty by him or I'll be the ruination of the child!** *(She exits, shaking her head.)*

TOM: My aunt Polly was patterned after Mark Twain's own mother, Jane Lampton Clemens, who was very good to him. My Aunt Polly was always good to me, in her own way, and took good care of me whether I 'preciated it or not. *(Looks off.)* **Here comes my friend, Huck Finn. There's no other boy in the world I'd rather hang around with.** *(HUCK enters, swinging a dead cat on a string.)* **Huck is the son of the town drunkard and he is cordially hated and dreaded by all the mothers in town because they think he sets a bad example by never going to school or church. He's idle, lawless, and vulgar, and his society is forbidden to us "respectable boys." He goes fishin' or swimmin' whenever he wants to. He sleeps on doorsteps in fine weather and inside empty barrels in wet, and he never has to wash or put on clean clothes or wear shoes. He can do everything that makes life precious to a boy and I wish I could be like him!** *(As HUCK approaches him)* **Hello, Huckleberry!**

HUCK: Hello, yourself, Tom Sawyer, and see how you like it!

TOM: What's that you got there, Huck?

HUCK: Dead cat.

TOM: Lemme see him. My, he's pretty stiff. Where'd you get him?

HUCK: Bought 'em off'n a boy.

TOM: What'd you give?

HUCK: A blue ticket and a bladder that I got at the slaughterhouse.

TOM: What's a dead cat good for, Huck?

HUCK: Good for? Why, to cure warts with!

TOM: Is that so? How do you do it?

HUCK: Why, you take your cat and go in the graveyard along about midnight after somebody that was wicked has been buried. Then when it's midnight, a devil will come, or maybe two or three, and when they're takin' the dead feller away, you heave your cat after 'em and say, "Devil follow corpse, cat follow devil, warts follow cat, I'm done with ye!" and that'll cure any wart!

TOM: Sounds right. When are you going to try it?

HUCK: Tonight. I reckon the devils will be comin' after old Hoss Williams.

TOM: But he was buried on Saturday. Didn't the devils get him Saturday night?

HUCK: Why, how you talk! How could a devil's charm work till midnight? And then it's Sunday. Devils don't slosh around much of a Sunday, I don't reckon!

TOM: I never thought of that. Say, Huck, lemme go with you?

HUCK: Of course, if you ain't afraid.

TOM: Me afraid? T'ain't likely! You just "meow" outside my window when it's time to go.

HUCK: All right. You be ready. *(He wanders off.)*

TOM: There he goes, off to do what he feels like doin'. But I have to go to school! Being in school is always a dismal time. I'm always wishin' I was fishin' or swimmin' or playin' somewhere out in the woods. 'Course, sometimes school isn't so bad 'cause Becky Thatcher's there. Then I can show off

and think about her and wonder who she's thinkin' about. She's the prettiest girl in the whole school. *(BECKY THATCHER enters and sits down on a bench, glancing shying at TOM.)* **As I was sayin', Becky is...special.** *(He crosses to her and sits beside her. For a moment they sit, neither speaking, just idly swinging their legs and looking shyly at each other. Then TOM suddenly blurts out:)* **Becky, do you love rats?**

BECKY: *(Making a face)* **No! I hate them!**

TOM: Well, I do, too, live ones. But I mean dead ones to swing around your head on a string.

BECKY: No, I don't care for rats much any way. What I like is chewing gum.

TOM: Oh, I do, too. I wish I had some now. *(More leg swinging and shy smiling)* **Say, Becky, was you ever engaged?**

BECKY: Engaged? What's that?

TOM: Why, engaged to be married.

BECKY: No.

TOM: Would you like to?

BECKY: I don't know, Tom. What's it like?

TOM: Like? Why, it ain't like anything! You just tell a boy you won't ever have anybody but him, and then you kiss and that's all. Anybody can do it.

BECKY: Kiss? What do you kiss for?

TOM: Why, that...you know...is to...well, they always do it!

BECKY: Everybody?

TOM: Everybody that gets engaged. Now, I'll whisper something in your ear and then you have to whisper the same thing to me. *(He whispers in her ear. She squirms and looks down.)* **Now you whisper it to me.** *(BECKY hesitates, then quickly whispers in his ear.)* **Now for the...** *(He quickly kisses her on the cheek.)* **Now we're engaged! And always after this you're to walk to school with me when there ain't anybody lookin', and you choose me and I choose you at parties, and you don't marry anybody but me and I don't marry**

anybody but you.

BECKY: It sounds nice, Tom. I never heard of it before.

TOM: Oh, it's lots of fun. Why, me and Amy Lawrence... *(He breaks off, clapping his hand over his mouth.)*

BECKY: *(Jumping up)* **Oh, Tom! Then I ain't the first you've been engaged to!** *(Begins to cry.)*

TOM: Oh, don't cry, Becky. I don't care for her anymore.

BECKY: Yes, you do, Tom. You know you do! *(Sobs louder.)*

TOM: No, Becky, honest! I don't care for anybody but you. *(He tries to take her hand.)*

BECKY: *(Slapping his hand)* **Tom Sawyer, I think you're just awful!** *(She flounces out, still crying.)*

TOM: But, Becky, what did I do? *(He turns away in disgust.)* **I didn't do anything so awful. Girls! She'll be sorry some day!** *(As he turns to leave, ALFRED TEMPLE enters, neatly dressed, wearing shoes and a hat, and looking spoiled and snobbish.)* **Well, lookee here! The new boy in town, Alfred Temple!** *(He and ALFRED eye each other scornfully and suspiciously and walk around each other in a wide circle. Suddenly they move in closer until they are nose to nose.)* **I can lick you!**

ALFRED: I'd like to see you try it!

TOM: Well, I can do it.

ALFRED: No, you can't, either!

TOM: Yes, I can!

ALFRED: No, you can't!

TOM: I can!

ALFRED: You can't!

TOM: Can!

ALFRED: Can't!

TOM: *(Backs off a moment.)* **Say, what's your name?**

ALFRED: T'isn't any of your business, maybe.

TOM: Well, I'll make it my business.

ALFRED: Well, why don't you?

TOM: If you say much, I will.

ALFRED: Much-much-much! There now!

TOM: Oh, you think you're mighty smart, don't you? I could lick you with one hand tied behind me, if I wanted to.

ALFRED: Well, why don't you do it?

TOM: Well, I will, if you fool with me! Smarty! What a hat!

ALFRED: You can lump that hat if you don't like it. I dare you to knock it off, and anybody that'll take a dare will suck eggs!

TOM: You're a liar!

ALFRED: You're another!

TOM: Say, if you give me much more of your sass, I'll bounce a rock off'n your head!

ALFRED: Oh, of course, you will!

TOM: Well, I will!

ALFRED: Then why don't you do it? Or are you afraid?

TOM: I ain't afraid!

ALFRED: You are!

TOM: I ain't! Go away from here! *(Shoves him.)*

ALFRED: Go away yourself! *(Shoves him back.)*

TOM: I won't!

ALFRED: I won't either!

TOM: *(Draws a line in the dust with his toe.)* **I dare you to step over that line, and I'll lick you till you can't stand up! Anybody that'll take a dare will steal sheep!**

ALFRED: *(Stepping over the line)* **Well?**

TOM: Don't you crowd me now. You better look out!

ALFRED: Well, why don't you lick me?

TOM: By jingo! For two cents I will! *(ALFRED smirking, takes two pennies from his pocket and holds them in front of TOM's face. TOM smacks the pennies out of his hand and jumps on ALFRED, knocking him to the ground. They roll and tumble, pounding and groaning, until finally TOM gets astride him and holds him down.)* **Holler 'nuff!**

ALFRED: *(Struggling)* **Let me up!**

TOM: Not till you holler 'nuff!

ALFRED: *(Furious, but helpless)* **Let me up! Let me up!**

TOM: Holler 'nuff!

ALFRED: *(Choking it out)* **'Nuff! 'Nuff!**

TOM: *(Lets him up.)* **Now that'll learn you! Better watch out who you're foolin' with next time!**

ALFRED: *(Sniffling, brushing off his clothes)* **You just wait! I'll get you next time!** *(As TOM makes a rush at him, he dashes out, squealing.)*

TOM: Guess I showed him! Whew! What a day! I'm all tuckered out. You can see how hard it is to be a boy – and this is only a sample of what Mr. Mark Twain put in his book about me. You'll just have to read the rest for yourself. Now, where did I leave that strawberry jam? *(He looks around, spots the jam jar, scoops it up, and runs off.)*

From

AROUND THE WORLD IN EIGHTY DAYS

By Jules Verne

Published in 1872, Jule Verne's delightful story of a determined gentleman's voyage *Around the World in Eighty Days* offers an incredible adventure on land, the sea, and in the air. It also introduces us to one of the most imperturbable characters in literature — Phileas Fogg, of No. 7, Saville Row, Burlington Gardens, London. On October 2, 1872, Mr. Fogg walked to the Reform Club, as he did every day, and, while sitting in the reading room with a copy of the *Daily Telegraph* before him, became involved in a conversation that would drastically change his life. Seated in the room with him were his friends and partners at whist, Andrew Stuart, an engineer, John Sullivan, a banker, and Gautier Ralph, a director of the Bank of England.

CHARACTERS: PHILEAS FOGG, a London gentleman; ANDREW STUART, an engineer; JOHN SULLIVAN, a banker; GAUTIER RALPH, a director of the Bank of England

SULLIVAN: Well, Ralph, what about that bank robbery?

STUART: Oh, the bank will lose the money, of course.

RALPH: On the contrary, I hope we may put our hands on the robber. Skillful detectives have been sent to all the principal ports of America and the Continent, and he'll be a clever fellow if he slips through their fingers.

SULLIVAN: There is a reward of two thousand pounds offered, plus five percent on the sum that might be recovered. That should certainly inspire the detectives.

STUART: But have you got the robber's description?

RALPH: In the first place, he is no robber at all.

SULLIVAN: What! A fellow who makes off with fifty-five thousand pounds from the Bank of England, no robber?

RALPH: No.

STUART: Perhaps he's a manufacturer, then.

FOGG: *(From behind his newspaper)* **The *Daily Telegraph* says that he is a gentleman.** *(He lowers the paper slightly, bows to his companions, then reads from the paper aloud.)* **"On the day of the robbery a well-dressed gentleman of polished manners, and with a well-to-do air, had been observed going to and fro in the paying-room, where the crime was committed. A description of him was easily procured and sent to the detectives who do not despair of his apprehension."**

STUART: I maintain that the chances are in favor of the thief, who must be a shrewd fellow, gentleman or not.

RALPH: But where can he fly to? No country is safe for him.

SULLIVAN: Oh, I don't know. The world is big enough to hide him.

FOGG: It was once.

STUART: What do you mean by 'once'? Has the world grown smaller?

RALPH: Certainly. I agree with Mr. Fogg. The world *has* grown smaller, since a man can now go round it ten times more quickly than a hundred years ago. And that is why the search for this thief will be more likely to succeed.

STUART: And also why the thief can get away more easily. You have a strange way, Ralph, of proving that the world has grown smaller. Just because you can go round it in three months —

FOGG: In eighty days.

SULLIVAN: That is true, gentlemen, only eighty days now that the section between Rothal and Allahabad, on the Great Indian Peninsula Railway, has been opened. Here is the estimate made by the *Daily Telegraph:* *(Reading aloud)* **"From London to Suez, by rail and steamboats, seven days; from Suez to Bombay, by steamer, thirteen days; from Bombay to Calcutta, by rail, three days; from Calcutta to Hong Kong, by steamer, thirteen days."**

FOGG: *(Reading aloud)* **"From Hong Kong to Yokohama, by steamer, six days; from Yokohama to San Francisco, by steamer, twenty-two days; from San Francisco to New York, by rail, seven days; from New York to London, by steamer and train, nine days. Total – eighty days.**

STUART: Yes, in eighty days! But that doesn't take into account bad weather, contrary winds, shipwrecks, railway accidents, and so on.

FOGG: *(Calmly)* **All included.**

STUART: But suppose the Hindoos or Indians pull up the rails? Suppose they stop the trains, pillage the luggage-vans, and scalp the passengers?

FOGG: All included.

STUART: Well, you are right, theoretically, Mr. Fogg, but practically –

FOGG: Practically also, Mr. Stuart.

STUART: I'd like to see you do it in eighty days!

FOGG: **It depends on you. Shall we go?**

STUART: **Heaven preserve me! But I would wager four thousand pounds that such a journey, made under these conditions, is impossible.**

FOGG: **On the contrary, it is quite possible.**

SULLIVAN: *(Excited)* **Well, why don't you make it then, Mr. Fogg!**

FOGG: **The journey round the world in eighty days?**

SULLIVAN: **Yes!**

FOGG: **I should like nothing better.**

RALPH: **When?**

FOGG: **At once. Only I warn you that I shall do it at your expense.**

STUART: **It's absurd!**

RALPH: **Calm yourself, my dear Stuart. It's only a joke.**

STUART: **It is not a joke. I said I would wager four thousand pounds, and when I say I'll wager, I mean it.**

FOGG: **Gentlemen, I have a deposit of twenty thousand at Baring's which I will willingly risk upon this venture.**

SULLIVAN: **Twenty-thousand pounds! You could lose it all by a single accidental delay!**

FOGG: *(Quietly)* **The unforeseen does not exist.**

RALPH: **But, Mr. Fogg, eighty days are only the estimate of the least possible time in which the journey can be made.**

FOGG: **A well-used minimum suffices for everything.**

SULLIVAN: **But, in order not to exceed it, you must jump mathematically from the trains upon the steamers, and from the steamers upon the trains again.**

FOGG: **I will jump – mathematically.**

SULLIVAN: **You are joking!**

FOGG: **A true Englishman doesn't joke when he is talking about so serious a thing as a wager. I will bet twenty thousand pounds against anyone who wishes, that I will make the tour of the world in eighty days or less; in nineteen hundred and twenty hours, or a hundred and fifteen thousand two hundred minutes. Do you accept?**

SULLIVAN/STUART/RALPH: *(All look at each other, consider a moment, then nod in agreement.)* **We accept!**

FOGG: Good! The train leaves for Dover at a quarter before nine. I'll take it.

STUART: This very evening?

FOGG: This very evening. *(Consulting his pocket almanac)* **As today is Wednesday, the second of October, I shall be due in London, in this very room of the Reform Club, on Saturday, the twenty-first of December, at a quarter before nine p.m., or else the twenty thousand pounds, now deposited in my name at Baring's, will belong to you, in fact and in right, gentlemen.** *(Taking out his pocketbook)* **Here is a check for the amount.** *(He writes the check and hands it to RALPH.)*

STUART: Will you go alone, Mr. Fogg?

FOGG: My valet will accompany me. I have just engaged him this very day, a young Frenchman by the name of Passepartout. We shall take no trunks, only a carpetbag with two shirts and three pairs of stockings for each of us. We'll buy our clothes on the way. I shall also take my mackintosh and traveling cloak, and some stout shoes, and a goodly roll of bank bills for expenses. It is all quite simple, gentlemen.

RALPH: I'm afraid this undertaking is impossible, Mr. Fogg, but I must admit your confidence is admirable.

FOGG Gentlemen, if you will excuse me, I must begin my journey. *(With a polite bow, he folds his newspaper, places it on the table, and walks out of the room.)*

STUART: A journey round the world in eighty days! It simply can't be done! Gentlemen, in eighty days Mr. Fogg's twenty-thousand pounds will be ours!

From

THE IMPORTANCE OF BEING EARNEST

By Oscar Wilde

Oscar Wilde's delightful comedy of English manners, *The Importance of Being Earnest,* was first presented in 1895, and focused on confused identities and two young ladies who place extreme importance on the name of the man they intend to marry. In the following two scenes, the importance of that name is explained in perfect detail, first by Gwendolen Fairfax, who, while visiting her London cousin, Algernon Moncrief, with her mother, Lady Bracknell, takes advantage of her parent's brief errand into another room to speak to her intended, Mr. Jack Worthing, also visiting Algernon and known to all as Ernest (for reasons of his own).

CHARACTERS: GWENDOLEN FAIRFAX, JACK WORTHING, CECILY CARDEW, ALGERNON MONCRIEF.

JACK: *(Seated on the edge of his chair)* **Charming day it has been, Miss Fairfax.**

GWENDOLEN: *(Seated opposite him)* **Pray don't talk to me about the weather, Mr. Worthing. Whenever people talk to me about the weather, I always feel quite certain that they mean something else. And that makes me so nervous.**

JACK: I do mean something else.

GWENDOLEN: I thought so. In fact, I am never wrong.

JACK: And I would like to be allowed to take advantage of Lady Bracknell's temporary absence...

GWENDOLEN: I would certainly advise you to do so. Mama has a way of coming back suddenly into a room that I have often had to speak to her about.

JACK: *(Rising, nervously)* **Miss Fairfax, ever since I met you, I have admired you more than any girl...I have ever met since...I met you.**

GWENDOLEN: Yes, I am quite well aware of the fact. And I often wish that in public, at any rate, you had been more demonstrative. For me you have always had an irresistible fascination. Even before I met you I was far from indifferent to you. *(JACK looks at her in amazement.)* **My ideal has always been to love someone of the name of Ernest. There is something in that name that inspires absolute confidence. The moment Algernon first mentioned to me that he had a friend called Ernest, I knew I was destined to love you.**

JACK: *(Seizing her hand)* **You really love me, Gwendolen?**

GWENDOLEN: Passionately!

JACK: Darling! You don't know how happy you've made me.

GWENDOLEN: My own Ernest!

JACK: But you don't really mean to say that you couldn't love me if my name wasn't Ernest?

GWENDOLEN: But your name *is* Ernest.

JACK: Yes, I know it is. *(Gently removing his hand from hers)* **But supposing it was something else? Do you mean to say you couldn't love me then?**

GWENDOLEN: Ah! That is clearly a metaphysical speculation, and like most metaphysical speculations has very little reference at all to the actual facts of real life, as we know them.

JACK: Personally, darling, to speak quite candidly, I don't much care about the name of Ernest. I don't think the name suits me at all.

GWENDOLEN: It suits you perfectly. It is a divine name. It has music of its own. It produces vibrations.

JACK: Well, really, Gwendolen, I think there are lots of other much nicer names. I think Jack, for instance, a charming name.

GWENDOLEN: Jack? No, there is very little music in the name Jack. It does not thrill. It produces absolutely no vibrations. Besides, Jack is a notorious domesticity for John! And I pity any woman who is married to a man called John. She would probably never be allowed to know the entrancing pleasure of a single moment's solitude. The only really safe name is Ernest.

JACK: Gwendolen, I must get christened at once! I mean we must get married at once. There is no time to be lost.

GWENDOLEN: Married, Mr. Worthing?

JACK: *(Astounded)* **Well, surely. You know that I love you, and you led me to believe that you were not absolutely indifferent to me.**

GWENDOLEN: I adore you. But you haven't proposed to me yet. Nothing has been said at all about marriage. The subject has not even been touched on.

JACK: Well, may I propose to you now?

GWENDOLEN: I think it would be an admirable opportunity. And to spare you any possible disappointment, Mr.

Worthing, I think it only fair to tell you quite frankly beforehand that I am fully determined to accept you.

JACK: Gwendolen!

GWENDOLEN: Yes, Mr. Worthing, what have you got to say to me?

JACK: You know what I have got to say to you.

GWENDOLEN: Yes, but you don't say it.

JACK: *(Places a sofa pillow carefully on the floor at her feet and kneels.)* **Gwendolen, will you marry me?**

GWENDOLEN: Of course I will, darling! How long you have been about it! *(Gazing at him adoringly)* **What wonderfully blue eyes you have, Ernest! They are quite, quite blue. I hope you will always look at me just like that, especially when there are other people present.** *(As the scene ends, they both gaze lovingly at each other.)*

***

In this scene, Jack Worthing's ward, Cecily Cardew, is courted by Jack's friend and Gwendolen's cousin, Algernon Moncrief who, having fallen in love with Cecily from Jack's description of her, has journeyed to her home in the country to meet her, posing as Jack's brother Ernest. This scene takes place in the garden, where Cecily is seated at a table with Algernon at her side.

ALGERNON: *(Taking her hand)* **I hope, Cecily, I shall not offend you if I state quite frankly and openly that you seem to me to be in every way the visible personification of absolute perfection.**

CECILY: I think your frankness does you great credit, Ernest. If you will allow me, I will copy your remarks into my diary. *(She opens her diary and begins to write.)*

ALGERNON: Do you really keep a diary? I'd give anything to look at it. May I?

CECILY: Oh no. *(Puts her hand over it.)* **You see, it is simply a very**

young girl's record of her own thoughts and impressions, and consequently meant for publication. When it appears in volume form, I hope you will order a copy. But pray, Ernest, don't stop. I delight in taking down from dictation. I have reached "absolute perfection." You can go on. I am quite ready for more. *(Somewhat taken aback, ALGERNON coughs nervously.)* **Oh, don't cough, Ernest. When one is dictating, one should speak fluently and not cough. Besides, I don't know how to spell a cough.**

ALGERNON: *(Speaking very rapidly)* **Cecily, ever since I first looked upon your wonderful and incomparable beauty, I have dared to love you wildly, passionately, devotedly, hopelessly!**

CECILY: *(Writing as he speaks)* **I don't think you should tell me that you love me wildly, passionately, devotedly, hopelessly. Hopelessly doesn't seem to make much sense, does it?**

ALGERNON: Cecily! You will marry me, won't you?

CECILY: You silly boy! Of course. Why, we have been engaged for the last three months.

ALGERNON: The last three months? But how did we become engaged?

CECILY: Well, ever since dear Uncle Jack first confessed to us that he had a younger brother who was very wicked and bad, you have formed the chief topic of conversation between myself and my governess, Miss Prism. And of course, a man who is much talked about is always very attractive. One feels there must be something in him, after all. I dare say it was foolish of me, but I fell in love with you, Ernest.

ALGERNON: Darling! And when was the engagement actually settled?

CECILY: On the fourteenth of February last. Worn out by your entire ignorance of my existence, I determined to end the matter one way or the other, and after a long struggle with

myself I accepted you under this dear old tree here. The next day I bought this little ring in your name, *(Shows her finger)* **and this is the little bangle with the true lover's knot I promised you always to wear.** *(She displays a bracelet.)*

ALGERNON: Did I give you this? It's very pretty, isn't it?

CECILY: Yes, you've wonderfully good taste, Ernest. It's the excuse I've always given for your leading such a bad life. And this is the box in which I keep all your dear letters. *(She produces the box from under the table, opens it, revealing letters tied up with blue ribbon.)*

ALGERNON: My letters! But my own sweet Cecily, I have never written you any letters.

CECILY: You need hardly remind me of that, Ernest. I remember only too well that I was forced to write your letters for you. I wrote always three times a week, and sometimes oftener.

ALGERNON: Oh, do let me read them, Cecily!

CECILY: Oh, I couldn't possibly. They would make you far too conceited. *(Replaces box under the table.)* **The three you wrote me after I had broken off the engagement are so beautiful, and so badly spelled, that even now I can hardly read them without crying a little.**

ALGERNON: Our engagement was broken off?

CECILY: Of course it was. On the twenty-second of last March. You can see the entry if you like. *(Shows page.)* **"Today I broke off my engagement with Ernest. I feel it is better to do so. The weather still continues charming."**

ALGERNON: But why on earth did you break it off? What had I done? I am very much hurt to hear you broke it off, particularly when the weather was so charming.

CECILY: It would hardly have been a really serious engagement if it hadn't been broken off at least once. But I forgave you before the week was out.

ALGERNON: *(Kneeling beside her)* **What a perfect angel you**

are, Cecily. You'll never break off our engagement again, will you?

CECILY: I don't think I could break it off now that I have actually met you. Besides, there is the question of your name.

ALGERNON: *(Nervously)* **Yes, of course.**

CECILY: You must not laugh at me, darling, but it had always been a girlish dream of mine to love someone whose name was Ernest. *(He rises; she rises also.)* **There is something in that name that seems to inspire absolute confidence. I pity any poor married woman whose husband is not called Ernest.**

ALGERNON: But my dear child, do you mean to say you could not love me if I had some other name?

CECILY: What other name?

ALGERNON: Oh, any name you like. Algernon, for instance...

CECILY: But I don't like the name of Algernon.

ALGERNON: Well, my own dear, sweet, loving little darling, I really can't see why you should object to the name of Algernon. It is not at all a bad name. In fact, it is rather an aristocratic name. Half of the chaps who get into the bankruptcy court are called Algernon. But seriously, Cecily, if my name was Algy, couldn't you love me?

CECILY: I might respect you, Ernest, I might admire your character, but I fear that I should not be able to give you my undivided attention.

ALGERNON: *(Suddenly taking up his hat from the table)* **Your rector here is, I suppose, thoroughly experienced in the practice of all the rites and ceremonials of the church?**

CECILY: Oh, yes, Dr. Chasuble is a most learned man. He has never written a single book, so you can imagine how much he knows.

ALGERNON: I must see him at once on a most important christening! I mean on most important business.

CECILY: Oh?

ALGERNON: I shan't be away more than half an hour.

CECILY: Considering that we have been engaged since February the fourteenth, and that I only met you today for the first time, I think it is rather hard that you should leave me for so long a period as half an hour. Couldn't you make it twenty minutes?

ALGERNON: I'll be back in no time. *(Kisses her and dashes off.)*

CECILY: What an impetuous boy he is! My darling Ernest! I must enter his proposal in my diary. *(She sits and begins to write, smiling happily.)*

INDEX

SCENES & MONOLOGS

(Listed by Country, Title, Author, Characters)

AMERICAN

BRITISH

SCOTTISH

FRENCH

SPANISH

RUSSIAN

ITALIAN

BELGIAN

GERMAN

IRISH

SWISS

INDIAN

DUTCH

MONOLOGS FOR WOMEN

MONOLOGS FOR MEN

SCENES FOR ALL WOMEN

SCENES FOR ALL MEN

SCENES FOR MIXED CAST

DRAMATIZED POETRY

ABOUT THE AUTHOR

Originally from Indianapolis, Indiana, Joellen K. Bland has lived in Lexington, Virginia, in the beautiful Shenandoah Valley, for the past twenty years. She is currently Director of the VMI Theatre at Virginia Military Institute, and also an editorial assistant at the George C. Marshall Foundation. A graduate of Purdue University, she has been active in all phases of community, children's, church, and college theatre, including directing, stage-managing, costuming, and acting. She has worked in public relations and educational television, and has had over forty plays published, mostly adaptations of classics. Her playwriting awards include the Shenandoah Valley Playwrights competition and the Festival of Firsts Playwriting Competition. She has been married to her historian husband, Larry, for thirty-four years, and has two grown sons, Neil and Ryan.

THE SCENEBOOK FOR ACTORS

by Norman A. Bert

Somewhere in this book is one or several *perfect* monologs or dialogs for your audition. Short cuttings from some of the very best scenes in theatre yesterday and today. Selections are by many of the world's leading playwrights including: Pinter, Goldsmith, Ionesco, Mamet and many more. Powerful moments. Some soft and quiet. Others strident and commanding. The choices are many. The book explains how to find the right audition monolog for your voice, your face, your style, your stage persona. Valuable tips on how to develop your audition monolog for performance and how to build a systematic file of scenes for your personal working repertoire. Recommended as a textbook supplement for acting classes.

Paperback Book (256 pages) ISBN #0-916260-65-8

ORDER FORM

MERIWETHER PUBLISHING LTD.
P.O. BOX 7710
COLORADO SPRINGS, CO 80933
TELEPHONE: (719) 594-4422

Please send me the following books:

_________ **Playing Scenes From Classic Literature #TT-B201** **$14.95**
edited by Joellen K. Bland
Short dramatizations from world literature

_________ **Multicultural Theatre #TT-B205** **$14.95**
edited by Roger Ellis
Scenes and monologs by multicultural writers

_________ **Playing Contemporary Scenes #TT-B100** **$14.95**
edited by Gerald Lee Ratliff
Thirty-one famous scenes and how to play them

_________ **The Scenebook for Actors #TT-B177** **$14.95**
by Dr. Norman A. Bert
Collection of great monologs and dialogs for auditions

_________ **One-Act Plays for Acting Students #TT-B159** **$14.95**
by Dr. Norman A. Bert
An anthology of complete one-act plays

_________ **Theatre Alive! #TT-B178** **$24.95**
by Dr. Norman A. Bert
An introductory anthology of world drama

_________ **Playing Scenes — A Sourcebook for Performers #TT-B109** **$14.95**
by Gerald Lee Ratliff
How to play great scenes from modern and classical theatre

These and other fine Meriwether Publishing books are available at your local bookstore or direct from the publisher. Use the handy order form on this page.

NAME: ______________________________

ORGANIZATION NAME: ______________________________

ADDRESS: ______________________________

CITY: ______________________________ STATE: ____________

ZIP: ____________________ PHONE: ____________________

❑ **Check Enclosed**
❑ **Visa or MasterCard #** ______________________________

Signature: ______________________________ *Expiration Date:* ____________
(required for Visa/MasterCard orders)

COLORADO RESIDENTS: Please add 3% sales tax.
SHIPPING: Include $2.75 for the first book and 50¢ for each additional book ordered.

❑ *Please send me a copy of your complete catalog of books and plays.*

ORDER FORM

MERIWETHER PUBLISHING LTD.
P.O. BOX 7710
COLORADO SPRINGS, CO 80933
TELEPHONE: (719) 594-4422

Please send me the following books:

_______ **Playing Scenes From Classic Literature #TT-B201** **$14.95**
edited by Joellen K. Bland
Short dramatizations from world literature

_______ **Multicultural Theatre #TT-B205** **$14.95**
edited by Roger Ellis
Scenes and monologs by multicultural writers

_______ **Playing Contemporary Scenes #TT-B100** **$14.95**
edited by Gerald Lee Ratliff
Thirty-one famous scenes and how to play them

_______ **The Scenebook for Actors #TT-B177** **$14.95**
by Dr. Norman A. Bert
Collection of great monologs and dialogs for auditions

_______ **One-Act Plays for Acting Students #TT-B159** **$14.95**
by Dr. Norman A. Bert
An anthology of complete one-act plays

_______ **Theatre Alive! #TT-B178** **$24.95**
by Dr. Norman A. Bert
An introductory anthology of world drama

_______ **Playing Scenes — A Sourcebook for Performers #TT-B109** **$14.95**
by Gerald Lee Ratliff
How to play great scenes from modern and classical theatre

These and other fine Meriwether Publishing books are available at your local bookstore or direct from the publisher. Use the handy order form on this page.

NAME: ____

ORGANIZATION NAME: ___________________________________

ADDRESS: ____

CITY: ______________________________ STATE: __________

ZIP: ______________________ PHONE: ___________________

❑ **Check Enclosed**
❑ **Visa or MasterCard #** _______________________________

Signature: __________________________ *Expiration Date:* ______________
(required for Visa/MasterCard orders)

COLORADO RESIDENTS: Please add 3% sales tax.
SHIPPING: Include $2.75 for the first book and 50¢ for each additional book ordered.

❑ *Please send me a copy of your complete catalog of books and plays.*